Wake

Critical Issues in American Education

Lisa M. Nunn, Series Editor

Taking advantage of sociology's position as a leader in the social scientific study of education, this series is home to new empirical and applied bodies of work that combine social analysis, cultural critique, and historical perspectives across disciplinary lines and the usual methodological boundaries. Books in the series aim for topical and theoretical breadth. Anchored in sociological analysis, Critical Issues in American Education features carefully crafted empirical work that takes up the most pressing educational issues of our time, including federal education policy, gender and racial disparities in student achievement, access to higher education, labor market outcomes, teacher quality, and decision making within institutions.

Judson G. Everitt, *Lesson Plans: The Institutional Demands of Becoming a Teacher*
Karey Harwood, *Wake: Why the Battle over Diverse Public Schools Still Matters*
Megan M. Holland, *Divergent Paths to College: Race, Class, and Inequality in High Schools*
Katie Kerstetter, *How Schools Meet Students' Needs: Inequality, School Reform, and Caring Labor*
Laura Nichols, *The Journey Before Us: First-Generation Pathways from Middle School to College*
Lisa M. Nunn, *College Belonging: How First-Year and First-Generation Students Navigate Campus Life*
Daisy Verduzco Reyes, *Learning to Be Latino: How Colleges Shape Identity Politics*

Wake

Why the Battle over Diverse Public Schools Still Matters

KAREY HARWOOD

Rutgers University Press

New Brunswick, Camden, and Newark, New Jersey

London and Oxford

Rutgers University Press is a department of Rutgers, The State University of New Jersey, one of the leading public research universities in the nation. By publishing worldwide, it furthers the University's mission of dedication to excellence in teaching, scholarship, research, and clinical care.

Library of Congress Cataloging-in-Publication Data

Names: Harwood, Karey, author.
Title: Wake : why the battle over diverse public schools still matters / Karey Harwood.
Description: New Brunswick : Rutgers University Press, [2024] | Series: Critical issues in American education | Includes bibliographical references and index.
Identifiers: LCCN 2023041242 | ISBN 9781978836563 (paperback) | ISBN 9781978836570 (hardback) | ISBN 9781978836587 (epub) | ISBN 9781978836594 (pdf)
Subjects: LCSH: School integration—North Carolina—Wake County. | Segregation in education—North Carolina—Wake County. | Educational equalization— North Carolina—Wake County. | Wake County Public School System—History. | Community schools—North Carolina—Wake County—History. | Community and school—North Carolina—Wake County—History. | Public schools—North Carolina— Wake County—History.
Classification: LCC LC214.22.N66 H37 2024 | DDC 379.2/630975655—dc23/eng/20231106
LC record available at https://lccn.loc.gov/2023041242

A British Cataloging-in-Publication record for this book is available from the British Library.

References to internet websites (URLs) were accurate at the time of writing. Neither the author nor Rutgers University Press is responsible for URLs that may have expired or changed since the manuscript was prepared.

♾ The paper used in this publication meets the requirements of the American National Standard for Information Sciences—Permanence of Paper for Printed Library Materials, ANSI Z39.48-1992.

rutgersuniversitypress.org

Dedicated to the public school teachers, staff, and students who do the work of integration.

Contents

1   Wake County's Example: What Happened Here
    Was Remarkable   1

2   Contested Values in Wake's Debate: Published
    Opinions, 2009–2011   21

3   Defenders of the Faith: Community Leaders
    Reflect on Diversity a Decade Later   45

4   Arguing from the Past, Fighting for the Future   73

5   Moral Logics and the Case for True Integration   101

    Appendix A: *News & Observer* Search Process   129
    Appendix B: Interviewees and Questions   131
    Appendix C: Key Participants   133
    Acknowledgments   137
    Notes   139
    Index   169

Contents

Wake

1

Wake County's Example

What Happened Here
Was Remarkable

On December 1, 2009, I along with dozens of my fellow citizens in Wake County filed into the old board of education building on Wake Forest Road in Raleigh. We were there to see the new school board members at their first public meeting after upset victories in a low turnout election that fall. Four Republican candidates running on a promise of "neighborhood schools" had swept their races. The neighborhood schools supporters joined Ron Margiotta, already serving a term on the board, to form a 5–4 majority. Before that night, I had never attended a school board meeting. I never had reason to. From my perspective as a relatively young parent whose children attended the Wake County Public School System (WCPSS), the district was doing an excellent job. Wake County's superintendent had won the National Superintendent of the Year Award just a few years prior, in 2004, when my oldest child was in first grade. In fact, in 2002 we turned down an opportunity to move from Atlanta, where I had attended grad school, to New Jersey, my home state, deciding instead on North Carolina because of the quality of the public schools. When we first moved to Raleigh, I did not fully understand how much the excellence of the schools in Wake County went hand in hand with their racial and socio-economic diversity. But as that reality became quickly apparent, I was both amazed and pleased: my children's public school experience in a southern school district was destined to be considerably more integrated than my own had been across three different districts in the Northeast.

An Awakening

Given my satisfaction with the schools, I never imagined I would be sitting among this agitated crowd and anxious about what the election results portended. What was at stake, what had drawn the big response, was concern that the newly elected board members would dismantle Policy 6200, the so-called "diversity policy" governing student assignment, one of many pieces in a decades-long effort to ensure racial and socioeconomic integration in Wake County's public schools. Many individuals delivered passionate speeches during the public comment period expressing their support for the school system and specifically for the diversity policy. But speeches turned to shouts and protest as it became quickly apparent that the new board members had met privately to discuss their plans in advance of the public meeting. Projected on a screen were the draft changes being proposed for Policy 6200, including the elimination of "Creating and maintaining a diverse student body" as a priority in student assignment. These words were struck through with a line. The proposal also replaced "Maintaining diverse student populations" with "Maintaining stable populations that consider proximity to home."[1]

I was not unaware of the discontent felt by some parents toward Wake County's student assignment policy. A small but energized group of parents had organized around their shared dissatisfaction with the system, particularly over what they perceived to be unwarranted and disruptive reassignment of students for the purpose of "social engineering"—that is, intervening through policy to avoid the creation of high-poverty schools rather than letting the chips fall according to neighborhoods and who happened to live in them. These were the parents who had recruited and campaigned for the four partisan Republican candidates, and who had mobilized voter turnout. As I left the meeting that night, I overheard Democratic board member Carolyn Morrison commenting to a reporter that the four newcomers had "awakened a sleeping giant." Aware of my own sleepy privilege in taking for granted the school system's success and staying power, the consequences of local politics jolted me awake. That December meeting served as my initiation to learning about the history of Wake County and North Carolina's public schools and the ongoing struggle to provide an equitable education to all children.

The Intervening Years

In his book, *Children of the Dream: Why School Integration Works* (2019), Rucker C. Johnson describes the "trauma" felt by supporters of school integration in Louisville, Kentucky, when they watched Wake County, a "pillar of defense," dismantle its successful integration plan.[2] What happened in Wake apparently emboldened politicians in the Kentucky state senate and other stakeholders to pursue more aggressive anti-integration efforts of their own. Despite what Kentucky took to be a death knell for integration, the battle in Wake County is by no means over. An equally dramatic school board election in 2011 wrested control of the board away from the Republican majority. After considerable grassroots organizing by energized parents and community members, five Democratic candidates won all five contested seats, including the one held by Chair Ron Margiotta. Although the board has never been able to reinstitute the full extent of the old Policy 6200, in many ways they have continued the work of resisting segregation. Among the core beliefs of WCPSS's strategic plan, for example, are these: "The Board of Education, superintendent, and all staff value a diverse school community that is inviting, respectful, inclusive, flexible, and supportive," and "Every child is expected to learn, grow, and succeed while we eliminate the ability to predict achievement based on socioeconomic status, race, and ethnicity."[3] These core beliefs inform policy decisions large and small, at both the school and district level.

Another sign that the battle continues is the robust landscape of organizations supporting public education in Wake County and North Carolina more broadly. Some of these organizations predate the 2009 school board election by decades; for example, WakeEd Partnership and the Public School Forum of North Carolina.[4] Some emerged in the aftermath of that watershed event or were created much more recently, such as Great Schools in Wake, Public Schools First NC, EdNC, Center for Racial Equity in Education, Dudley Flood Center for Educational Equity and Opportunity, Every Child NC, and A Better Wake: Dismantling Systemic Racism.[5] These organizations have different missions and priorities. They are not all singularly focused on racial and socioeconomic integration of schools per se, but most include equity in education as part of their core mission or advocate for North Carolina to make good on its state constitution's commitment to provide a sound basic education for all children.[6] What is most significant is that these various groups keep the conversation about public schools going—through their publications, webinars, in-person events, and outreach efforts to inform and engage citizens. The conversation about public school integration is now more nuanced and less combative than it was during the most intense period of 2009–2011, but it is no less robust. Inside schools, through school equity teams, and in other spaces of civic engagement, there is a willingness to tackle the difficult subject of racial equity that may not have existed a decade ago.

The battle also continues because schools and districts are not static. The WCPSS enrolled 161,907 students in the 2019–2020 school year, which represents a near tripling of its student population since 1980.[7] People often say that Wake County was a victim of its own success. The schools were great, and taxes were low, so people moved here. WCPSS is now the fifteenth-largest school district in the nation and the largest in North Carolina. Its total number of schools grew from 159 to 191 during the last decade, from 2009–2010 to 2020–2021, even as the public schools faced increasing competition for students from the rapid growth of charter schools enabled by the North Carolina state legislature, which lifted the statewide one hundred charter school cap in 2011, and a private school voucher program initiated by the state legislature in 2013 and given increasingly more funding since.[8] Still, despite its large size, WCPSS is nothing like the large, intensely urban school districts of New York City, Chicago, or Los Angeles. At 857 square miles, Wake County spreads its population of 1.1 million (2019) across a dozen cities and towns, including the state's capital, Raleigh.[9]

While current demographic profiles of the schools in Wake County show some troubling trends toward racial and socioeconomic segregation, the district has held the line in important respects. For example, 72% of schools as of the 2021–2022 school year still met the original benchmark of the old diversity policy, which was to have no more than 40% of students in a school qualifying for free and reduced-price lunch (FRL), a standard used to make sure each school had a "healthy" balance of low- and high-needs students. This is similar to—and slightly better than—where things were in 2009–2010, when 67% of schools met that benchmark.[10] Figure 1.1 shows the change over time (between 2009 and 2022) in the percentage of Wake County public schools meeting the benchmark of less than 40% FRL.

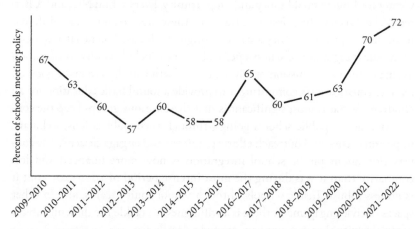

FIGURE 1.1 Wake schools meeting old diversity policy (less than 40 percent free and reduced-price lunch), 2009–2022. (Data from Wake County Public School System, August 2022.)

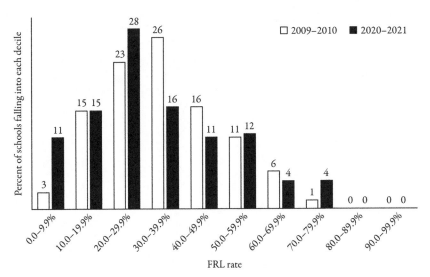

FIGURE 1.2 Distribution of Wake free and reduced-price lunch (FRL) rates. (Data from Wake County Public School System, August 2022.)

Still, in the 2020–2021 school year, 30% of schools had more than 40% of students qualifying for free and reduced-price lunch. Of those schools, 21 out of 191 (or 11%) were in the 40–50% FRL range, 22 (11.5%) were in the 50–60% FRL range, 8 (4.2%) were in the 60–70% FRL range, and 7 (3.7%) were in the 70–80% FRL range. At the time, none were over 80% FRL. Those with higher FRL numbers are higher poverty schools. Figure 1.2 shows the distribution of FRL rates by decile, comparing the percentage of schools falling into each decile in 2009–2010 and 2020–2021. Percentages have been rounded to whole numbers.

A significant change from a decade ago is that the number of schools in the 70–80% FRL range increased from 2 to 7 schools (or from 1.3% of schools in 2009–2010 to 3.6% of schools in 2020–2021). In all 7 of these schools, the largest ethnic group is Black (ranging from 50.0 to 70.6% Black).[11] The next largest group is Latino, who make up an average of 27.1% of the student population in these higher poverty schools. Figure 1.3 shows the average racial makeup of schools in the highest FRL decile existing in WCPSS, which for the 2020–2021 school year was 70–80% FRL.

On the other end of the wealth spectrum, the number of public schools in Wake County with very few students qualifying for free and reduced-price lunch has also increased over the last decade. In 2009–2010, only 4 out of 159 schools (2.5% of schools) had less than 10% of their student population qualifying for free and reduced-price lunch. By contrast, in 2020–2021, 21 out of 191 schools (11% of schools) were below 10% FRL. Interestingly, while white

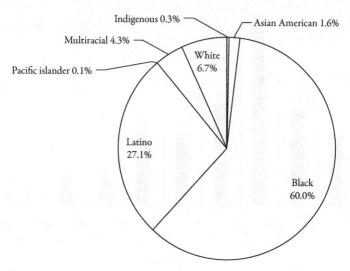

FIGURE 1.3 Average racial makeup of schools in highest free and reduced-price lunch decile (70–80 percent), 2020–2021. (Data from Wake County Public School System, August 2022.)

students were the largest ethnic group in 4 out of those 4 high-wealth schools in 2009–2010, white students were the largest ethnic group in only 10 of the 21 high-wealth schools in 2020–2021 (ranging from 44.7% to 81.8% white in those 10 schools; averaging 50.1% across all 21 high-wealth schools). Asian students were by 2020–2021 the largest ethnic group in 11 of the 21 high-wealth schools (ranging from 37.5% to 62.8% Asian in those 11 schools; averaging 32.3% across all 21 high-wealth schools).[12] Most of these schools are located in the western part of the county, which is closest to Research Triangle Park, a major hub for research and technology companies. Figure 1.4 shows the average racial makeup for these high-wealth (lowest FRL) schools in 2020–2021.

These more recent statistics suggest some polarization of the student population in Wake County, with increases at either end of high and low socioeconomic status. But it is important to remember how well Wake still compares to other large school districts and to the country as a whole. Apples to apples comparisons are tricky, but there are numerous examples around the United States where city school districts are high poverty and neighboring suburban school districts are not. Wake County Public Schools, by consolidating Raleigh City and Wake County schools into one unified district in 1976, has used its size to share its wealth and buffer smaller towns and their schools from economic stresses. According to nationally reported data on the country's

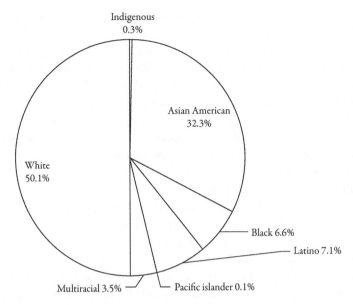

FIGURE 1.4 Average racial makeup of schools in lowest free and reduced-price lunch decile (0–10 percent), 2020–2021. (Data from Wake County Public School System, August 2022.)

120 largest school districts, Wake County's poverty rate of five-to-seventeen-year-olds in 2017 was 11.1%, whereas, to name just a single example in a commonly repeating pattern across the United States, the city of Baltimore school district's poverty rate of five-to-seventeen-year-olds was 29.2% while Baltimore County school district's was 9.5%.[13]

As for racial segregation, Wake County still does considerably better than the country as a whole. For example, Wake has *no* intensely segregated schools, defined as 90–100% nonwhite (or white) students. In the United States overall, 40% of Black and 41.6% of Latino students attend intensely segregated nonwhite schools.[14] Indeed, Wake's school demographics are a striking contrast with many districts in the Northeast, which has some of the most racially segregated schools in the country.[15] Wake's countywide structure also contrasts with the far more typical structure of small school districts that align with a town's borders.[16]

To take one example, the school district where I attended grades ten through twelve in Westfield, New Jersey, sits four miles down the road from the town of Plainfield, New Jersey. In 2018–2019, thirty years after I graduated from high school, Westfield and Plainfield were still the inverse of each other in terms of white and nonwhite student populations, although if anything, Westfield has more racial diversity than it did when I lived there. In 2018–2019, the West-field Public School District served just 6,304 students, pre-K through twelfth grade. Its student population was 80% white, 3% Black, 8% Latino, and 7% Asian. In the same year, the Plainfield Public School District served 9,363 students, pre-K through twelfth grade. Its student population was 9% white, 40% Black, 45% Latino, and 1% Asian. Westfield spends a generous $19,839 annually per pupil, and the source of 83% of its total revenue is local, from the town of Westfield, while only 16% comes from the state and 1% from the federal government. Plainfield spends $21,928 per student, but 81% of its total revenue comes from the state and 5% from the federal government. The remaining 14% comes from Plainfield.[17]

In contrast to both Westfield and Plainfield, Wake County Public Schools serves nearly 162,000 K-12 students, 44.5% of whom are white, 22.4% Black, 18.6% Latino, and 10.4% Asian.[18] Wake's per pupil expenditure is $9,670, not even half what is spent in these New Jersey towns; 61% of Wake's revenue comes from the state, 32% from local sources, and 7% from the federal government.[19] Districtwide, just under 30% of students qualify for the free and reduced-price lunch program.[20]

There are periodic demands to break up the WCPSS into multiple smaller districts. This desire is not surprising for at least two related reasons: (1) Wake County is one of the fastest growing counties in the United States, which has created understandable challenges for the school system, and (2) a significant number of people who have moved to Wake County in recent decades are relocating from other states, including northeastern states like New Jersey, New York, and Pennsylvania, where the structure of school districts is not centralized.[21] To date, Wake County resists those demands, citing both pragmatic and moral reasons: economies of scale create efficiencies and savings, and a single countywide system enables the opportunity for meaningful integration.

Case Studies of Wake County Schools

The Wake County Public School System (WCPSS) has provided a rich case study for social scientists and journalists alike, given its complex history and prominent role in seeking a pathway to racial and socioeconomic integration. Studies over the past twenty years have described some of that history and analyzed key policy decisions and their impact.

For example, a chapter by education reporter Todd Silberman in the Century Foundation's report *Divided We Fail: Coming Together through Public School Choice* (2002) describes the key student assignment policy decisions in Wake County since the merger of city and county school systems in 1976. He includes the late 1970s policy to balance schools by race (no more than 45%

minority and no less than 15% minority in each school at a time when the county's overall enrollment was approximately 70% white and 30% Black), the opening of the first magnet schools in the early 1980s to encourage voluntary integration, and the decision in 2000 to use socioeconomic status rather than race as a factor in student assignment.[22] Silberman also provides crucial context for the challenges facing the school system at the turn of the millennium, including explosive population growth during the 1990s, a decade that saw a 48% increase in Wake County's total population and dramatic shifts in demographics in some of its smaller towns. For example, Holly Springs grew nearly tenfold and shifted from 78% Black to 77% white. Apex grew fourfold and shifted from 90% Black to 7.5% Black. Significantly, he points out signs of trouble, such as white families choosing majority-white environments where available (e.g., year-round schools when first introduced), affluent families leaving a school (Joyner Elementary) when more poor children were assigned to it, families in Apex protesting the assignment of their own children to poorer schools, and affluent neighborhoods in the western part of the county demanding the construction of new schools in lieu of commuting to downtown magnets.

Sociologist Gerald Grant's *Hope and Despair in the American City: Why There Are No Bad Schools in Raleigh* (2009) tells a dramatic tale of two cities: his hometown of Syracuse, New York, and Raleigh, North Carolina. Compared to Syracuse, which is held up as the emblematic northern city that never integrated across city and suburb district lines thanks to the 1974 U.S. Supreme Court decision in *Milliken v. Bradley*, Raleigh is presented as a remarkable success and beacon of hope. Grant's primary evidence for the success of Wake County schools is gathered from the 2000s, when the district fully committed to a goal of having 95% of all K-8 students achieving at or above grade level by 2003. With the collective effort of teachers, principals, and community members, the number of third graders passing the state's math and reading tests rose from 71% in 1994 to 91% by 2003. Notably, the percentage of Black children in grades 3–8 who were passing the state math test rose from 57% to 81%. The scores of white students also rose, while the gap between white and Black students shrank from 37 to 17 points. Similarly, the gap between Latino and white students narrowed from 28 to 11 points.[23] In striking contrast to Wake County, only 25% of eighth graders in Syracuse passed state achievement tests in reading and math in 2003, while an affluent suburb of Syracuse boasted 84% passing.[24] Lest anyone be tempted to dismiss the difference between Syracuse and Wake County as attributable to easier tests in Wake and lower standards in the South, Grant is quick to point out how well Wake County students did on national tests such as the SAT.

Grant's book was published on the eve of the 2009 election, and although he was cognizant of some parent discontent and the challenges of a growing population, he was hopeful that "those with grievances" would use their voice in the democratic forum rather than exiting for greener suburban pastures as so many white families in Syracuse had done.[25] He writes, "The protesters turned out to be a small vocal minority, but their letters to the Raleigh *News & Observer* and the responses of those who disagreed proved that democracy was alive and well in Wake County, NC."[26]

Toby Parcel and Andrew Taylor's 2015 book, *The End of Consensus: Diversity, Neighborhoods, and the Politics of Public School Assignments*, picks up the story where Grant left off and presents an alternate point of view, focusing on the watershed 2009 election, its causes, and the immediate aftermath. Like Grant, these authors employ social capital theory to frame and interpret their findings. But where Grant focuses on the benefits of sharing of educational resources and opportunities across city and suburb district lines, Parcel and Taylor use social capital theory to describe what was lost to students and their families in Wake County during the years of frequent student reassignment—lost connections to peers and teachers, lost investments in a specific school community, reduced or impeded parental involvement in schools.[27] Student reassignments were largely triggered by population growth and the need to fill newly constructed schools, but they were also governed by the diversity policy and the goal of maintaining balanced or "healthy" schools across the entire district. In Parcel and Taylor's reporting, typically no more than 5 percent of students in a given year were reassigned, but the policy nevertheless created uncertainty, anxiety, and resentment among some parents.[28]

Parcel and Taylor's book offers a nuanced account of attitudes toward Wake's school assignment policies and a closer look at the political landscape that led to the Republican takeover of the school board. Notably, their research complicates the assumption that support for neighborhood schools and support for diversity were mutually exclusive. On the contrary, rather than being polarized positions, these attitudes overlapped. Their survey data showed that "many individuals favored neighborhood schools, but a subset of them were also strongly committed to diversity."[29] Their survey also illuminated that attitudes were not monolithic within racial groups. Socioeconomic class—and "reserves of social capital"—played an important role in how easily a family could weather the disruption of reassignment or travel to a more distant school, for example, and correlated with more or less critical attitudes toward the district's policies. Among their findings, the authors note: "Affluent African American residents with large reserves of social capital were [diversity's] most vocal supporters. Poorer African Americans who lived in central Raleigh were considerably more ambivalent. It was children in their neighborhoods who were often bused long distances in the policy's implementation."[30]

Significantly, according to the authors, neighborhood schools garnered more support from people with burdensome work and family demands, including those with longer household work hours and single-headed households.[31] Criticisms of the district's policies were also understandably stronger among parents whose children were assigned to different calendar tracks; for example, one child assigned to a school with a year-round calendar and another child in the same family assigned to a school with a traditional calendar with summers off.

One of Parcel and Taylor's key conclusions is that a student assignment policy incorporating both diversity and stability would be likely to garner the greatest public support. Indeed, the work of the school board since 2011 reflects this more tempered approach. The authors also affirmed Wake's historic uniqueness: "Alone among large districts across the nation in persisting with a diversity policy as a central feature."[32] Wake's diverse population and "robust civic life," in their analysis, have supported a "broadly participatory" and "vibrant public debate about and political competition over public school policies."[33]

Education policy scholar Sheneka Williams uses Wake County as one of three case studies in "The Politics of Maintaining Balanced Schools: An Examination of Three Districts," in *The Future of School Integration: Socioeconomic Diversity as an Education Reform Strategy* (2012). Like almost everyone who has written about Wake County's recent history, Williams notes the significant impact of newcomers to the area. One of her main recommendations is as follows: "Districts need to constantly communicate to members of the public about the rationale for socioeconomic school integration policies," especially when districts experience growth, because the audience for the message is always changing. "It cannot be assumed that parents are long-time residents who know the history of and the rationale for diversity policies."[34] She also concludes that "choice" is more politically sustainable than compulsory reassignment, and that a community's political will to support integration can be strengthened through intelligently designed policies.

Many education policy scholars have examined Wake County's student assignment policies in great depth, using empirical data to measure the success of the socioeconomic-based school integration policy in achieving racial desegregation.[35] Their core research question, which the case of Wake helps them articulate, is simply this: Do socioeconomic-based plans work as well as race-based plans in desegregating a school district? Some studies additionally seek to measure whether Wake's socioeconomic-based assignment policy improved student achievement, although there has been less research on this specific question.[36] Perhaps the most comprehensive study to date compares Wake County's socioeconomic-based assignment policy to a purely residence-based assignment policy—a "counterfactual" reality created with data to simulate what students would have experienced in the 2000s in the absence of the diversity policy. The authors of this study, published in February 2020, conclude on the basis of a comprehensive statistical analysis that the assignment policy employed throughout the 2000s "substantially reduced racial segregation for students who would have attended majority-minority schools under a residence-based assignment policy."[37]

In other words, without the diversity policy in place during the 2000s, public schools in the center of Raleigh would have looked a lot more like urban districts around the country: intensely segregated by race.[38] Significantly, they also found that for the typical Wake County student, not much would have changed with a purely residence-based assignment. The policy worked in a targeted way to bring the most benefit to the most racially isolated students, in terms of both reducing their racial isolation and exposing them to more advantaged peers, while having the political benefit of having a negligible effect on most everyone else. The authors conclude that "political realities often result in broad-based policies bestowing educational benefits on advantaged student populations while doing little to change the schooling contexts of their less advantaged peers. WCPSS' school assignment policy arguably does just the opposite." Or it did until 2010. Astutely, the authors also note that "advantaged families wield disproportionate power in school district politics, and an assignment policy that resulted in the typical student's schooling context involuntarily diverging from their residential context would likely be unsustainable from a political standpoint."[39]

The sudden discontinuation of Wake County's diversity policy in 2010, the community reaction it triggered, and the policy decisions then faced by the newly elected board of education is the subject of "The End of a Diversity Policy? Wake County Public Schools and Student Assignment," an award-winning teaching case. The case is rich with empirical data and charts, as well as helpful historical background and a brief explanation of factors leading to the 2009 election.[40] It also tackles the question of values, beginning the conversation that I build upon in this book. The teaching case distills the essential conflict to a clash between the values of stability and diversity: "Throughout the spring and summer of 2010, the values of these two groups were pitted against one another. The key dispute was over which group's values were more important; it seemed to both sides that encompassing all of these values in the new assignment plan was impossible."[41] However, more helpful in conveying the complexity of the controversy and the diversity of interests is the appendix, containing a list and description of key stakeholders, as well as a list of Great Schools in Wake Coalition Partners—43 in total—a coalition that was a major force in the community's push to retain its commitment to integration.[42]

Finally, in addition to this brief sampling of secondary sources that analyze Wake County's school policies, it is important to note that the controversy drew national media attention, including articles in the *Washington Post* and the *New York Times*.[43] Even Stephen Colbert took notice, deriding the Republican school board in January 2011 for abolishing the diversity policy.[44] After briefly describing Wake County's efforts at racial and socioeconomic integration and noting that 94.5 percent of surveyed parents were satisfied with their children's school ("Clearly a tragic triumph of government intervention"), Colbert lampooned school board member John Tedesco by name, showing a clip of him at a Wake County Tea Party rally railing against the "social engineers and bureaucrats who wanted to for a generation control the hearts and minds of our children." With his characteristic sarcasm, Colbert retorted, "Sure, integrating schools may sound benign, but what's the use of living in a gated community if my kids go to school and get poor all over them?"

Locally, the *News & Observer* in those years was saturated with daily coverage of the Wake County school board and its antics. An additional side conversation took place through the WakeEd blog, an online platform run by the *N&O* where news items would be posted by education reporter T. Keung Hui and a deluge of often heated and sometimes rancorous public comment would ensue. (The blog comments have not been saved in the archive.) Compelling as it is, Wake County's story is just one piece of a much bigger debate about public schools in the United States.

The Larger Landscape of Scholarship on School Integration in the United States

Sociologists, education policy experts, and others writing today about the well-being of America's public schools in the twenty-first century often focus on segregation or "re-segregation."[45] Many school districts across the United States are becoming more, rather than less, segregated. This trend has been driven by a multitude of factors, including key court decisions, the lifting of court-ordered integration plans, the voluntary "secession" of smaller, racially homogeneous school districts from larger racially mixed ones, and what is broadly referred to as "privatization," or the "school choice" movement, which includes the growth of charter schools and private school voucher programs.

The literature on this topic is vast and comes from a wide range of disciplinary perspectives. Broadly speaking, studies of the problem of school segregation tend to fall into the following categories:

- Statistical analyses of school demographics and segregation for a changing country that is becoming more multiracial and less white.[46]
- Legal analyses of significant court decisions, including the United States Supreme Court's 1954 decision *Brown v. Board of Education* and its legacy, the *Swann* and *Milliken* decisions of the 1970s, and the more recent *Parents Involved* decision in 2007, to name just a few.[47]
- Historical case studies of cities like Richmond, Charlotte, and Louisville, and states like North Carolina and Georgia, and how

they have handled school integration efforts over time, as well as the costs of integration for African American communities.[48] Broader historical analyses of government policies that fueled segregation, like redlining, and histories of white resistance to integration.[49]

- Sociological studies of educational inequality and related structural inequalities in American society.[50] Studies of student outcomes that assess the educational and long-term benefits of school integration, as well as the challenges of in-school segregation and tracking.[51]
- Economic and public policy studies of the impact of privatization on public schools, including the tendency of charter schools to increase self-segregation by both whites and Blacks.[52]
- Comprehensive journalistic accounts of segregation, most notably by *New York Times* reporter Nikole Hannah-Jones, in districts from New York City to Tuscaloosa, Alabama.[53]

Almost every scholar or journalist writing about public school segregation engages with or at least references *Brown v. Board of Education* to legitimate the value of integrated schools.[54] Most commonly, scholars seek to bolster the moral authority of *Brown*—in essence, the idea that separate cannot be equal—with quantifiable evidence demonstrating that integration works to create tangible academic and lifelong benefits for students who experience it. Few other than legal scholars and philosophers linger on the values discussion itself to probe the idea of equality more deeply or to interrogate why the older, disproven formulation of "separate but equal" still seems to hold so much allure.

This book frames the challenge to integrated schools in Wake County in terms of values. While it is informed by the prodigious literature referenced earlier, as an ethicist, I am interested in how some people think and reason about the value of integrated schools, and I see the example of Wake County as an especially intriguing case for understanding this conversation.[55] Alongside studies of education policy, this book offers instead a discussion of public moral arguments. This is not to say that opinion research is not plentiful. Many studies are based on large-scale surveys that ask people's opinions about public education and integration in the United States. Survey data has the benefit of being concrete and quantifiable, but it cannot tell the whole story. To get at what people think, it is useful to hear their own words.

One fascinating study by scholars affiliated with the Making Caring Common Project at the Harvard Graduate School of Education asks, "Do Parents Really Want School Integration?" Survey data say they do, at least in principle, but their actions say otherwise. When given more choice, white parents choose whiter schools, and schools become more segregated generally. Torres and Weissbourd used interviews and focus groups to try to find out what "beliefs and biases might be deterring advantaged, white parents from sending their children to integrated schools?"[56] Probing more deeply led to some interesting if not surprising revelations; for example, that it is "hard to bridge differences" in integrated schools, where "children become acutely aware of wealth differences," and that, at the end of the day, parents prioritize school quality more than they do integration. White parents, rather than investigating the full picture of a school's quality and whether it is truly a good fit for their child, tend to rely on simplistic school rating systems, the advice of people they know in their own social circle, and simply "the number of other white, advantaged parents at a school as an indicator of school quality."[57]

What I admire about this study is that it does not shy away from the ethical aims of its inquiry. It frankly implores white families to do better, to consider the reasons for integration more seriously, but crucially, it does not characterize this call as some kind of "service to low-income children and children of color."[58] On the contrary, this way of thinking, they explain, would mischaracterize integration. Instead, they embrace the following vision: "Integration is most accurately characterized as a collective act that is likely to benefit one's own children, other people's children, and the country as [a] whole."[59]

Although I encountered the Harvard study after I had concluded my own research, I take inspiration from its willingness to consider difficult questions and to explicitly share the authors' own normative commitments and considered judgments. The late Robert Bellah once explained that the researcher's task is always "to listen, to reflect, to respond"—with the goal of contributing to greater understanding.[60] The researcher, he argues, is not outside or above the society being studied. I was very much part of the community I study in this book, and my aims and methods are also "to listen, to reflect, to respond" to public moral arguments surrounding school integration.

Aims and Methods of This Project

A significant motivation behind this research is to understand why Wake County has maintained, however imperfectly, a commitment to school integration. Is this commitment likely to endure, or is change already under way, with Wake County falling in line with national trends? Because there is a widely shared perception at the national level that our country's commitment to integration is weak, it is important to ask whether the political will exists anywhere to commit to integrated public schools. Only through examining public moral arguments can this question be coherently answered—not through survey data but rather through seeking out and interpreting the richly textured moral themes and vocabulary used by diverse individuals. While data can tell an interesting story, it provides information about "what" people think but not much about the "why."

No studies that I have been able to find on Wake County have specifically held up public moral argumentation for deeper discussion and analysis, though more than one has noted Wake's robust civic life. My primary interest is to investigate the normative values that underlie this community's investment (however robust or not) in public school integration. The normative values of community members and leaders, although difficult to specify, are nonetheless significant driving forces in private choices and public policy decisions. Only through talking with people about their own choices and justifications can values be identified, including beliefs about the role public education should play in knitting together people of disparate backgrounds, in preparing them to be functioning citizens in a democracy, and in providing equality of opportunity for the next generation. Thus, a major focus of the research for this book involved conducting in-depth, individual interviews. Complementing in-person interviews was archival research of newspaper opinion pieces, as well as listening to recorded speeches from public meetings.

Over the course of 2018–2019, with a research grant from North Carolina State University and after obtaining institutional review board (IRB) approval, I interviewed twenty-two racially diverse individuals who were community leaders/activists or school leaders/elected officials in Wake County. Community leaders/activists included individuals who were previously and/or currently involved in the PTA (parent-teacher association) at the school or county levels, members of various WCPSS advisory committees, members of citizen-led advocacy groups, representatives of prominent think tanks based in Wake County, members/chairs of BACs (board advisory councils), and past school board candidates or campaign managers. School leaders/elected officials included current and former board of education members and a former school superintendent. Lasting approximately one hour, the interviews were audio-recorded and transcribed.

With the help of a research assistant, I also collected a set of 411 articles published in the *News & Observer* during the years 2009–2011. The focus here was on a moment when moral arguments about integration took center stage—sustained, explicit, public disagreements during the years of greatest controversy over the diversity policy. Only opinion articles were selected for content analysis, including letters to the editor, op-eds, and editorials. These articles were coded for themes and managed with the qualitative data analysis software NVivo. I also reviewed recorded speeches given at public meetings during the years 2009–2011, many of which I had personally attended. These recordings are still publicly available through the local news outlet WRAL's archive.

To identify subjects for the qualitative interviews, I started with people I knew and branched out through recommendations. I was able to reach well beyond my personal networks to interview individuals who held a variety of viewpoints on the issue of school integration and the policies of Wake County schools. The goal was to identify individuals who had direct involvement with the Wake County public schools in some way that brought them into the public conversation about the diversity policy specifically or school integration more generally, with a focus on the years 2009–2011 and attention to the years since.

The interviews were semi-structured.[61] I asked the same basic set of questions of everyone, but the interviews were conversational. I listened to the recorded interviews, corrected the transcriptions, and engaged in an initial round of open-ended coding. I then reread transcripts while grouping together similar codes and pulling out representative quotes, looking both for moral logics in how people understand the issue of school integration while also listening to how people "tell the story" of events that happened here. I made choices about what themes to highlight based on my interest in the philosophical question of integration as a value and the historical question of Wake County's uniqueness. I also drafted analytic memos as part of the process of reviewing the transcripts. I preserved the confidentiality of interviewees. However, for some interviewees who are public figures, I obtained their permission to identify them and give attribution for their quotes. I undertook the analysis with the explicit acknowledgment that to tell the story of a single school district in one southern state does not necessarily make for generalizable knowledge. The goal instead is for a rich, grounded, humanistic description of how one American community has negotiated and continues to negotiate the role and value of integrated public schools.

As a matter of transparency, I must be clear that my way into this research was personal. Sometime shortly after the first meeting of the new school board in December 2009, I found myself sitting in the basement of the Fairmont United Methodist Church in Raleigh. I am no stranger to church basements, having grown up in the United Methodist Church, but this was not my church and the people who gathered there were mostly not its parishioners. That first meeting at Fairmont was a remarkable conglomeration of highly concerned citizens, almost none of whom had ever met each other before. There were parents, activists, white and Black, many women and more than a few men. We had gathered—dozens of us—to try to organize some way to stop the dissolution of the diversity policy. Out of the cacophony of voices was a pervasive feeling of "all-hands-on-deck" in a moment of crisis. The solidarity that emerged sorted tasks naturally according to people's skills and strengths. There was no jockeying for "position," just a willingness on everyone's part to lend a hand to save something special. This group was the beginning of what would become Great Schools in Wake, a key group, or coalition of groups, that connected PTAs with the NAACP, faith-based groups, and many others in what would be a pitched battle to "save" diversity. My own involvement included speaking at school board meetings as a concerned parent and citizen, participating in private LISTSERV conversations of community members, writing a few letters to the editor and op-eds, and ultimately taking an approved leave from my university job for a year and a half to work for a new nonprofit organization called Public Schools First North Carolina.

As with most research and most researchers, there is no way for me to claim neutrality or disinterest and no pretense of being a detached outsider. However, in addition to the easily demonstrated claim that all research is infused with prior commitments and values, two additional points are worth making: (1) Many years have passed since my personal involvement, which gives me distance, perspective, and greater objectivity, and (2) it is inherent to my understanding of research as an ethicist that multiple points of view are necessary for a more accurate picture of reality. This is more than a stance of self-serving convenience, but part of a constructivist (rather than objectivist) approach to research that views data as "co-constructed" between researcher and research participants, and that assumes "observers' values, priorities, positions, and actions affect his or her views of data."[62] My project is an immersive, focused examination, or "close reading," informed by personal experience but with distance and hindsight. A benefit of my personal involvement was access to and credibility with interviewees; a liability is my own bias in favor of integration because of positive experiences with Wake schools under the diversity policy and my own personal values.

Recap of Rationale and Overview of Chapters

Why look at the public debate of one school district? To take an in-depth look at one community helps us to see democratic deliberation in action. If, as Bellah argues at the end of *The Good Society*, "democracy means paying attention," then there is value in paying attention to the articulation of ideas and their impact on the course of events.[63]

On one level, I am engaging in what some call "values clarification," only on a community-wide scale—to understand why we think what we do and how it relates to our history and self-understanding as a community. On another level, I am interested to compare this public debate to the most persuasive philosophical arguments that I have found that promote true societal integration as "imperative," or the best way forward for individuals to meet each other as equals. Because of these interests, I have listened for arguments that connect the value of integration to democratic ideals such as equality or equality of opportunity. However, as an ethicist, I am also listening for what other people value, including when their values differ from mine, and trying to understand their values in context. I recognize the limitations of this study, which is only a snapshot of an ongoing conversation.

The themes that emerged from my interviews and other textual analyses were grouped into three broad categories: core understandings of the purpose of public education; different perspectives on integration based on race, ethnicity, and personal experience with public education; and different perceptions of the community of Wake County and its history. These three categories inform all the remaining chapters.

More specifically, chapter 2 contains the content analysis of 411 opinion articles published in the *News & Observer* during the time frame of 2009–2011. Its primary aim is to describe the major themes in these opinions, including competing conceptions of equality, competing appraisals of "separate and equal," and differing ideas about whether to conceive of public education as an individual or a public good.

Chapter 3 features interviews conducted in 2018–2019 with twenty-two community members. These interviews delve more deeply into core understandings of public education and how these understandings are informed by race, class, and personal experience. Even while acknowledging shortcomings, defenders of past and present integration efforts expressed a commitment to the idea that diverse schools are stronger, healthier schools. More fundamentally, "defenders of the faith" expressed a belief in the radical equality of all children and their right to receive an education.

Chapter 4 situates the Wake County case within a broader historical context and asks what difference it makes for a community to understand its own history. I come to this question as a relative newcomer to the area myself—recognizing that it took time to learn about and appreciate the history of Wake County. This chapter reviews North Carolina's decidedly mixed record on racial equality and school integration in order to contextualize why some members of the public found the school board's disinterest in the state's segregationist past so irresponsible. This chapter describes how school choice and privatization have evolved in more recent years and explores whether an embrace of individual choice has recapitulated "separate and equal" under the guise of race-neutral "color blindness."

Chapter 5 summarizes and responds to competing "moral logics" that circulated in the public debate, with the goal of bringing underlying values into the open for discussion. Individualism and pragmatism were prevalent, but so was civic idealism, I argue, which involved genuine openness to the benefits of true integration. This civic idealism was an important aspect of the Wake debate, setting it apart and setting an example.

Throughout the book, I look for signs that the will still exists to support integrated schools, knowing that what happened in Wake County in 2009–2011 was "remarkable": energized citizens pushed for neighborhood schools and then equally energized citizens pushed back successfully in the name of diversity.[64] Parents seeking stability for their children's school assignments clashed with parents and community members invested in imperfect gains and the idea of diversity, creating the space for a rich, complicated, and ongoing debate.

2

Contested Values in Wake's Debate

Published Opinions, 2009–2011

Public education in the United States carries the weight of many deep philosophical disagreements. It is a container for disputed understandings of our national identity and character, and it mirrors who has power and privilege.[1] It is the embodiment of very personal aspirations for our own children and collective aspirations about the strength, health, and fairness of our democracy. Not uncommonly, communities across the United States erupt in controversy over their public schools.[2] Thus, paying attention to these controversies can be quite illuminating. What are the conflicting ideas that underlie hours of angry public comments when parents fill a school auditorium?[3] Whose interests are being served by school policies, by decisions about where boundary lines are drawn, how students are assigned to schools, or which curricula are taught?[4] What do we learn about ourselves when we listen more carefully to the quieter voices as well as the ones commanding our attention?

A Larger Context for the Conversation

Throughout most of the country, the ideology of private property frames how people understand access to public education. Families expect the public schools their children attend to be tied to their address, whether they own or rent their home.[5] Real estate listings include the district elementary, middle, and high schools zoned for the property—and homeowners take issue when those connections cannot be relied upon or guaranteed.[6] Beyond this common expectation for how school access is determined, the ideology of private property is a common framework for understanding what public education is and why it has value. Like the ownership of a house, public education is seen as a commodity to be purchased and possessed. It can signal status or exclusivity. It can confer opportunity. This framework for understanding access to a particular public school as more like a private possession, something that can be purchased and linked to one's personal wealth, has profound implications. Arguably, it subverts the meaning of *public* education. It also directly affects the issue of school integration. Nevertheless, this framework for understanding access to public education is usually taken as a given without any deeper discussion of its merits. "If I can afford to buy into an affluent neighborhood, I deserve access to better schools," the thinking goes. This is the normative landscape assumed by many Americans, a landscape they assume to be settled and fixed, and upon which they go about living their lives.

Take, for example, the phenomenon of policing school boundaries. A 2012 news article described a school policy in Greenwich, Connecticut, that required parents or guardians registering their children for school to present a notarized affidavit testifying to their address. If parents lied about being residents of Greenwich, a town just over the border from New York State, they could be criminally prosecuted. Why such a punitive approach by the Greenwich Public Schools, serving not quite nine thousand students at the time? According to school administrators, "Taxpayers are increasingly vigilant about how their dollars are spent... unwilling to pay for students whose families may be tricking the system to get a better education."[7] There were sixty-one investigations in a single year, each one tracking down the legitimacy of a student's residency, each one stemming from complaints by people (i.e., fellow parents) who suspected certain students did not belong, usually based on out-of-state license plates or other unspoken reasons—although school officials said "they were being careful not to single out minority students for scrutiny." Superintendent William McKersie described his moral obligations thus: "We have a fiduciary responsibility to the taxpayers of Greenwich to ensure that the students attending Greenwich Public Schools are in fact legitimate residents of Greenwich." Kristen Laczkowski, a parent who camped out in the school parking lot and took notes on license plates of cars coming and going, stated her logic plainly: "If I pay property taxes in Greenwich, then I am entitled to the perks of being in Greenwich.... If you belong to this neighborhood, you belong to this school," she said. "If you don't belong to this neighborhood, you shouldn't be in the school."[8]

In 2016, New York City Mayor Bill de Blasio, embroiled in his own controversies about New York City's segregated public schools, was asked why the city did not redraw some of its school attendance lines to encourage integration. He framed his response in terms of property rights, specifically the property rights of affluent parents who buy into certain neighborhoods with the expectation that their purchase entitles them to high quality (perceived as heavily white) schools: "You have to also respect families who have made a decision to live in a certain area," he said, "because families have made massive life decisions and investments because of which school their kid would go to."[9] Beyond expressing sympathy for the homeowners, the mayor suggested he was powerless to correct the problem of school segregation because it was tied tightly to housing segregation, which itself is the legacy of decades of discriminatory policies. "This is the history of America," he said.[10] Whether the tight connection between school access and property ownership is morally legitimate, or whether property rights deserve presumptive priority, was not up for debate.

Passively accepting the claim that housing segregation ineluctably determines school segregation, much the way topography determines where cities are built, is nothing new. Most famously in 1974, the U.S. Supreme Court in *Milliken v. Bradley* missed a crucial opportunity to acknowledge and address the consequences of decades of discriminatory housing policies—man-made government policies, not the natural landscape, that fostered racially segregated neighborhoods across the country. Specifically, the Court missed the opportunity to acknowledge that de facto segregation in the city of Detroit, Michigan, and its surrounding suburbs was not merely the innocent result of people choosing where they wanted to live based on their own individual and freely chosen preferences but rather the direct and predictable result of government policies that gave home loans and homeowners insurance to white families, subsidized the growth of suburbs for white families, and enabled the accumulation of wealth for white families.[11] If the Supreme Court had decided in *Milliken* that de facto segregation (i.e., segregation in fact, segregation that exists but results from multiple causes) were indistinguishable legally from de jure segregation (i.e., segregation in law, segregation that is the direct result of a law requiring it), then cross-district busing would have been allowed, enabling substantial school integration between city and suburb. Instead, by only targeting de jure segregation as warranting correction, as it had done in *Brown v. Board of Education* in 1954, the Court created a situation in which only those states that had legally sanctioned segregation—that is, southern states during Jim Crow—were ever required to make a change and face their segregation problem. By turning a blind eye to de facto segregation and all its causes (such as redlining), the Court allowed many school districts, but especially northern school districts, to be essentially let off the hook from having to deal with the problem.[12]

The American tendency to conceptualize public education as more like a private good, a positional good whose value depends on its exclusivity, has meant that we tolerate enormous levels of inequality of access, resources, and quality.[13] This tendency is even more pronounced in our approach to private school education, where the freedom of wealthy individuals to buy advantages for their offspring is on full and unapologetic display.[14] The difference between our approaches to private and public school education is perhaps more a matter of degree than kind. Similarly, a deep respect for the freedom of private choices lies behind the legal legacy of viewing de facto segregation as beyond the purview of government correction—that, plus deeply embedded structures of white supremacy. Given this backdrop, given these particular American priorities and tendencies, it was remarkable that Wake County, North Carolina, was having a different kind of conversation about its public schools when controversy over its student assignment policy erupted after its school board election in 2009. The path Wake County took to get to that moment in time looks very different from the histories of Greenwich, New York City, Detroit, Syracuse, and many other American school districts, both in the North and South. It is a story that deserves its own telling and will be the focus of chapter 4.

What was remarkable is simply this: By virtue of having a countywide system, Wake County public schools challenged and destabilized one of the most basic (one might even say sacred) understandings of public school access in America—that you go to school in your neighborhood, and that the better the neighborhood, the better the school. Even though the vast majority of students in Wake County attended then and still attend the school closest to their home, the assignment policies of the first decade of the 2000s disrupted the assumption that the connection between neighborhood and school was automatic. There were magnet schools, for example, that drew students from across the county to voluntarily attend a school farther from home. And there was the nonvoluntary assignment of some students from low-income neighborhoods to higher-income neighborhood schools farther away—what opponents referred to as "forced busing"—in order to maintain a system of schools where none was overwhelmed by poverty. There was also nonvoluntary reassignment of a small percentage of students each year to help fill newly built schools and to maintain, again, a system of schools where none was overwhelmed by poverty and all had a fighting chance of being good. Setting aside the minutiae of the assignment policies themselves, which involved comparing demographic data (specifically family income) and student achievement data between "nodes," a unit of measurement smaller than a neighborhood, the important point is that the tight connection between property ownership and school access had been loosened. Also, and perhaps even more significantly, integral to the school system's approach was an intentionality about its goals: efficiency, integration, and excellence.[15]

Simply put, policies had been devised with the good of the whole in mind, and "the whole" had been defined capaciously enough to include affluent, middle-class, and poor neighborhoods, old-time residents and newcomers, suburbs and city, and all resident racial and ethnic groups. It was an example of social purpose politics in action: people subsuming narrow self-interest into a larger vision for the good of the community.[16] It was also what philosophers call a communitarian vision and something that might have seemed utterly strange to a person unfamiliar with it or steeped in a different ethos. The vision had its shortcomings, as all visions do when translated into reality. Nevertheless, the terms of the debate when controversy erupted were already on a different terrain.

The Public Debate in Wake (2009–2011)

We were shocked by the torrent of negative feedback about reassignments on various Triangle message boards. . . . There is even a book on Amazon.com called "Wake County's Big Secret" that details the effects of this diversity policy. The message is clear to any prospective transplant: The Triangle is great, just be sure to avoid Wake County schools at all costs.[17]

This letter to the editor appeared in our local newspaper, the *News & Observer*, in January 2009, many months before the October election that ushered in the new Republican majority. I confess I was not paying attention. Apparently neither were many other people who might have disagreed with the sentiments expressed by the letter writers. For that reason, the "pro-diversity" school board candidates did not carry the day in what was a low-turnout municipal election. The winning school board candidates each garnered about four to six thousand total votes, out of 482,580 registered voters.[18] Soon enough, however, it was clear that the residents of Wake County—at least the ones who took an interest in the public schools—were ready for an energized debate connected to real-life decisions. By energized debate, I do not mean the siloed sounding-off on the internet of individuals unknown to each other, now commonplace on social media—although that happened too.[19] Instead, the "main stage" debate took the form of month after month of letters to the editor, op-eds, and editorials. On more than a few occasions, school-related letters and op-eds dominated the opinion pages of the *N&O* to the exclusion of other topics, and it was not uncommon for an editorial or op-ed to draw a response or several responses a few days later from letter writers who disagreed with the original article, creating the back and forth of a debate, even though it was not instantaneous.

A parallel debate took place on the *News & Observer*'s WakeEd blog, an online platform maintained by education reporter Keung Hui. News items were posted there several times per week, raw meat added to a shark tank, and readers would respond both to the news item and to each other. Crucially, no one was required to use their real names while commenting. Most people opted for pseudonyms, like "Sideburns," though if they were frequent commenters, like Sideburns was, it was generally known who they were. Individuals' posts on the blog often echoed their speeches during public school board meetings, creating the impression of one continuous conversation. Anonymity permitted and arguably encouraged very personal attacks on the WakeEd blog. By contrast, the actual N&O opinion pages required that authors sign their own names to their letters and op-eds. The newspaper also upheld some standards: "We edit for brevity, clarity, accuracy, grammar and civility."[20]

In addition to the N&O and the online WakeEd blog, at least two other local newspapers were covering the controversy in Wake County at the time: The Indy, a weekly progressive independent newspaper published in Durham, and The Carolinian, "North Carolina's Twice-Weekly African-American Newspaper," published in Raleigh. Bob Geary covered the Wake County schools saga for The Indy, as did Cash Michaels, "the Triangle's foremost black journalist," for The Carolinian.[21] These two journalists did important work reporting on the story as it developed. But neither of their publications hosted the range or sheer quantity of letters and opinions that were published by the N&O, a daily newspaper with a larger circulation.[22]

Beyond printed and online outlets, individual opinions were also voiced during the in-person public comment period of school board meetings, which could last for hours. Overwhelmed by the public's response to the changes they were proposing, the new school board instituted a system by which individuals had to sign up in advance if they wanted to speak at meetings. They also had to sign up if they wanted to attend the board's work sessions. According to one community member, "I remember waiting outside for an hour and a half or two hours to get in. In the middle of the day. Again, the meeting was going to start at noon. You had to get there at 10:00 A.M. to line up. Tickets. Margiotta instituted tickets to get into school board meetings."[23] At first, ticketholders were not allowed to leave the building if they wanted to keep their seat or their opportunity to speak, although the board was pressured to drop this requirement. The line to speak sometimes stretched out into the hallway, and on at least one occasion, pizzas were ordered and delivered to those who were waiting.

What took place in the school board meetings was, in turn, commented upon in letters to the editor published in the N&O, such as when one parent complained during the public comment period that she did not want to send her child to "the ghetto" in order to access the benefits of the county's magnet schools, or when the actions of the board members themselves during the meeting drew criticism, or when a letter writer hoped to influence the actions of board members: "I hope the newly elected Wake County school board is reading the N&O, especially the Oct. 18 Point of View article from the Charlotte

PTA president who shared her dismay at the effects of resegregation in the Charlotte-Mecklenburg schools."[24] It is more than fair to describe the civic engagement as "robust," as Parcel and Taylor did in their 2015 book.[25] But the intensity and messiness of the debate went beyond any typical or predictable ideological stances. At the time, the content of what people were actually saying was already interesting to me as an ethicist.

Themes in the *News & Observer*–Published Opinions

My research for this project began with the realization, which occurred to me as the controversy was unfolding, that the opinions being expressed by members of the public warranted analysis. Wake County's size and cohesiveness as a single school district were significant factors in my decision to study it: small enough to constitute a focused conversation but large enough to encompass diverse ideas. Wake County also appeared to be a microcosm of important national controversies, and by some accounts, a test case for national political strategies.[26] However, it was not until 2018 that I set about trying to systematically study the content of the conversation. I decided to limit the scope of my initial examination to the period of time between January 1, 2009, and December 31, 2011: an arbitrary snapshot encompassing the buildup to the 2009 election, the ensuing two years of controversy, and the 2011 election. I also focused on the *News & Observer* because of the quantity and range of views published there, recognizing that this decision itself was a circumscription of the public debate. The *N&O* did not encompass every Wake County opinion, but it represented the closest thing to a centralized forum.

To find content previously published in the *News & Observer*, which is no longer freely available on the newspaper's own website, we (my research assistant and I) used NewsBank Inc.'s America's News archival software. Early on, we set aside any ambition of studying the WakeEd blog, as the reader comments were not saved in the America's News database. We also did not collect and analyze in a systematic way the many news articles that reported on the actions of the Wake County school board. There were simply too many. Instead, we focused on collecting opinion articles that pertained to the Wake County school board and issues related to student assignment, integration, diversity, busing, and the like. Opinion articles included letters to the editor, op-eds, and editorials. (See appendix A for a fuller description of the search process, including search terms and exclusion criteria.) Our goal was to collect a reasonably representative sample that was still a manageable size for content analysis. Mindful that we were drawing our sample from a regional newspaper that is perceived by some to have a liberal bias, we took pains to make sure we selected a range of views for our analysis.

The search process involved several rounds of collection and refinement, but eventually we arrived at a set of 411 distinct articles: 91 articles for 2009, 220 articles for 2010, and 100 articles for 2011. My research assistant and I independently read batches of articles and developed a list of codes based on common themes we were each seeing. We specifically read the articles with an eye for the values that were underlying individual arguments. What seemed to be the priority, principle, assumption, or belief that drove the author's main point? After much comparison and discussion, we arrived at the following codes, listed here alphabetically:

- Choice as a benefit: An explicit reference to the desirability of having options or choices between different kinds of schools (e.g., neighborhood school vs. magnet school, traditional public schools vs. charter schools, public vs. private schools, etc.).
- Community benefits: An explicit reference to tangible benefits (demonstrated or anticipated) to the entire community of having good schools, including things like attracting businesses, attracting new employees, tax revenues, property values, and so forth.
- Diversity as a value: Includes references to substantive benefits of having a diverse student population inside the school; diversity valued in and of itself; diversity as an aid to social cohesion; and diversity in the community.
- Equality as a value: Includes statements or judgments about equality or inequality, including references to "separate but equal" or explicit references to discriminatory housing, racial segregation, unequal resources, and poverty.
- Greater good: Includes references to the "common good" or religious language (e.g., love of neighbor); explicit reference to the value of what's good for the community as a whole, though not necessarily opposed to what's good for the individual; explicit idealism (e.g., responsibilities of citizenship).
- Pragmatic management: Includes references to planning for growth in the county, efficient use of resources, and good stewardship of resources, specifically pertaining to the management of the school system.
- Procedural fairness: Includes references to good governance, transparency, fair representation, and respect for rules, specifically pertaining to the school board.
- Self-interest: Includes explicit references to protecting and prioritizing the family's well-being and promoting the best interests of one's own child.

- Student performance: Includes references to academic achievement, outcomes related to test scores, long-term well-being of students, including later economic productivity, and mental health. May include student-centered references, but can also refer to things that lead to improved student performance, like stability in assignment and high-quality teachers.

We read each of the 411 articles and coded them at the sentence level. Unsurprisingly, individual articles frequently contained more than one code, as an author's arguments often articulated more than one important value. Sometimes, the same sentence embodied more than one value, in which case it was coded for both. We used NVivo 12 software to facilitate the coding process and to keep track of the distinct references, but it was never our intention to make quantitative analysis the goal of our work beyond simply noting the frequency of codes in the entire set of articles.

RANKING OF CODE FREQUENCY BY NUMBER OF ARTICLES:
1 Equality as a value—256 articles
2 Student performance—215 articles
3 Pragmatic management—186 articles
4 Procedural fairness—161 articles
5 Greater good—85 articles
6 Self-interest—75 articles
7 Community benefits—64 articles
8 Choice as a benefit—49 articles
9 Diversity as a value—39 articles

The process of coding the articles provided helpful perspective on the "big picture" of public opinion. Not everybody prioritized diversity, for example, but many people cared about student performance. The process of coding also enabled us to see the differences of opinion that existed within a single code— to see the variety of views about equality, for example, by reading all the references for that code and looking more carefully at what was being said.

Because the code "equality as a value" was very broad by design, encompassing both criticisms of inequality and positive mentions of equality, it applied to a great many things, including arguments about graduation rates, test scores, teacher quality, school funding, housing, poverty, busing, and more. Still, the fact that "equality as a value" was the most coded theme suggests that it was a central focal point of the public debate. Sixty-two percent of all articles mentioned it. Student performance was the code with the second highest frequency, with just over half of articles mentioning it. Notably, these two values often went hand in hand: someone whose argument was based on the importance of student achievement was often also basing their argument on their interpretation of equality. Thus, the most frequent individual reference overlap was between "equality as a value" and "student performance."

Competing Conceptions of Equality

Individual letter writers, op-ed authors, and the editorial staff of the *N&O* generally agreed that they wanted a public school system in which every child received an excellent education. "Our community must insist on equal educational opportunity," wrote one letter writer.[27] "And remember our main goal here: a good education for every student!" wrote another.[28] Rick Martinez, a contributing columnist for the *N&O* and consistent critic of the diversity policy, also agreed, despite some sarcasm: "In Wake County, just about every parent group, teacher (ahem) 'association,' civil rights group and liberal and conservative think tank supports the goal that every child should receive a high-quality education."[29] At the time, these statements may have seemed like easy platitudes. Who doesn't want a good education? But I believe they were significant for at least two reasons: (1) they suggested an openness to civic engagement, a willingness to look for some common cause that would bring opposing sides together into a common conversation, and (2) they acknowledged, whether implicitly or explicitly, that public education is a *public* good. Some constraints (or incentives) had emerged in the community's conversation that at the very least motivated people to frame their arguments with attention to every child. This is no small thing in a society that often views public education more like a private or individual good—where you can be criminally prosecuted for trying to get a better education for your child than you "deserve" based on where you are able to afford to live.[30] Whether this attention to every child was sincere or simply window dressing, I cannot say, but the conversation brought competing conceptions of fairness and equality into the open for consideration.

Beyond surface-level agreement, different visions of how to achieve an excellent public education for all students in Wake County—what equality ideally looks like—were sharply contested. Common conceptions of equality included equality of treatment (e.g., who gets into magnet schools, who is bused across town) and equality of outcome (e.g., good graduation rates, good test scores), though these conceptions were interpreted and applied differently. For example, in using equality of outcome as an ideal, the opposing camps marshaled conflicting sets of facts and conflicting interpretations of reality to support their arguments. The pro-diversity-assignment group argued "our outcomes will get worse if we abandon the diversity policy," while the anti-diversity-assignment group argued "our outcomes are currently terrible."[31]

In addition, opponents of the diversity policy used both equality of treatment and equality of outcome as justification for demanding change. By contrast, supporters of the diversity policy tended to focus on equality of outcome and rarely pushed for equality of treatment. They were more likely to frame their arguments in terms of equality of opportunity. This difference might reflect a fundamental disagreement about how different backgrounds should be fairly accounted for and addressed in the educational system. Equality of treatment seems to be based on the idea that all children should be treated the same. Equality of opportunity is willing to take steps to offset socially created or systemic disadvantages.

Arguments that take equality to mean treating people the same tended to frame student achievement as a universal goal that can and should transcend student assignment policies. Claude Pope Jr., chairman of the Wake County Republican Party at the time, described the goal of student achievement thus: "The new board's community school policy is designed to create schools focused on achievement, where parental and community involvement in our children's education becomes the norm rather than the exception and where one's color, nationality and economic background are irrelevant."[32] In asserting the irrelevance of color, nationality, and economic background, Pope deemphasized structural factors that disadvantage some kids and elevated the individual responsibility of insufficiently involved parents. He implied that dramatic differences between students' preparedness for school could simply be absorbed by a focus on "achievement" in the classroom. But the evidence from high-poverty schools shows the opposite: students' economic background has a significant impact on academic performance. Similarly, another letter writer described student achievement as a goal that transcends differences between students: "The desire to handle diversity in a way that is positive for all is not anti-diversity. It is pro-everyone. It is looking out for each student and providing a quality education for all."[33] When differences between students were acknowledged, the role of individual responsibility loomed large: "When students do not respect authority, do not care about how they should behave in school, do not want to learn and are not held responsible by their parents for poor results in school, we should not expect the schools to be able to educate them."[34] In this view, parents play the primary role in preparing a child to achieve—not schools, assignment policies, or social structures: "I've seen many struggle because they lack support at home—something that cannot be fixed by driving them across the school system to sit next to more privileged kids."[35]

Arguments that take equality to mean treating people the same also tended to take issue with the magnet program. Magnet schools were introduced in Wake County in 1982 for the purpose of encouraging voluntary integration and fully utilizing schools that were then experiencing declining enrollments. Schools in the center of Raleigh were "magnetized"—given special themes (like "academically gifted"), unique offerings (like orchestra or dance), and strong leadership to draw in affluent, white students from the suburbs.[36] Over time, magnets had grown increasingly desirable, supply had not kept up with demand, and access was increasingly perceived as unfair. Some parents wanted the special offerings at magnets to be available at all schools: "Provide magnet programs in all areas, [do] not provide magnet programs only in low income areas to bribe students to be bused there."[37] Others wanted equal access to existing magnets: "While every school inside Raleigh's Beltline is either a magnet and/or under 40 percent low income, high poverty schools outside the Beltline are largely ignored and the students assigned to them denied equal access to the academic opportunities in magnet schools."[38] And parents complained that the system was unfair: "In the current system, every student does not have an equal chance of getting into a magnet program."[39] Access was not, in fact, uniformly equal but was weighted to favor an outcome of socioeconomically balanced schools in all areas of the county—a county that was and still is struggling to keep all its schools well resourced. Rather than spurring non-magnet schools to "up their game" and keep their base population of students satisfied, magnets had stirred resentment and envy. Notably, it was a white family suing over being denied access to a magnet school in Charlotte that led to the demise of the pro-integration busing program in the Charlotte-Mecklenburg school district, causing that district to rapidly resegregate at the turn of the millennium.[40]

A very different conception of equality was just as prevalent in published letters and opinions in the N&O and found frequent articulation in columns written by editorial page editor Steve Ford.[41] This conception takes equality to mean treating people fairly, not necessarily the same. Fairness requires acknowledging morally relevant differences between people and taking steps when necessary to ensure a level playing field. Not everyone arrives at kindergarten equally ready to read, for example, as some have been able to attend high-quality preschools and others have not, so extra instruction may be required to assist the less well prepared. Equity rather than equality is the goal in this worldview, which sees individuals as both free and responsible for themselves and also shaped by the society into which they were born, including its systems of privilege and oppression. As explained by philosopher Elizabeth Anderson, "The proper negative aim of egalitarian justice is not to eliminate the impact of brute luck from human affairs, but to end oppression, which by definition is socially imposed. Its proper positive aim is not to ensure that everyone gets what they morally deserve, but to create a community in which people stand in relations of equality to others."[42] Many letter writers explored this question of where to draw the line between "brute luck" and socially created oppression (in their own words, of course), and asked more generally what we owe one another in order to provide equality of opportunity. For example, this parent questioned whether equal treatment can be achieved without taking account of socially created inequalities:

Public education in America is predicated on the belief that a good education for all is the best hope for our collective future. To the extent that all are given the same opportunity to learn, we live up to our ideal of equal treatment regardless of social and economic advantage. A kid from a poor neighborhood is entitled to the same public school educational opportunity as a kid from a rich neighborhood. But this raises questions: How far should our society go to ensure that people of varied backgrounds and economic means have the same opportunity? What are we willing to spend and how should our investment in school facilities, teachers and administrators be apportioned to give all students an equal shot at a decent future? If some students are advantaged outside the school system, should the school take that into consideration as it tries to give all the same educational opportunity?[43]

This parent did not have the answers himself, but he posed these important questions to the school board directly, imploring them to gather more information and use better analysis.

Steve Ford's many columns during the timespan of our study overtly defended this conception of equality as fairness and argued in favor of policies that leveled the playing field: "People simply can't be treated as if the bad luck of their impoverishment should be compounded by shortchanging them at the opportunity counter."[44] He disagreed strongly with the school board's decision to end the diversity policy in the spring of 2010: "It was a pungent irony that the board's climactic vote occurred a day after the anniversary of the 1954 Supreme Court ruling that outlawed segregated schools because of their inherent inequality. Even if resegregation is unintentional in the sense that it isn't enforced by law, it still could have a discriminatory effect in putting poor and Black students in schools where they would have diminished chances of success."[45] And he believed that high-poverty schools diminished opportunity: "As it happens, public school enrollments throughout the South are becoming more heavily poor, according to the Southern Education Foundation. In North Carolina, half of all students are regarded as low income, and 45.6 percent of students last year were black, Hispanic or other people of color. Poverty and ethnicity are sadly intertwined. And increasingly, Black students are concentrated in schools with largely Black enrollments."[46] By the fall of 2010, Ford expressed his concern about the rise of charter schools: "If better achievement for all students is the goal, as it must be, any approach that tends to separate students into schools for the well-off and schools for the less well-off cannot work. And if charter schools reinforce that pattern, they are not part of the solution but of the problem."[47]

Competing Facts, Unequal Outcomes

As mentioned above, part of the contentiousness about equality in the public debate was a function of opposing camps marshaling conflicting sets of facts and conflicting interpretations of reality to support their arguments. "You're entitled to your own opinion but you are not entitled to your own facts," the saying goes, but different facts were nevertheless used to support a variety of claims. A large body of social science evidence supports the claim that racially integrated schools improve student outcomes and narrow achievement gaps between students.[48] Indeed, as education reporter Nikole Hannah-Jones noted in a 2018 speech, "Nothing has closed that racial achievement gap like actually getting Black and white kids in the same classrooms together, and poor and wealthier kids in the same classrooms together."[49] She elaborated:

> Educators in this room know, sociologists in this room know, there's only been one thing that's ever worked on scale to close the racial achievement gap and to also bring about societal equality—or as close to it as we've gotten in this country for Black kids. But that is the one thing that is always automatically off the table. We'll give those schools more money. We'll break those schools up into four small high schools . . . We'll do all of these other reforms, but we can't speak the name of the one thing that works. And that is actually getting Black and white kids into the same classrooms together. Integration has been off the table, and we have to ask ourselves why.[50]

There is substantial evidence that high-poverty schools create acute challenges, like a high teacher turnover rate. Supporters of the diversity policy certainly had these facts on their side. But opponents of the diversity policy repeatedly pointed to lower graduation rates and test scores of minority students and inferred a causal connection between the diversity policy and these unequal outcomes in Wake County.[51] Even without definitive evidence, they used these outcomes as justification for abandoning the policy.[52] They also tried to claim that busing for diversity caused the lower academic achievement of those bused.[53]

Unimpressed with the results of Wake County's integration efforts, contributing columnist Rick Martinez returned again and again to the issue of graduation rates: "Diversity supporters, including the state NAACP, say the [diversity] policy is needed to keep Wake schools from racially resegregating, as if that were the most important issue facing minority students. . . . Unfortunately, Wake's diversity policy has become a major-league diversion from the foremost civil rights challenge confronting blacks and Hispanics— lagging student achievement. Diversity supporters may find it comforting that Wake schools are racially diverse. But they use that solace to shield them from the reality that the district's educational output is anything but equal."[54] Notwithstanding considerably worse outcomes in other urban districts around the country, it was hard to dispute that there was a problem with Wake's graduation rates, regardless of cause: "According to Wake County schools' own data published in October, the overall graduation rate for Black students fell from 69.9 percent in 2006 to 63.4 percent in 2009. For Hispanics, it dropped from 57.7 to 51.1 percent. For Black males, the graduation rate in 2009 was 57.4 percent, and it was a paltry 45.5 for Hispanic boys."[55]

Arguments from the editorial board of the N&O, scholars in the community, and other citizens were not enough to dissuade the school board from ultimately voting to abandon the diversity policy, but the prevalence of these voices in the public debate kept the evidence-based harms of resegregation front and center.[56] From an editorial in March 2010: "Yet even taken at their word that they have the best interests of all the county's students at heart—even those from poor families, many of whom are African-American—members of the board majority are setting the stage for a school system that is backsliding toward separate and unequal."[57] And from another editorial that same month: "Members of the Wake school board's conservative majority say the right things about wanting to improve academic outcomes for poor students, many of whom are African-American. But the momentous change they are poised to make today runs a high risk of just making matters worse."[58] From two local historians: "The old school assignment plan would not have ended poverty, but the new plan will surely make matters worse for the poor. Why? Because poor people lack the political power to demand their fair share of resources."[59] And from a parent: "If Wake County's schools are allowed to become as segregated as schools in most other cities, we can expect the graduation rate for our low-income students to drop as low as the rates in those cities."[60]

Separate and Unequal

Closely connected with the battle over competing facts was an ideological battle over "separate but equal." Some people had adopted the message of *Brown v. Board of Education*, which is that separate is inherently unequal: "In a country built on racial caste, separate cannot be made equal."[61] Others seemed to work from the discarded framework of *Plessy v. Ferguson*, believing that separate can be equal if everyone is provided with enough resources or as long as people choose it voluntarily. Whether people made these arguments in bad faith or believed that separate could be made equal was not always clear.

The frequent comparison of Wake County to the Charlotte-Mecklenburg school district was used to argue both sides: separate can and cannot be made equal. The dispute seemed to turn entirely on dueling sets of facts, as if there were no moral core to the requirements of equality, only a cost-benefit analysis with varying degrees of accuracy. Some said Charlotte-Mecklenburg was doing better than Wake on key measures, others said Wake was doing better than Charlotte-Mecklenburg, and still others said they were doing about the same, but Wake was arriving at similar outcomes while spending less. According to one news report comparing the two districts: "Instead of busing kids to balance out the level of low-income students at each school, the [Charlotte-Mecklenburg] district pours millions of dollars into these high-poverty schools each year to boost the performance of academically disadvantaged students. . . . Despite the different approaches, the academic results among minority and at-risk students are very similar in both districts, with only a narrow gap in test scores."[62]

Bob Luebke, senior policy analyst at the conservative Civitas Institute, interpreted the Charlotte-Mecklenburg example in a favorable light and used it to defend the board majority's move toward neighborhood schools: "That CMS minority students are bucking the conventional wisdom of those who oppose the current direction of Wake County schools is yet more evidence that demography is not destiny."[63] Continuing with the same theme later that year, Luebke wrote, "The success of many public, private and charter schools with large minority populations shatters the notion that academic success is tied to a school's racial composition. . . . A public school's No.1 goal is to educate students in an environment that values both the student and learning. Wake's diversity policy fails these goals. It sends an emphatic message that minority students can't learn or succeed without the help of others."[64]

The Reverend Dr. William J. Barber II, then serving as the president of the North Carolina chapter of the NAACP, and who rose to national prominence initially through his involvement in the Wake schools controversy, interpreted the risks of segregation very differently: "Diversity is the law, but more than that, the reality is that 'separate but equal' doesn't work. The current school board's policies will lead to resegregated schools, and with those, you get high teacher turnover, low teacher experience . . . and they're underfunded. Anywhere there is resegregation, we can show you that there is poverty, and experienced teachers don't want to be there. Segregation is against history, and it's against the law."[65] In fact, by the fall of 2010, a complaint had been filed before the U.S. Department of Education Office of Civil Rights (OCR), alleging that the Republican-controlled school board was in violation of Title VI of the Civil Rights Act of 1964: "Complainants seek remedies for intentionally discriminatory acts by the respondents which include making specific changes to the school system's student assignment policies with the intent to assign students to schools on the basis of their race, color and national origin, and to establish and maintain single-race schools."[66] The OCR complaint clearly arose out of fear that ending the diversity policy would lead to resegregation, which in turn would lead to exacerbated inequality—or what had been labeled "academic genocide" by Judge Howard E. Manning Jr., in reference to Charlotte's lowest-performing high schools just a few years prior.[67]

In addition to tangible harms, some noted the symbolic harm of embracing separate and equal: "Segregated schools were that symbol, the highest fence that divided people. It took a long time to tear it down and build a school system that would be the community's strongest symbol of progress. No wonder so many citizens are standing up for it."[68] It felt like moving backwards and forgetting history—a topic I will address at greater length in chapter 4. However, most people gravitated toward practical solutions and deemed the "separate but equal" debate to be ultimately intractable. From the executive director of the Wake County Democratic Party at the time, there was, again, a call to focus on student achievement: "We can all agree that we need a rational plan beyond politics that protects magnets, addresses costs and stability concerns, acknowledges the value of diversity, gets our focus back on student achievement and puts an end to this separate but equal circus."[69]

Whose Interests? Which Voices?

As we have seen, people had different takes on how to interpret or apply the value of equality. Most of the disagreement stayed at the level of facts and how to interpret them. Some of it was deeply rooted in ideological differences. But this was not an abstract philosophical debate waged on the merits of ideas alone. Arguments were also rooted in divergent perspectives and divergent experiences. Whose interests were being served? Which voices were gaining traction?

In the lead-up to the 2009 school board election, a news article by Kristin Collins, "Black Voices Quiet," noted that white parents were largely driving the conversation about the public schools: "With the election just days away, Black residents have had only a small voice in a noisy campaign season."[70] However, Collins investigated Black residents' concerns through several interviews: "Some Black parents say they fear voters don't know what's at stake. If busing is abolished, they envision a two-tiered system in which many minority children cluster in high-poverty schools, dropout rates soar and good teachers flee. Even middle class Black parents whose children are not bused for diversity are concerned."[71] After the election, Black parents spoke up at school board meetings and wrote letters to the editor: "If Tedesco wants to prove his devotion to Black women, he should protect our children. Preserve diversity. End high-poverty schools, don't make more of them. Help us address the achievement gap."[72] And activist groups like the NAACP and NC HEAT (Heroes Emerging Among Teens) continued to press their case to save the diversity policy, through legal channels, public speaking, and protests. But the fact that white parents dominated the debate sometimes raised questions about motive.

In our analysis of printed opinion pieces, the well-being of poor and minority students was used as justification by multiple interest groups. (For example, various groups claimed one or more of the following: poor and minority students are not graduating in sufficient numbers, poor and minority students are being bused farther than white students, poor and minority students perform better in healthy schools, poor and minority students need more funding.)

What did it mean that many of those claiming to advocate for poor and minority students did not hold those identity markers themselves? Notably, articles written by people who identified as Black or Hispanic, the two demographic groups most often cited for their lagging academic performance in WCPSS, offered a more pragmatic view: "we support whatever it takes for our students to succeed."[73] While Black activists certainly expressed fear about returning to segregation, their comments seemed to come from a place that recognizes that the benefits of integration do not derive from sitting next to a white kid per se, but because the presence of white students likely indicates an environment with more resources.[74]

White parents and activists traded frequent accusations of disingenuousness, claiming that each side was cynically using evidence to further their own self-interest, especially as the months of controversy wore on. The anti-diversity-assignment crowd was accused of wanting neighborhood schools with no poor children bused in; the pro-diversity-assignment crowd was accused of wanting to keep their "inside-the-Beltline" (central Raleigh) magnet schools to themselves. Sometimes these accusations were quite angry: "It is crystal clear to everyone now that the cries of 'keep diversity' from this crowd were never about helping others. Rather, these magnet parents and students just want to keep a good thing going. They feel entitlement to the academic riches at Enloe and will not let anything get in their way—even the education of those they've pretended to care about."[75] Sometimes letter writers defended their motives: "Ford painted the opposition as merely inconvenienced spoiled parents. That's convenient for his argument. I know many defying that definition who would provide interesting interviews."[76]

Perhaps the strangest and most common accusation was that through its efforts to achieve socioeconomically balanced or "healthy" schools throughout the district, the Wake County Public School System had been intentionally "hiding" its low-performing students to make itself look better.[77] Poor test scores were "diluted" or "masked" by moving low performers in with high performers. Students were "shuffled" between schools to keep up appearances. This letter hit all the points: "I've seen many struggle because they lack support at home—something that cannot be fixed by driving them across the school system to sit next to more privileged kids. Diluting their concentration in schools only masks their struggles. . . . The easy fix is to play a shell game shuffling low-performing kids around the district so they don't skew school achievement statistics."[78] There seemed to be a fixation with unmasking or revealing a con to get at the truth.[79] Supporters of the Republican school board members viewed their efforts as bringing much-needed honesty and directness to a shameful problem: "Instead of shuffling ED [economically disadvantaged] students around the county, the new board majority intends to provide excellence in education for all children."[80] Taken to its logical extreme, this line of reasoning seemed to suggest that the best way to deal with low-performing students was to put them all together in a low-performing school where their problems could get the direct and explicit attention needed. It was this idea, in fact, that earned the school board majority the searing mockery of Stephen Colbert on *The Colbert Report* in January of 2011.

Locally, plenty of people questioned the school board's claim that the system had been "hiding" students: "I don't understand this argument. Why hasn't the school board majority been challenged about this strange justification? My question is: Why do we need to isolate low-performing children in order to serve them? Why do we need to separate them out into low-performing schools? Why is going to school with everybody else referred to as 'hiding'?"[81] Some rejected it outright: "John Tedesco claims that economically disadvantaged students are hidden. This is utter nonsense. Under No Child Left Behind, the academic performance of many demographic groups is closely tracked and addressed at all schools."[82] And others continued to question motives and intentions: "John Tedesco's latest proposal seems a reaction to opponents: mean, because it ghetto-izes those already sequestered in marginalized areas; cynical, because it is proposed in the name of these very communities, as if conceived primarily to benefit them (as opposed to his political agenda)."[83] A less common but notable objection was to ask why school integration could not be better solved through integrated housing: "But why should we be dealing with the poverty effect on schools solely by shuffling kids around while we continue to allow grown-ups to get away with creating economically segregated enclaves—developments carved out whole for certain income groups, with apartments or duplexes relegated to other schools' districts. How are poorer groups ever going to fit into this style of development?"[84]

Overall, it must be underscored that there were a variety of views held by people with a variety of identity markers. Some saw their priorities for their own children as aligning with the priorities of the district, others did not. Some viewed the school board as genuinely attempting to do good, others saw quite the opposite.

Good Governance as Area of Agreement

In our analysis, one area of wide agreement centered on what we originally coded as "procedural fairness," but which is better described as "good governance." During a very divisive time, the school board antics seemed to give moderates something to agree on. There were a significant number of opinion articles focused solely on how the board conducted business, rather than the policy issues at hand.[85] Complaints were directed at rushed decisions, lack of professionalism, secrecy or lack of transparency, conflicts of interest (e.g., Ron

Margiotta was on the board at Thales Academy, a private school), insufficient analysis of data and evidence, and hyper-partisanship. For example, after Democrats swept all five contested seats in the 2011 election, the lame duck school board, with the cooperation of Superintendent Anthony Tata, moved ahead to instate a Choice Plan for the following school year rather than waiting to allow the newly elected board members to weigh in.

Individual or Public Good?

One final theme worth holding up is the tension between what we coded as "self-interest" on the one hand and "greater good" or "community benefits" on the other. This tension mirrors the tension between viewing public education as a private, individual good and viewing it as a public, shared good. Several writers echoed the communitarian vision that had been the hallmark of the Wake County system, including former school board member Tom Oxholm, who was clearly paying attention to the growing discontent leading up to the 2009 election.

> If you want every child to go to the closest school and have great teachers and a supportive parent group, you can have that in some of our community's schools. But you will also get just the opposite in many other parts of our county. The Board of Education is well aware of this tradeoff, as is the Wake County Board of Commissioners. For years the boards have chosen the path that was best for the whole community despite the complaints of parents who want what is best for their children. I hope they will continue to support what is best for the whole county.[86]

This tradeoff was not made to "keep up appearances" but rather as an effort to grapple with the tension that naturally exists between these questions: "What is best for each child? What is best for our community?" Oxholm recognized and understood that a parent's first obligation is to look after their own child's best interests. He also recognized that the obligations of the school system required its leaders to ask a little more from families, including some degree of inconvenience and disruption, for the sake of a greater good, which if accomplished successfully, would also redound to their individual benefit as well: "The goal is to have every school be healthy, which means that parents should be happy to have their children go there."[87]

Parents themselves grappled with this apparent conflict between individual self-interest and the common good. One of the parents interviewed for the article "Black Voices Quiet" gave her perspective: "With neighborhood schools, Evans said, her child would probably go to a good school where many students were white. But Evans said she worries about children in poorer neighborhoods, who might end up in failing schools similar to those in cities such as

Philadelphia and Baltimore. 'I just think it's very selfish and very shortsighted,' she said, 'to care only about your child.'"[88]

Some parents refused the frame of the common good altogether, or at least insisted that the individual good of student achievement was the sole responsibility of the school system. Allison Backhouse, a leader of the parent group that had helped elect the Republican majority and frequent letter writer to the N&O, made the case for a binary choice between education or diversity: "Wake Schools Community Alliance supports innovative solutions that get academic results. Clark says that WCPSS's diversity policy is not for diversity's sake. It is, however, not for education's sake, either. Isn't it time for our school system to make education the priority?"[89] She reiterated the point later that year: "Even the school system's diversity policy is being repackaged and sold to the public as a moral policy, an ethical policy and an economic policy—without mention of the policy's failure to increase student achievement."[90]

Others refused this characterization of student achievement and what they called a "false choice" between either student achievement or diversity. Amelia Lumpkin, herself a product of the Wake County schools, wrote: "I was dismayed to hear Superintendent Anthony Tata state that he refuses to trade student achievement for diversity, as though it were a choice. This is a false choice. Instead, a well-rounded achievement plan demands diversity."[91] Given the relentless focus on test scores, graduation rates, and other assessment data, voices that attempted to articulate some of the more intangible (or not immediately quantifiable) benefits of diversity had an uphill battle with an incredulous audience. Letter writers certainly mentioned the benefits of students learning from each other or preparing for a diverse world, but very rarely could a persuasive case be made on the basis of democratic equality—as someone like philosopher Elizabeth Anderson has described it—meaning placing students from disparate backgrounds into relations of equality with one another.[92] Such arguments could find no foothold when graduation rates were lagging. Also, and perhaps more importantly, most people were not readily able to see how white students would be harmed by predominantly white environments. The harms were always assumed to run in the other direction, from being excluded from predominantly white environments.

Yet there were some, including, reliably, columnist Steve Ford, who could articulate at least the value of social solidarity: "What [the Wake County school district] must avoid is a splintering into subcommunities neglectful of the fact that a chain is only as strong as its weakest link. Those who struggle to sustain hope and equal opportunity throughout Wake's schools aim to keep our citizens who already face the steepest odds from becoming the link that breaks, to the detriment of all."[93] In a community where people felt accountable to each other, that message resonated.

Conclusion

Our analysis of the public debate over the Wake County schools during the years 2009–2011 suggests a few tentative findings, to be explored further in chapter 3. First, as with national debates in the United States, most people found it easier to talk about the individual benefits as opposed to the social benefits of public education. (What besides student achievement matters?) Likewise, the struggle to define what is a matter of justice rather than a matter of misfortune was present here, just as it is nationally. (What is the scope of the school system's responsibility? What is a matter of private choice and what should be a matter of collective will?) And the tendency to think of education like a commodity to possess was just as prevalent too. (How can we see equality in relational terms as opposed to merely distributive terms or who gets access to valuable educational assets?)

And yet, the debate in Wake County was still remarkable for keeping the communitarian vision alive, for challenging individualistic arguments, and ultimately for electing a very different slate of candidates in the 2011 election, two tumultuous years after the 2009 "takeover." Despite considerable disagreements, Wake County residents managed to sustain an earnest and probing conversation about what it really means to provide an excellent education to every child. Although messy and often unsatisfying, the process of democratic deliberation flourished.

That the conversation was not confined by a "property rights" mentality is itself noteworthy. The robust pushback of numerous citizens and organizations who challenged the direction of the Republican school board changed the terms of the debate and enlarged it. At the same time, some might say that both pro- and anti-diversity crowds were making whatever argument they needed to make in the moment to preserve their own interests. Since white parents have a remarkable track record of looking out for their own interests above all others, this criticism must be taken seriously, even while it is not allowed to become a justification for abandoning imperfect efforts at integration.[94]

Many academic discussions of public education in the United States begin with a quote from philosopher John Dewey, but here I will conclude this chapter with his insights as a way of summarizing the most salient theme of our discussion: the relationship between the individual and the common good. Dewey's description of public education is as relevant now as it was in the early twentieth century.

> We are apt to look at the school from an individualistic standpoint, as something between teacher and pupil, or between teacher and parent. That which interests us most is naturally the progress made by the individual child of our acquaintance, his normal physical development, his advance in ability to read,

write, and figure, his growth in the knowledge of geography and history, improvement in manners, habits of promptness, order, and industry—it is from such standards as these that we judge the work of the school. And rightly so. Yet the range of the outlook needs to be enlarged. What the best and wisest parent wants for his own child, that must the community want for all of its children. Any other ideal for our schools is narrow and unlovely; acted upon, it destroys our democracy. All that society has accomplished for itself is put, through the agency of the school, at the disposal of its future members. All its better thoughts of itself it hopes to realize through the new possibilities thus opened to its future self. Here individualism and socialism are at one. Only by being true to the full growth of all the individuals who make it up, can society by any chance be true to itself.[95]

Dewey understood that what we most easily see and what we can more easily measure are the individual benefits of education—usually for our own children. Yet, he was attempting to persuade his audience to keep in mind the broader social goods as equally important. A society can be only as healthy and successful as "all the individuals who make it up." To think of education as a positional good in a zero-sum game would mean certain children would be shortchanged. And then, as Nikole Hannah-Jones has pointedly asked, "Whose children do we sacrifice?" Such an individualistic approach would be self-defeating in the long run as it undermines the overall health of society, a shared loss for everyone.

3

Defenders of the Faith

Community Leaders Reflect
on Diversity a Decade Later

On a sunny day in late February 2019, when redbuds and other early blooms were signaling the beginning of spring in Raleigh, I met the Reverend Nancy E. Petty for an interview in her senior pastor's office of Pullen Memorial Baptist Church. Spacious with high ceilings and original built-in bookshelves and cabinetry painted white, the office was tidy, welcoming, and full of history, in the way of old buildings (especially churches) that have been maintained and loved but not significantly modernized. Founded originally in 1884 by John T. Pullen, the church moved to its current location on Hillsborough Street in 1923 and dedicated its new sanctuary in October 1950 at a service featuring a sermon by the renowned liberal preacher Harry Emerson Fosdick of Riverside Church, New York City.[1] Pullen remains one of the most progressive Christian churches in the country and is a standout in the South for its longstanding commitment to civil rights and LGBTQ activism. In 1992 its open acceptance of gay and lesbian Christians earned Pullen exclusion from the Southern Baptist Convention, the Baptist State Convention of North Carolina, and the Raleigh Baptist Association. But for decades prior, Pullen was already known as a "liberal" church for its public stances on race relations, organized labor, and other issues.

Notable former pastors in a long line of liberal and outspoken pastors stretching back to the Social Gospel Movement include J. A. Ellis, who led Pullen for a decade beginning in 1919, Edwin McNeill Poteat Jr., who served Pullen in two separate stints in the 1930s and 1940s, and William Wallace Finlator, who was Pullen's pastor from 1956 until his retirement in 1982. Poteat was a talented, much-admired preacher who drew in many nonmembers. He was also unafraid to challenge local norms at the time. In 1936, while serving as Pullen's pastor, Poteat sharply criticized the *News & Observer* for an editorial endorsing racial separation.[2] Among his many accomplishments, Poteat helped organize the North Carolina Council of Churches in the 1930s; served as president of Colgate-Rochester Divinity School in Rochester, New York, in the 1940s; served on the board of Shaw University in Raleigh; and was founder and president of Protestants and Other Americans United for Separation of Church and State.[3] For his part, William Wallace Finlator was already a public figure when he wrote a letter in 1955 to then Governor Luther Hodges urging him to embrace desegregation in the wake of the *Brown v. Board of Education* decision.[4] Finlator was a charter member of the ACLU and a strong defender of civil liberties, from within the Baptist dissenting tradition.[5] Finlator was senior pastor when Pullen adopted a new constitution in 1958, declaring itself open to all people regardless of race; when it joined the more progressive American Baptist Churches USA in 1967; and when it became part of a network of organizations called the Community of the Cross of Nails based at Coventry Cathedral in England in 1977.[6] The Community of the Cross of Nails' three guiding principles—"Healing the wounds of history, learning to live with difference and celebrate diversity, and building a culture of peace"—resonated well with Pullen's own enduring values.[7]

Thus, when Nancy Petty became senior co-pastor in 2002 and sole senior pastor in 2009, she inherited a liberal tradition of leadership that has come to seem increasingly rare in American Christianity, particularly among predominantly white Christian churches.[8] She has persisted in articulating a radically inclusive vision of Christianity committed to social justice, strongly defending marriage equality, for example, in the years before *Obergefell v. Hodges* legalized same-sex marriage in 2015. She was also deeply involved in the fight to maintain integrated public schools in Wake County, catching the attention of Rev. William Barber—not yet the national figure that he is today—with her January 2010 op-ed in the *News & Observer* about resegregation and being arrested more than once for civil disobedience later that summer. I had come to her office that springlike day in 2019 to talk with her about her experiences protesting the school board and her reflections on Wake County's present and future.

Her first arrest came in June 2010 after she and three other activists occupied the seats of the Board of Education members and refused to leave. She was protesting the board's decision to end the diversity policy and was joined by Reverend Barber, Duke University professor Tim Tyson, and Wake County parent Mary Williams. They had planned in advance of the meeting to give speeches during the public comment period. The last person to speak, Tim Tyson, would give a history lesson about segregation and deliberately go past his time limit, a brief two minutes. Petty recounted the events of that evening as follows:

> I think Mary spoke first, I spoke second, Rev. Barber spoke, and we just kept our time. We didn't go over. And then Tim got up there. Tim got up to speak, and they tried to cut him off. He was trying to give a history lesson. That was his role, [to] talk about the history . . . the whole busing language and the neighborhood schools. . . . Well, Tim kept going, the crowd got into it. The room was packed. School kids, parents, it was packed, down the hallway was packed. . . . Margiotta slinging that thing [the gavel] saying, "Time's up. Time's up!" And then everybody starts singing, and Tim's still going, and it's getting, you're getting that feeling. The intensity is just going up. And everybody knew something was getting ready to happen. At the time, I still didn't know what's going on, what was going to happen . . . but the intensity was so high, and Margiotta banged [the gavel]. . . . They got scared. It was that kind of feeling, you know, like something's going to go down here. And they were vulnerable. The school board, they were all sitting up there in those chairs. So Margiotta called for recess.

As the school board members filed out of the room for a recess, Petty, Barber, Tyson, and Williams moved to the front and took over the board members' high-backed swivel chairs. Now facing the cameras, they conducted a teach-in, which was live streamed on the local news station, WRAL. As they had anticipated and planned, they were arrested for their actions, but hoped it would bring greater attention to the dissolution of the diversity policy: "Our actions woke people up." Indeed, the community took notice, including business leaders who were eager to maintain Raleigh's reputation as a progressive, attractive place to live.[9]

I remembered the arrests. I also remembered that the four had written something akin to Martin Luther King Jr.'s "Letter from Birmingham Jail."[10] As I was asking her questions and she was recounting details, Petty went over to one of her built-in cabinets with its original turn-latch and pulled out a scrapbook. She had saved everything: newspaper clippings, her op-eds, the magistrate's order. After a subsequent arrest, they were banned from school property, at Margiotta's direction, which posed a difficulty for Petty and Williams, who still had children attending Wake County public schools. When they were no longer allowed to attend school board meetings, "then we just kept on holding rallies." These rallies were a tributary that fed into the Moral Monday Movement, led by Barber, which would be in full swing by the summer of 2013.[11]

As I sat with Petty and listened to her describe her experiences, I was struck by the idealism in her defense of integration and in her understanding of the core purpose of public education. It resonated with what many of my interviewees had shared, exemplifying some of the motives behind Wake County's efforts at integration. In some ways, her distinctively religious voice distilled this idealism to its essence.

> Before you do anything to discourage a child, stop and ask that question, "What would God see if God was standing here looking at that child?" God would see potential regardless of [whether] the kid can't read or add two plus two. God would see potential and find some way to lift up whatever gift that kid had inside of him or her. That's what education should be about. That is what education should be about, but it's not. It's about the fittest survive and get ahead.[12]

In other words, she described education not as a positional good, something that feeds individual competitive striving, but as a means to human flourishing. At the same time, even while holding up the positive potential of education and defending the importance of diversity in principle, she fully recognized that integration had come at a cost.

To illustrate, she told me the story of a man who had heard her speak about racism and education just the previous week on a local news program (WRAL's *On the Record*) and then contacted her by email to share his negative experience with integration. Petty hunted for his email on her computer and then read it aloud. The man had grown up in the Franklinton area, north of Raleigh, and had been enrolled in a white school against his will in the late 1960s. Even though his mother had signed "freedom of choice papers" for her son to remain at a "Negro school," their choice was not honored. "The feds" who visited his home in the summer of 1968 informed him: it was "white school or no school at all." When his mother asked to make a change, she was told "Negroes don't have any rights in America." The experience had a deep, lasting impact. He wrote the following in his email to Petty:

> Attending white school was a nightmare. Only having soldiers on campus kept us alive. At home our cotton fields were burned. Kerosene was poured on our vegetable gardens, as well [as] poisoned woods near our house set on fire, and many other attacks. At school most teachers refused to teach us, putting us in detention. My college dreams ended as well as our farming. My mother and [my] names was printed in the newspaper [claiming] that mom and me insisted I be enrolled in white school, which was a lie. After that, we had trouble borrowing money. . . . Farm stores would no longer sell to us. I feel like it was a nightmare that never ended. Over the years I have asked feds, was it true Negroes have no rights in America? I have never got an answer.[13]

Petty was moved by this story, clearly pained by the losses this man had suffered, which caused her to reframe her support of integration in a more realistic light: "I'm up here saying integration's the right way. We got to integrate. Now that was 1968, but for that man, *integration ruined his life*, as he sees it. He wanted to stay in Negro school." She acknowledged that the white schools were unwelcoming and, more than that, they "didn't want to teach Black kids, so they just sent them to detention." She recognized that talking about integration is one thing, "but if the schools are not going to treat kids equally that's a whole other issue."[14]

Analysis of Interviews

Nancy Petty was one of twenty-two interviews that I conducted over the course of a year with the help of a grant from North Carolina State University in 2018–2019. I had a rapport with many of the people I interviewed because I had met them in the aftermath of the 2009 election—either through attending school board meetings or through my own volunteer efforts with Great Schools in Wake, the grassroots group that sprang up to fight for diverse schools. I knew Petty directly because I am a member of Pullen Church, although not a regular attendee. Notwithstanding years of personal immersion in the conversation about Wake County schools, I ventured beyond my networks while conducting my research to interview several people whom I did not know personally. These included former superintendent Bill McNeal (the superintendent who happened to be in charge of WCPSS when my oldest child began kindergarten in 2003), as well as current and former school board members and longtime community leaders. I also interviewed Republican activists and the founder of the conservative John Locke Foundation. Almost everyone I interviewed had had a child attending the Wake County schools at some point in time. However, my primary strategy was to seek out individuals with a variety of viewpoints who had been or were still actively engaged with the schools and the public debate about school integration. In other words, this was not a random sample of ordinary parents but a focused subset of community leaders and activists. (See appendix B for more information about my interviewees.)

We have seen the major themes of the public debate as it unfolded in the local press within the bounded timeframe of 2009–2011. In this chapter and the next, individual interviews are my main source for reflecting on what transpired in Wake County. Some of the people I interviewed have memories and direct involvement that stretch back for many decades and were therefore uniquely situated to offer a broad perspective on Wake County. Others were recently involved and well situated to speak about future directions. All my interviews were deeply interesting, and the substance of these interviews is woven into my discussion. However, I chose only a few individuals to spotlight and name. I received their permission to do so. The rest of my interviewees were promised anonymity, so I have withheld identifying details.

I asked the same set of questions of everyone I interviewed, but conversations were open-ended and tracked the interests and experiences of my interviewees. I made a point of asking broad questions about public education before getting into the specifics of Wake County's history and the issue of school integration. For example, I asked, "What are some of the qualities of public schools that are most important to you, and why? If you chose to send your child(ren) to Wake County public schools (as opposed to another alternative, such as private school or home school), what are some of the reasons why you made this choice?" These questions gave people a chance to articulate their values—what was important, what were their reasons—which provided a helpful context for their views on integration. To probe views on integration, I asked directly, "How important is it to have schools that are racially or socioeconomically diverse? What are your reasons?" (See appendix B for a complete list of my questions.)

By looking at the differences between my interviewees' core understandings of public education and integration, I highlight how these understandings can be informed by different perspectives based on race, class, and personal experience. To make the analysis more concrete, I discuss interviewees' recollections of the "golden age" of Wake County schools, when the diversity policy was perceived to be working well and achievement gaps were narrowing. I then consider responses to one specific criticism leveled against integrated schools—that they are often "two schools in one."

"Education Goes beyond the Books": What Is the Purpose of Public Education?

When asked to talk about why they value public education, most of my interviewees had a lot to say. Many had considered carefully their views on public education and had deeply held beliefs about its role in American society and our local community. For example, there was broad respect for the ideals of equality of opportunity, equality of access, and the ability of public education to provide social mobility. There was also full recognition that the United States falls far short of these ideals in many places and across many subgroups of students.[15] Still, people articulated what was important to them about public education based on what they believed ought to be the case.

For many, there was a mixture of idealism and pragmatism in their views: public education should ideally provide equality of opportunity, yes, but also preparation for the real world. Racially and socioeconomically diverse schools, it was felt by many, are best situated to accomplish this goal. Across all my interviews, everyone understood that public schools exist in order to provide an education to anyone who walks through their doors. In North Carolina, providing a sound basic education is, at least on paper, a constitutional duty.[16] But opinions diverged over whether the delivery of academic content can be conceptually or practically disconnected from the civic dimensions of public education—what Dewey held together as the individual and social goods of public schools. Opinions also diverged over how well public schools are now succeeding at any of the aims attributed to them.

In early 2019, I interviewed Yevonne Brannon, a community leader who has been working for decades to support public education in Wake County and North Carolina. Currently chair of Public Schools First North Carolina, a statewide nonprofit launched in 2013, she was a founding member of Great Schools in Wake in the aftermath of the 2009 election and a former Wake County commissioner from 1996 to 2000. Of all the people I interviewed, Brannon spoke the most directly about education as a human right, deeming it foundational in the same way that health is foundational. It is the good that underlies other goods. Without an education, she explained, very little else is possible: "Human and civil rights are connected around education and through education." Like many people I spoke with, her personal experiences—in this case as the child of parents who had not graduated from high school—colored her perception.

> I had the right to be taught to read, to write, to think, to be able to have a door opened to participating in democracy. So that I could learn a trade, I could learn how to negotiate in the world, I could get a loan, I could get a driver's license. I could get an opportunity to participate. To vote. Education is it. We know how directly correlated your education is to everything in your life, including the length of your life and your health. It is everything. Maybe it is valued more by people who feel the urgency of that, than those who take it for granted. I don't know. I felt the urgency of knowing that my parents had not graduated from high school. The urgency of knowing that nobody in my family had been to college.[17]

She described public education as the key to opportunity, pointing out that schools can do more than parents alone to broaden children's horizons, to provide what parents cannot, to make up for disadvantages. In these ways, schools are a pathway, at least in theory, for social mobility. But more fundamental than advancement in a hierarchy was basic participation in society and participation in democracy. She emphasized that public school must be equally open to everyone, a point echoed by several of my interviewees.

In fact, equal access was described by several people as *the* defining feature of public schools. "The most important values of public schools [are] that they accept everyone," said one parent activist.[18] To explain this foundational belief, she and other interviewees simply referenced "the blueberry story" without elaboration. The blueberry story, I have learned, is a parable of sorts that telegraphs the message that a school cannot or should not be run like a business. I am unsure of the true origins of the blueberry story, but the version in circulation explains that unlike a successful ice cream business, which uses only premium ingredients and rejects subpar blueberries, public schools must accept all children. According to the story, a teacher admonishes a businessman: "We can never send back our blueberries. We take them big, small, rich, poor, gifted, exceptional, abused, frightened, confident, homeless, rude, and brilliant. We take them with attention deficit hyperactivity disorder, junior rheumatoid arthritis, and English as their second language. We take them all. Every one. And that . . . is why it's not a business. It's school."[19] The profit motive finds no foothold in this view of education. Instead, a different motive undergirds the teacher's sense of duty: an implied commitment to the inherent, non-commodifiable value of all children and also, perhaps, an implied commitment to future generations and the shared responsibility of upholding human society.

Alongside these idealistic visions of public education, several people talked about the role that diverse public schools play in preparing children for the real world, particularly through exposure to difference. This benefit was almost always framed pragmatically, as an aspect of their child's preparation for adulthood that would more likely make them successful in life. Significantly, both white and nonwhite interviewees named this as a benefit. For example, an African American dad and community leader described diversity as an instrumental good, not merely an abstract good in itself: "Not just diversity for diversity's sake, but public schools prepare students for what the real world is like. The work world is the same. You're in a public space, a public company, you've got to collaborate with folks that you may know, may not know. Don't look like you, don't have anything in common with you, but you're here for a common goal or a common task."[20]

Similarly, an African American mom and community leader spoke of the benefits of diverse schools for her son: "It helped him to be more engaging and acceptable of people of different cultures, races, and backgrounds as opposed to being in an isolated, segregated environment where you don't have those kinds of kids. If you're exposed to diverse backgrounds and cultures at an early age, that better prepares you for [a] global society, which is what we're supposed to do."[21]

In addition to preparing students for a diverse work world in a global society, diverse schools also enable interracial friendships, which were deeply valued: "That type of friendship that's priceless. . . . Those kinds of opportunities and friendships that last a lifetime."[22] Or from another African American mom and activist: "If you're in an environment from early on, then you move with ease from one place to another. You have more of a richness in the friendships that you develop and appreciation of other people."[23] And from the dad quoted above: "Students get an appreciation for different cultures, different values. That in almost itself is a learning experience for students. . . . And they have friends from again, different communities, different neighborhoods, different nationalities or what have you."[24]

A white mom and activist likewise saw the value in diverse public schools and described the harmful consequences of avoiding diversity: "Unless you want to live in a bubble, and you can, maybe this is a harsh term, you can protect yourself from dealing with people who are unlike you in whatever way. You are heading *your* children on a path that actually will hamper their success. . . . There is so much value in understanding the other person's perspective."[25]

Building on this point, several people drew a contrast between private and public schools, describing the diversity of public schools as an asset that was not typically replicated in a private school setting. Words like "bubble," "silo," and "gated community" were used to describe white families separating themselves from the rest of society, such as in this quote from Nancy Petty: "And if you're white and going to an all-white school where . . . the family income's $250,000, and you're living in gated whatever-ville, [once] you get out of that, you're going to have a real hard time. I don't think those parents realize what a detriment that is to that child. You know, all at the expense of thinking, I want my child to have the best. And the best means only being with people like us."[26]

In the words of both white and Black interviewees, private schools were said to teach the "corrosive value" of exclusivity, and to foster homogeneity: "The folks who I know who go to some of the private distinguished schools, again, I just find it so homogeneous. . . . They're missing out on a lot."[27] Private schools were also described as inadequately preparing students for the real world: "And then you're quarantined off, so to speak, in this bubble, where you go and spend eight hours a day. And I'm sure they'd be catered to, but again you're in a bubble that's a select environment and everything is about you for that. And then you come back out and you're out here in the real world. Public school prepares you for that, as opposed to private school. So in that, you gain the benefits then of more diversity, I think increased opportunities for a deeper, a broader socialization with others."[28]

But not everyone I interviewed shared these valuations of diversity. For example, one person (white dad, Republican activist) said that diversity was important, but not as important as other things, like graduating on time with skills.[29] Another person (white mom, former school board candidate) raised the question of what counts as diversity, noting that schools in her part of Wake County were already diverse in terms of other factors, like ethnicity, religion, and life experience: "At Davis Drive Elementary, there was 22 nations. My kids didn't know who was Indian, Chinese, Korean, Japanese. They didn't know. There was so many shades of brown. They didn't know. They didn't care. . . . Don't tell me we're not diverse."[30]

Another divergence in my interviews surrounded the relative importance of academic achievement compared to the civic dimensions of public education. For example, one of my interviewees emphasized that public schools remain one of the only institutions in our society that bring people together into community and prepare them to be engaged citizens in a democracy. A (white) contributor to a liberal news outlet, Rob Schofield described how he framed "redistricting" to his daughter when she was assigned a different middle school to meet the needs of the school district.

> Obviously, you want schools that do a good job educating your children, but to me of course, public schools are a lot more than that. They are about being one of the very few places where we actually come together as a society and instill sort of civic values into our children and make them aware that they're a part of a community. To me, all those things are a very, very important part of what schools do. I remember when [my daughter] got redistricted. [Her sister] had gone to Martin, and [my younger daughter] got redistricted to Daniels. She was really grumpy about it, 'cause we're going to have to drive by Martin every day on the way to Daniels, and all of her friends were going to Martin. I remember saying you know, that school, I don't think she bought it, but I was like, that school needs us. They need you, they need our family. That's the way schools work, it's not just a, you're not just a consumer, you're a stakeholder in all this. I was trying to, you know, pie in the sky.[31]

By contrast, some people believed it was unrealistic or inappropriate for schools to take on additional civic tasks, or at least not as important as student learning. From a (white) community leader in a conservative think tank, Terry Stoops:

> I mean, for me, it's about student achievement. If I'm asked about the qualities that are important to public school, it's about kids learning. I know that there's a lot of folks that make arguments about what public schools should be and their larger social and philosophical significance and political significance, as a place where people come together and learn from each other. But for me, I want kids to actually learn. I think that that is the basic function of a school, is to teach something, and for kids to learn something. So, all of those other goals, while important, I think are secondary or maybe even tertiary to student learning.[32]

A few people tied these points together, noting that the strength of our country depends on a well-educated workforce of engaged citizens. On the whole, everyone agreed on the primacy of providing a good education to students. The starkest disagreement was over whether "education goes beyond the books"—whether it is exclusively a private good to be consumed or (also) a web of relationships to be experienced.[33]

It was helpful to hear my interviewees talk about their values regarding public education, but of course my research focused on investigating the Wake County example. As our conversations turned to questions about Wake County's experiences with integration, a story of struggle, progress, and community pride emerged.

"I Became a Believer": The Golden Age of Wake County Schools

As with the public debate that unfolded in the *News & Observer*'s opinion pages during the 2009–2011 timeframe, community leaders held a range of opinions about the strength of Wake County schools and the success of its student assignment policies. For those with a more negative appraisal, criticisms were similar to what was discussed in chapter 2—reassignments were burdensome, busing was problematic, access to magnet schools was unfair, and so on. For those who viewed the county's track record more positively, and (crucially) had a longer history of community activism, there was almost a religious zeal about the success of the system during what more than one person referred to as the "golden age" of Wake County schools, an era that spans roughly from the introduction of magnet schools in the 1980s through the early to mid-2000s, depending on whom you ask. Thinking back to when he first moved to Wake County in the early 1990s, Schofield expressed genuine pride: "I was aware that I felt like we had come to a really good place. I remember thinking, somebody figured this out. What happened, they integrated the schools, whatever, it had been 15 years before, 20 years before and I remember feeling some sense of pride, even from an early time. You know, bragging about it to people who were living in other parts of the country, my friends, and saying, you guys might be surprised to know how good things are here in this city where I live. They've kind of figured some stuff out."[34]

Notably, several people associated the "golden age" with Bill McNeal, the superintendent of Wake County public schools from 2000 to 2006. One school board member who had served in the 1990s explained how McNeal (then associate superintendent for instructional services) and other district leaders had mentored her about how the school system worked and what it was trying to accomplish. "I became a believer," she said, "a solid believer in what Wake County was about with their integration plan . . . almost fiercely and passionately."[35] She added that McNeal "could talk anyone into anything. . . . He's a good listener, but he also explains the big picture really well." He clearly impressed people with his leadership skills and ability to inspire: "McNeal has an aura. You know, he's a great communicator. If you've got a leader who is a great communicator, who can communicate with anyone in any walk of life, that speaks volumes. It's about selling your ideas. Making one believe that those things can occur. How can you benefit? How can businesses benefit when we're in a global setting? How will Raleigh? He has that aura, he can sell. . . . He can make people believe or show them how they fit in and how they can benefit."[36]

After his name came up in several of my interviews, I decided to reach out to him directly. Even though his tenure as superintendent came to an end before the controversies that were the focus of my research, I suspected his long perspective would be valuable. He graciously agreed to meet with me for well over an hour, and his interview did not disappoint.

Now retired, Bill McNeal spent from 1974 to 2006 working for the Wake County Public School System, starting as a middle school teacher and steadily working his way up. I first became aware of McNeal in 2004, when a school district newsletter arrived in my mailbox announcing that he had been named National Superintendent of the Year by the American Association of School Administrators. This seemed like an incredibly big deal at the time, and it had the effect, I well remember, of providing tremendous reassurance. Our oldest child was just in first grade, and here we were in this thriving, nationally recognized district. We had chosen well. Never did I imagine I would one day be interviewing Bill McNeal in a study room of the Cameron Village Regional Library, ten years after the school board "takeover" that shook the foundations of the district, asking him questions about school integration.[37]

McNeal was every bit as charming and persuasive as had been reported. When I asked him to specify the exact years of this "golden age" that other people had talked about, he said with a smile, "Well obviously during the years I was superintendent," before broadening his answer to say the mid-1990s through the mid-2000s. The son of a Baptist minister, McNeal, who is Black, attended segregated schools in Durham, North Carolina, during an era when Black schools were socioeconomically mixed, with children of Black middle class professionals learning alongside poorer students. Teachers and principals also lived in the community of the school and were deeply invested in their students' success. He had a clear-eyed perspective on then and now, recognizing that the key factor in any school system's success, above all others, is avoiding high-poverty schools.[38] High-poverty schools are unable to retain good teachers, attract strong principals, or provide models of excellence. He supported the benefits of integration, including greater social cohesion, but spoke most directly about schools simply being better and healthier when integrated. In this formulation he seemed to have combined idealism and pragmatism in equal measures.

In talking about the 1976 merger of Wake County and Raleigh City schools, he emphasized the pragmatic: "So economics drove that. I know some people look at it and say, 'Well you know, they were trying to integrate schools . . .' No. It was purely economics that drove it. It was the right decision, but economics drove it. And it was done. . . . I don't think you've ever heard about people bat-tling, and fighting, and picketing. It was done rather quietly."[39] Before the merger, Wake County schools were overcrowded while Raleigh City schools were underenrolled and falling into disrepair. The Raleigh City Schools were also found to be in violation of Title VI of the Civil Rights Act and under pres-sure from the U.S. Office of Civil Rights (OCR) to integrate. The merger solved all these problems, efficiently using existing school buildings and creat-ing racial balance across the district. The benchmark became 15–45 percent minority enrollment at each school at a time when the minority population districtwide was 30 percent. Race was explicitly used as a factor in assignment to achieve this balance.

In his book, coauthored with Tom Oxholm, McNeal described the courage of leaders who pushed for the merger: "During the period of the merger, the business community was a strong advocate in favor of merger. While OCR may have provided the impetus for merger, once the notion was entertained, the business community appreciated the economics of merger, including stemming white flight from the inner city schools, keeping all schools fully enrolled, and providing an equitable and quality education for all students."[40] Indeed, a commitment to equitable and quality education for all students seems to be the ingredient that made the merger work by garnering that most elusive but precious resource: parent loyalty.

McNeal spoke about the "business of academics" during our interview, explaining that delivery of academic content to students was the school's pri-mary responsibility. However, his emphasis on academic achievement did not come at the expense of the civic dimensions of public education. On the con-trary, the "business of academics" seemed to foster a sense of community or soli-darity because it was something "all parents can relate to." All students need to be educated, all parents want to see their children learn. In describing what made Wake County different, he said this:

> I thought we were different in this sense. . . . We didn't come at integration or
> desegregation from the lens of just putting the children together, and children
> getting to know each other. We came at it from the lens of how do we improve
> the academics of all our children, and I think that to me was a different lens
> than some other places, even though I believe in the pieces of it that talks
> about getting to know the best of one another, and there's less rancor when
> you become adults and that kind of thing. I believe in all of that. . . . But,
> indirectly we're in that business . . . we're really in the business of academics.
> And all parents can relate to that and buy into that, and they don't want you
> to be talking about any kind of a social construct that you now put in play,
> because at some point and time they're gonna tear that down, but it's harder
> for them to go after the academic piece.

He correctly ascertained that all parents want strong academics for their children. He also knew to tap into parents' natural tendency to look out for their children's best interests and that this motivation was stronger than a commitment to integration in the abstract: "It's not the driver to say that I want your Black child sitting beside a white child. Lots of communities try to paint that picture, but parents are gonna tear that down at some point. Because to me, that's not gonna be strong enough. That can be a secondary reason for doing it, but our reason was we want strong schools. We want schools that are excellent for all children, and how do we do that? We try to stay out of what we call identifiable poverty schools. That's it."[41]

What seemed to make his leadership so effective was his ability to inspire community-wide buy-in to a common goal. "When you put that goal out there, every parent can see their child, every parent." In a society with a long history of underestimating the abilities of minority students and underestimating the care and investment of minority parents, this seemingly anodyne commitment to create strong schools that improve the academics of all children was a profoundly influential organizing premise. It placed all parents on equal footing, working toward the same thing.

So, in 1998, a little over twenty years after the merger, when McNeal was serving as associate superintendent for instructional services and primarily responsible for students' academic progress, he played a key role in creating what was called Goal 2003, or the 95% goal: "By 2003, 95 percent of students tested in Grades 3 and 8 will be at or above grade level as measured by NC End-of-Grade (EOG) tests."[42] This was perceived as an ambitious, even audacious, goal. Some people worried it would set the district up for failure. But notably, the goal was set before the era of "over-testing" and harsh accountability ushered in by the No Child Left Behind Act, widely criticized for pressuring schools to "teach to the test" and strip their curriculum to its barest essentials to serve that utilitarian goal.[43]

Under McNeal's direction, in the late 1990s, the 95% goal was an inspiration that forged a sense of purpose among teachers and community members. There was supplemental pay for teachers to provide extra support to students after school and even on Saturdays (the ALP—accelerated learning program). There were tutoring programs run through the faith community, including the one McNeal started at Martin Street Baptist Church in southeast Raleigh. It was an astute strategy because it created a sense of ownership by the community. It also reduced the sense of tradeoffs being made between students—that some kids might be sacrificed for others' advancement. All students of all backgrounds, including the ones identified as academically gifted, were expected to improve.

Under McNeal's leadership, employing business principles did not involve rejecting "subpar blueberries" but rather demonstrating respect for teachers, the system's most valuable employees, transparency with the public, and measurable goals that would be meaningful to parents. Accountability was not punitive but rather a means to shore up an already solid work ethic. He spoke with great pride about the number of teachers in Wake County who were nationally board certified, and he clearly revered veteran teachers who had stayed with the system for decades: "We had a significant number of teachers who stayed 32, 35, 40 years, because they bought into what was being done, and they felt that they were a part of something special. We used to have annual economic summits, and the purpose of the summit was to bring the community together, and we talked about the state of the school district. How are we doing with your children? So the whole point was, everyone played a part. If they don't believe they are a part of [it], then they don't have allegiance to it." McNeal was able to earn the loyalty and trust of the teaching staff and to foster a sense of collective investment in what he promoted as "world class schools."[44]

He was also an excellent communicator and would meet directly with parents who had complaints. As the son of a Baptist minister, he noted, "I am very familiar with being in the pulpit," and he is as good at listening as he is at persuading. For example, he told me about a time when as superintendent he met with over two hundred mostly African American parents who had invited him to hear their concerns about long bus rides. He met with them downtown, at Moore Square Middle School. After hearing them out, he was able to allay their concerns by refocusing attention on the quality of the education their children were receiving. In essence, his message was that distance is no concern when excellence is the destination.

> They had the floor first, and they went through a litany of issues, primarily centered around long bus rides, and the fact that they couldn't get to the school because they were at work, or they didn't have transportation, and all of the problems created, and the fact that their child's standing beside the road at a stop in the morning, and the child's five years of age, and how could I do that to children. Oh my gosh! So they went on, and I listened intently. So, I surprised them, 'cause I stood up, and I said you know what, that's not even my issue. Well, that surprised and shocked them. Who is this guy? I said, "Let me tell you what my issue really is, my issue is: Have we done the best job of educating your child, so that your child can compete successfully anywhere, anytime, and anywhere they go?"

After telling them a story about a daycare in North Raleigh that was so highly coveted for its quality that parents drove from all corners of the county to get their children to this facility (and would camp out overnight to try to get the first slots), he said, "I want your child in an outstanding school. Where the teachers do a superior job, where the principal does a superior job, and your child comes home happy, and your child is achieving and learning. I said, 'That's where I live.'"[45] He said what was important to him was "what happens at the end of that bus ride." He had brought charts to show the parents data on student achievement, including gains for African American students. "Seems to me there's some significant work being done that falls in a positive category, and given that, what's your issue?" When he left, he said, "I got a standing ovation."[46]

One crucial piece of the system's success—what McNeal referred to as the "secret formula"—was the role played by the magnet schools. Magnet schools had special themes or unique offerings that would attract students from across the county. Their explicit reason for being was to promote school integration. However, magnet schools also served to spur a healthy competition between schools: Non-magnet (or "base") schools would have to find creative ways to "kick their program up a notch" in order to keep their students from being drawn to the magnets. However, just as the goal to have 95 percent of students at or above grade level was launched before the era of No Child Left Behind testing, the magnet program in Wake County was launched before the rapid growth of charter schools, before the introduction of North Carolina's private school voucher program, and before the squeezing of school funding created conditions of scarcity—never a good context in which to spur competition. It was a different time, with different pressures and different assumptions. The competition between magnet and base schools was healthy because it was manageable, affordable, and part of a collective effort to strengthen the system as a whole. In McNeal's words: "I thought that was our competitive edge, and created the kind of academic performance in our kids, because they [base schools] were always looking at evolving their programs and making it better. We never talked about that. The media never figured that out, but we used that internally in order to continue to improve our schools."[47]

When Walter Marks was hired to bring magnet schools to Wake County in 1982, the population was also much smaller and roads were less congested, making travel time between city and suburbs feasible. However, the seeds of later trouble, including "magnet envy," were arguably sown from the beginning. For while the pursuit of excellence was admirable, especially in a country that often relegates its public institutions to second best, it created a demand that outstripped supply and fostered a covetousness for the most exclusive and best school.[48] For example, McNeal explained that one way the magnets were marketed early on was through the "crowning" of master principals, who were all sent to be principals of magnet schools the following year: "Walter Marks came up with an idea of crowning master principals. You know, the best principals in Wake County. He chose nineteen. I was among the nineteen. I was the youngest at that time among the nineteen. So, in many ways it was a stroke of genius. For this, we never received one dollar more, not one."[49]

These master principals created publicity and excitement around the anticipated quality of the magnet schools because: "The quality of your principal dictates the quality of your teachers, because great principals hire great teachers, and they let great teachers do what great teachers do." However, he admitted they may have "oversold it" because "people got mad [when] they didn't get in."

It seems that, at least for a time, the promise that "we're not only gonna educate your child, but we're gonna give your child an edge," as he put it, was perceived to apply across the board, to all Wake County public schools, as a shared goal. But McNeal seemed to recognize the problematic tendency of parent-consumers to make comparisons and strive for better. Parents, especially white parents, were often angling for an advantage: "If you gonna stand around the water cooler at the bridge club you gotta say that your kid's in one of those magnet schools downtown. . . . Then after that it became the magnet schools among the magnets. So, Hunter fit that profile. Ligon, and then Enloe." He said when parents could not get their child into Hunter, they would be offered an alternative, but it was often deemed unsatisfactory. He would say to the parents, "'Well, you didn't get into Hunter, but we can get you into Fuller.' It's not the same thing. Because at the bridge club, everybody talks about Hunter." There was also the separate criticism that magnet schools brought white students in from the suburbs but didn't foster true integration: "It did bring kids downtown, but remember the argument with magnet schools. Two schools in one."

McNeal oversaw a significant period of the school system's history. He was superintendent as the system transitioned at the beginning of the new millennium from a race-based student assignment plan to one based on socioeconomic status and academic achievement, a preemptive change in policy that anticipated legal developments restricting the use of race in school integration plans; for example, what ultimately culminated in the U.S. Supreme Court decision in the *Parents Involved* case (2007) that ended school districts' efforts to integrate through the explicit use of race as a factor. He oversaw the ambitious and largely successful 95% goal that galvanized the district. He also oversaw the development of the "healthy school index" that measured a number of factors, including the integration of the student body, the quality of teachers and principals, the quality of the curriculum, the quality of school facilities, and safety and security. His professional memory stretched back to the beginning of the merged district in the 1970s, so he could explain some of the factors that helped launch the new WCPSS, including support from both Republicans and Democrats on the school board, support from the business community, and the fact that the community's elite sent their children to the public schools after the merger. He was also well aware of some of the more recent challenges. Although he still believes Wake County is a strong school system, competing mostly with itself and its own previous reputation, he says, "I do refer to that period as the golden age of Wake County, because I don't believe that Wake County will ever be able to reach the level of achievement during that period of time ever again."

WCPSS continued to have a strong market share until the 2010s, according to McNeal. So, what changed then? Among an array of factors, parent unhappiness played a significant part: there were "parent groups that became extremely angry and worked to unravel things, and their work included making sure they had their people on the school board who would support neighborhood schools." A focal point of the discontent was the fast-growing western part of the county, including "an organized group out of Apex that didn't like the fact that we were busing kids in from Raleigh to Apex schools." According to McNeal, the parents were not always forthright about their motives: "They're not gonna be that plain. They're not gonna come out and say, 'I don't want these children coming to school.' . . . Their complaint would be, 'Why is my child moved out?' Well, your child moved out because as we bring kids here, and we move your child over there. That's really what the complaint was. What they really wanted was, 'Don't bring those kids here. Let my child stay right here, and life is good.' But if . . . Now there's a courageous part about it. If we're going to have room at those schools downtown, we gotta move some kids here, then your children may move two miles down the road." Some parents were unmoved by this argument.

The 2009 school board's narrow focus on neighborhood schools meant the system languished, according to McNeal. He did not mince words about the board's choice of Anthony Tata, a retired brigadier general of the U.S. Army, to serve as superintendent: "What did Tony Tata know about a child's ability to read?"[50] But even after pro-diversity candidates retook the school board in 2011 and a new superintendent was hired, other changes were set in motion at the state level. The Republican takeover of the North Carolina General Assembly in 2010 ushered in several controversial laws, including lifting the cap on charter schools, introducing a private school voucher program, and eliminating longevity pay and master's degree pay for teachers. As they proliferated, charter schools hurt the market share of traditional public schools because, in McNeal's view, they did a better job marketing themselves and playing to parent demand, all while not having to follow many of the same regulations that traditional public schools must follow in North Carolina (like providing lunch or transportation or hiring certified teachers). Charters gave parents more power to make threats to leave WCPSS if they did not get the assignment they wanted. He noted that teachers also have more leverage now and can readily move to charters or private schools: "A number of those teachers have been siphoned off by charter schools." Private schools can attract stronger teachers by offering better salaries, as teacher pay for public school teachers in North

Carolina has stagnated. "Schools are over a barrel." When WCPSS had greater market share, a stronger reputation, and stronger funding, it was not as vulnerable to teachers' and parents' threats to leave. McNeal elaborated as follows:

> We have a different school system today, and as kids have left and gone to charters, private, parochial, virtuals, we've lost a lot of what I would consider to be great teachers as a result, and we now see schools that are becoming more racially identifiable. We're seeing them become more economically identifiable, and as a result, I see the things that we knew then would create problems, and that is then more and more kids leave, and when it becomes that identifiable, can you answer the question whether or not you have the best staff, the best administration?

As will be discussed further in chapter 3, charters are but one piece of a larger trend toward privatization and the disinvestment in traditional public schools. Recent research by Helen Ladd of Duke University's Sanford School of Public Policy and others has shown that charters have demonstrably worsened racial segregation in North Carolina, providing avenues for families to self-select more homogeneous enclaves based on race and class.

McNeal helped me to see more clearly those things that made the "golden age" of Wake County schools so golden. For one, there was support for high-quality integrated schools from all levels—from the school board, state legislators, the state's Department of Public Instruction, the business community, and the faith community. There was also a commitment to "providing an equitable and quality education for all students," respect for teachers, respect for professionalism, and (perhaps most importantly) a greater sense of community and community buy-in: "Wake County could not have done what we did without community support." In his summary of the more recent past, McNeal felt that waning political support, a shift in values, and new laws from the NC General Assembly "started affecting schools in a way that I consider detrimental."

"A School within a School": Facing the Problem of Racial Inequity

Of course, not everything was perfect during the "golden age," a point that I felt was important to investigate more carefully for the sake of balance and thoroughness. One criticism that surfaced both in the *N&O* opinions and my interviews was the claim that the integrated schools of Wake County, especially magnet schools, were internally segregated within themselves—or "two schools in one," as McNeal had put it. More commonly, this phenomenon was referred to as "a school within a school." This phrase describes the racial separation that exists inside a school building through academic tracking, self-segregation in social spaces, unconscious bias, and discrimination. The criticism was point-edly directed at magnet schools in Wake County, especially during the con-troversies of 2009–2011, and it was used in arguments as a justification for dismantling the diversity policy. But outside that political fight, the "school-within-a-school" observation has been a concern for some time. Indeed, many schools around the country, insofar as they have racially mixed student popu-lations at all, replicate the pattern of having white students overenrolled in hon-ors and AP courses and Black and brown students overenrolled in regular or remedial courses. U.S. public schools also suspend and expel Black and brown students at far greater rates than white students, significantly contributing to the school-to-prison pipeline and affecting who feels valued in the school.[51]

One of my interviewees, a white woman and transplant from the Northeast who had run for the Wake County school board in the 2010s, criticized what she felt was the hypocrisy of placing magnet schools in affluent white neigh-borhoods that did not need special offerings to draw in students from the sub-urbs. It added insult to injury to allow internal segregation within the school: "Martin does not need to be magnetized anymore. Come on. There's some of those that have cars that go through their parking lot. Come on. You know darn well that the kids that are in the basement classes, versus the kids that are in the other ones. It's two separate schools. They're joking themselves. Enloe, two separate. The kids may be in homeroom together, but there's no integration there. I'm sorry."[52]

In her comments, she conflated Martin and Enloe, two different schools in two different parts of Raleigh with markedly different "base populations" of students. Lumping them together undermined the validity of her initial criticism. But what really caused me to question her argument was her cynical interpretation: "Yeah. Maybe 10, 15 years ago, these were low-income areas. They're not now and you're just protecting your own database. Yeah, sorry. Close down the school. Oh, golly gee, you're going to drive five miles more too, just like the rest of us out here [in western Wake County]. Put the money where the growth is and you can make money by selling those ITB [inside-the-Beltline] schools' land."[53]

Though her comments seemed born of resentment, as well as a desire to divert resources to her part of the county, she had noticed something others had noticed too: the physical separation of students through tracking. Because the criticism of a "school within a school" was used so often by opponents of the diversity policy in 2009, I made a point of asking about it in my interviews if it did not come up on its own (as it had above). First, was the criticism of "school within a school" valid? Second, if schools were internally segregated, did that problem warrant jettisoning the student assignment policy that had sought to integrate Wake County's schools? These questions led to some important conversations, especially with my interviewees who were African American.

In a nutshell, according to the people I spoke with, the racial separation of students inside Wake County's public schools has unquestionably been a problem. However, no one deemed the "school-within-a-school" criticism to be a valid justification for ending the diversity policy or otherwise rolling back integration efforts systemwide. "The school-within-a-school criticism is absolutely justified," said one parent, but "you don't throw the whole thing out" because of its flaws, said another.[54] One African American mom who had served as a PTA officer at her child's elementary, middle, and high schools shared several relevant observations and experiences with me. About tracking, she said, "You do the tour of the magnets, and you see all these wonderful programs, you look in the classrooms and then you see the general classes and it's mostly Blacks and browns."[55] Although she had enrolled her child in magnet schools for her entire K-12 career, and readily admitted her daughter "got a great education," she was honest about her criticism and spoke up directly to school leadership: "I did not like that the magnet schools were a microcosm of a school within a school. That bothered me a lot. And it was a concern that I expressed to every principal that I dealt with."[56]

More specifically, this parent described the biases and processes that fed the "school-within-a-school" problem, including underestimating the abilities of children of color and a testing regime that sorts children by ability early and rigidly. She was also keenly aware that parent advocacy, or lack of it, can have an outsized impact: "I was not a believer that poverty equals . . . lack of intelligence. There were kids that were in the quote unquote general population who were just as bright as my daughter and others, [but] because their parents were not involved, [their children were not placed in more challenging classes]. . . . A lot of Black parents in the neighborhood were intimidated to come into the school unless their kids were in trouble and everything. And so they really didn't know how to advocate for their children."[57]

Incidentally, a white mom and parent activist whom I interviewed shared similar observations. This person had taught high school in Wake County for a number of years and saw firsthand how tracking plays out. In her experience, there were white students who did not belong in the honors track. In this case she was speaking about two eleventh grade (white) boys: "They were lazy. They barely should be in my honors class and they wanted to go into AP and I did not approve them. Guess where they ended up? In the AP class."[58] At the same time, there were Black students in the regular track who were missing the opportunity for greater challenge: "What really irritated me is in the 9th grade classes there were kids who were very smart, very capable and they were just there because they'd been tracked there. It wasn't effectively academically tracked. And so right away there was this gal, this African American girl in my 9th grade class. I was like why is she in this class? And so I had her moved to the next level. And she did fine. She did fine. But it wouldn't have happened without intervention."[59]

For her part, the African American mom and former PTA president had given a lot of thought to the role of testing in determining academic tracking. She said the process of identifying academically gifted children was "almost like a little secret society." To improve the process, she argued that testing should be done more broadly, and "if the teacher has seen that students are doing well . . . give more kids a chance." If students are "marginal" or "on the cusp" of being identified as academically gifted, "stretch them a little bit" and offer them the challenge. She rejected the idea that socioeconomic status was somehow the root of misidentifying children of color and directed her criticism at white teachers and school administrators: "This is a perception problem that Blacks and browns are not going to succeed as much as white kids. It is a perception problem."[60]

Other interviewees echoed these observations, providing examples where students were set up for failure (e.g., the "quick fix" of moving students directly into advanced classes without solid preparation from kindergarten) or underestimated (e.g., no intervention was considered necessary because mediocre grades or scores were "good enough" for children of color). Parents also talked about the problem of their children feeling isolated—being the only or one of only a handful of Black students in an AP class for example. An African American dad, lamenting this isolation, emphasized the importance of self-confidence and strong self-esteem to navigate a predominantly white environment. Poignantly, one mom described how the loneliness of being the only Black student in an advanced class played out at prom.

> Well, it was a very sad time, because it's one of those things where I could not . . . I mean, she ended up, which I'm glad of, going with a group of friends and that was fine but no boy invited her to the prom. And she says, "Mom, you have to understand that I'm in a lot of honors and AP classes." And I think when she was a senior she was in all AP classes. She says, "There are no Black boys in these classes." And, she said, "You know, the white boys won't invite me. They're my friends but they won't invite me to the prom." So, she said, "What's wrong with me? Why am I so . . ." That was . . . That tore my heart out. That tore my heart out, because there's nothing I can do about it. She's where she should be, she should be in the advanced classes, where she's being challenged and everything. But from a social standpoint, the few kids of color who are in those classes are somewhat isolated. Are really somewhat isolated.[61]

Another African American mom and activist framed her observations in terms of diversity versus inclusion, and underscored that everyone benefits when environments are authentically inclusive: "Diversity is sticking different people in a room but what about beyond that? What about inclusion? That's what I'm talking about with the classes. These people are in AP classes and these are in standard classes and that and how do you become a more inclusive environment so that really then everyone does get the advantages from all folks being included?"[62] This parent also mentioned that the school-within-a-school problem can be mitigated by the arts, a focus of many magnet programs in Wake County that encourages broad student participation. And yet, even here, she noted, the choices (e.g., of plays and musicals) often feature white leading roles, white storylines. In discussing parallel student clubs that exist to feature Black students and talents, she noted: "That is steeped in our history of when Black people couldn't participate in stuff, they created their own and that continues."[63]

So, given all these legitimate concerns—the underestimation, misidentification, missed opportunities, isolation, and more—why did my interviewees not agree with the critics of the diversity policy who wanted to retreat from the system's integration efforts? There were myriad reasons, most of them flowing from a pragmatic commitment to improve an imperfect system, an informed consideration of their children's best interests, and a long-range faith in incremental progress. The "school within a school" is, in fact, a problem and speaks to the incomplete nature of true integration, but diverse schools are still healthier schools: "I was not swayed by any of those arguments, I think there's still value in having schools that are diverse. . . . [Even with segregation inside the school], you still have a healthy environment that you know, in one respect, [is] attracting good teachers. A high-needs school that is either all free or reduced lunch, or racially identifiable, is a more difficult environment, certainly for learning outcomes."[64] When the 2009 school board voted to dismantle the diversity policy, the risks of racially identifiable high-poverty schools were plainly apparent to activists representing the NAACP and a youth-led group called NC HEAT (Heroes Emerging Among Teens).[65] In September 2010, their complaint with the U.S. Office of Civil Rights under Title VI of the Civil Rights Act of 1964 alleged "the Board's decision to reassign certain students was made with the discriminatory intent to satisfy a small and vocal set of parents and those student reassignments have an unjustified disparate impact on students because of their race, color, and national origin." They also alleged intent "to establish and maintain single-race schools."[66] Although impactful politically at the time for shining a bright light on the actions of the 2009 school board, the complaint was eventually dismissed at the request of the new board elected in 2011, after it had "reinstated diversity considerations in its student assignment policy."[67]

I had been aware of the OCR complaint in 2010, but talking directly with parents and community leaders nearly a decade later helped me to appreciate the complex pragmatism of fighting to preserve gains in a system despite its shortcomings. In the words of a Black mother, "I felt that we should fix the flaw, versus throwing everything out, because what happens when, if they had thrown everything out, then we would have schools closed in Wake County."[68] The school system was an imperfect human endeavor, but it was worth improving. These African American parents did not want their children in either all-Black or all-white schools, and thus supported the magnet program and related integration efforts. They sought high-quality academic opportunities for their children, as all parents do. And, as seen earlier in this chapter, they supported the richness of learning other people's cultures and preparing for a diverse global society. However, what stood out for me were remarkable instances of "both/and" thinking—being able to hold together two seemingly disparate ideas or stances—and a resilient, hopeful expectation of incremental progress.

For example, with regard to "both/and" thinking, one of my interviewees both empathized with teachers and criticized them. She talked about how much is expected of teachers, how their roles are stretched unreasonably in an effort to address students' basic, unmet needs: "I don't know how we can fix this. This is not a school problem. This is a societal problem. My opinion is that teachers are being asked to do more than teach. They have to be counselors, they have to make sure these kids are fed. . . . The teachers are worn out."[69] She expressed deep respect for the profession of teaching and the work of teachers. At the same time, she noted many specific ways that white teachers lack cultural competence for working effectively with children of color. Teachers interpret rambunctiousness as aggression, for example, and are at a loss for how to be authoritative and directive while also being supportive and caring. "I think because so many teachers, particularly a lot of the white teachers, never have to deal with us except in that environment. They come to school, they work with kids of color, they go back home, they go to their neighborhoods. There's nobody in their neighborhood that looks like us. They don't have anybody in their church [that] looks like us, and the only time they have to interact is when they were in school."

Many of my interviewees mentioned the problem of overdisciplining of children of color, a well-researched phenomenon in public schools, and yet also talked about the positive impact of having more teachers and principals of color—something that has been a priority for the downtown magnet schools in particular. Gretta Dula, for example, Ligon's principal from 2009 to 2019, made it a priority to hire teachers of color.

With regard to a resilient expectation of incremental progress, many of my interviewees contrasted their own school experiences with those of their children. For example, one mom said it was important to her that her children have a diverse experience because she herself had been the only Black child in an all-white school district growing up in New Jersey. Another mom spoke about her upbringing in segregated schools of Virginia, how her husband never had a Black teacher until he was in college, and how different their daughter's experience had been at Enloe, considered the most diverse high school in Wake County. She said she loved the study groups and group projects that would come over to her house to work, and she always provided food.

> I go up to my bonus room and it looks like [the] United Nations. I'm serious. It looks like the United Nations, and I said, "This is the way it's supposed to be." You got kids, a lot of Indians from Cary and Morrisville, you got North Raleigh, you have Southeast Raleigh, Knightdale. It looked like [the] United Nations. My daughter, for example, joined the Indian dance group. We were at the Diwali festival 'cause she's doing Indian dance. I'm like, "Okay," but the kids are fine with it. It's when they go home and put their feet underneath the table and start having the dinner conversation with their parents, because the parents have those biases.[70]

This mom said she and her husband had made a conscious effort to view her daughter's experiences with fresh eyes, or with what seemed to be genuine openness to the possibility of change: "So when I would say some things I remember, just make an odd comment, and my daughter would say, 'Well Mom, that doesn't matter to me,' or 'That's not my experience,' and so we had to really make sure our conversation was different and that we were not giving her the baggage that we had because of how we had to live."[71] This mom's past educational experience seemed to make her especially appreciative of what had been built in Wake County. She actually paused to ask me where I was from before criticizing the northern transplants on the 2009 school board who had sought to dismantle it.[72]

Some changes to the school system, especially as we move into the 2020s, have been good. Foremost among the positive developments has been greater explicit and constructive attention to the school-within-a-school problem: "We've gotten to a point now, especially at Enloe, where people, not just recognize it, but are ready to talk about it. And both teachers and students are asking questions about it."[73] Students are leading the way in conversations about equity through school equity teams. A recent video produced at Enloe features students of color answering the question, "What is something valuable you got out of taking an AP, IB, or honors course?"[74] Different perspectives based on race, class, and personal experience with public education have brought greater awareness of the school-within-a-school problem and a willingness to confront it. Rather than abandoning the magnets, students and parents continually push to make them more inclusive and fair.

Conclusion

At the time I conducted my interviews in 2018–2019, there had been nearly a decade to reflect on what transpired in Wake County in 2009–2011. Long-term resident Rob Schofield deftly enumerated the various causes of the school board takeover, referencing low voter turnout, energized conservatives, and complacent progressives.

> I think it was clearly, as was the 2010 election, it was a reaction to Barack Obama. It was the pushback. It's the same thing with Donald Trump, really. I mean, I think it was. . . . We were still in the depths of the tough economic times, and . . . Republicans and anti-Obama people were very energized. . . . Meanwhile, the people who would've been natural defenders of the faith were sort of asleep at the wheel and kind of, I think everybody was kind of depressed. It was when the recession was going on, and I just think there was a lack of action and mobilization amongst progressives. Sort of asleep at the wheel in those '09 elections.[75]

Setting aside the accuracy of his political analysis of the causes of the takeover, I was struck by the use of the term "defenders of the faith." Faith in what?

Without question, some of the people I interviewed articulated a faith in the secular ideal of equality of opportunity, which is broadly associated with the purpose of public education in the United States. Yvonne Brannon, leader in grassroots organization Great Schools in Wake, articulated this value directly: "I want to have faith that we still have a strong contingency of people who believe in the American dream. The American promise. Of free and equal opportunity and free and equal education for all. I'm just not going to give up on it."[76] A leader from the business community, perhaps the person with the longest-term involvement in supporting the Wake County schools of anyone I interviewed, likewise shared his understanding: "That's the deal. That's a deal we have in the good ole USA, and that is everybody has the same opportunity and that's the deal. That's who we are. That's the work we're supposed to be doing."[77]

There were also those who explained their commitment to equitable public education as a function of their religious faith. Rev. Nancy Petty did this most explicitly: "And for me, I can't separate out my faith's position on that, that we're all created equal and that we all carry the image of God in us. And that we're all God's children."[78] But so did school board member Christine Kushner.

> I'm an avid churchgoer, so it's been . . . tested lately, but I have a deep faith. . . . Sometimes the Holy Spirit's the only part I believe in, and that is that we have

communion with each other as children of God, for lack of a better description. I believe that deeply, because every religion talks about loving your neighbor as yourself. I'm getting emotional. So that drives me as a person, so it drives my politics, as a board member, I have to think of the practical, the brain science, the cost-effectiveness. But what drives me is my [belief in the] value in our connection to each other.[79]

Even without reference to religion, some people reiterated the idea that schools are the place where lessons of equality are best learned. School is the "best learning laboratory" for teaching that most basic rule—that all people are created equal.[80]

Looking at these quotes, one might surmise that "defenders of the faith" were highly idealistic progressives, all of whom happened to be white. But pragmatic voices, like that of former superintendent Bill McNeal and the African American parents I interviewed, expressed faith in the ideal of equality as well. Pragmatically, integration makes for stronger, healthier schools. It is an instrumental good that creates other goods, like student achievement, preparation for the real world, and community prosperity. But the foundation upon which integration rests is still the ideal of equality. Parents' criticisms of the flaws in the school system—the school-within-a-school problem and other inequities—existed alongside their idealism, including their expectation that progress was possible. This "both/and" mindset of idealism and pragmatism seemed more realistic and durable, as compared to the keen disappointment felt by some of the most passionate idealists who believed the important gains of the "golden age" were destroyed overnight by the 2009 school board.

Idealism sometimes suffers the keenest disappointment, as reality so often falls short of the vision. However, idealism that sits alongside pragmatism, noticing and addressing problems, may be more durable. This approach does not jettison ideals so much as it appreciates the long game to get there. I believe this is an important distinction, as faith in the possibility of high-quality, integrated public schools is at an all-time low nationally, as is faith in the democratic ideal of equality. The challenges faced now by Wake County and districts across the country are formidable. Christine Kushner, who was serving the final years of an eleven-year term on the school board at the time of our interview, described the situation as follows:

In the United States we're creating two tiers of education, where the public is not as robustly funded and not as strong an education as the private sector, in some parts of the country. I would argue that's not the case in Wake County. But in many parts of the country, public schools are left to flounder and those who can afford to get out of public schools, do. And that's just in the long term detrimental to all children, including those who go to private schools.[81]

The effects of the COVID-19 pandemic have only worsened the problems of public schools. Divisions are deep. Disillusionment is real. According to one of my interviewees, some people resent public schools if they are good enough to have comparable prestige to private schools, or they want the benefits of the best public schools kept only for themselves and "their group of people."[82] It is to these tensions that I now turn.

4

Arguing from the Past, Fighting for the Future

Nearly eighty members of the public signed up to address the Wake County Board of Education on March 23, 2010, the night the board ultimately voted 5–4 to adopt a "Directive for Community-Based Assignment." The new directive prioritized proximity between home and school in any new student assignment plan—making way for the promised "neighborhood schools"—and removed diversity as an explicit goal. It also prioritized stability in school assignments. With his distinctive New Jersey accent, immediately recognizable to my ears and incongruous amidst North Carolina Piedmont accents and the highly educated intonations of residents of the Research Triangle, Chair Margiotta read out the names of the speakers in batches.[1] Individuals walked to the podium one at a time, often with written speeches in hand and visible emotion, and addressed their comments to the nine board members seated around a semicircle of tables at the front of the room. Board attorney Ann Majestic and interim superintendent Donna Hargens sat at the front as well. As a last-minute change, Margiotta had reduced the time allotted for an individual's public comment from three minutes to two. Adding to the tension, a timer warned with accelerating beeps and a red blinking light when each person's two minutes of speaking time were about to be up. The boardroom was packed, with people standing in the hallway, but Margiotta had denied earlier requests to move the meeting to a larger venue.

"I Dreamed That We Had Made Progress Here"

By a margin of 4–1, speakers during the public comment period argued against the new directive, imploring the board members to consider history, personal experience, and educational research before jettisoning a system that took years to build. Jim Henderlite, a grandfather of a Wake County elementary student, had driven from his home in Charlotte to warn against embracing neighborhood schools, using Charlotte's experience with resegregation as a cautionary tale. By contrast, those arguing in support of the directive were more likely to criticize aspects of the current system than to argue the merits of community-based schools outright. Charles Campbell of Apex, for example, explained his preference for neighborhood schools by contending that busing was too costly and time-consuming.[2]

But the most notable speaker that evening, tenth on the list, was a gray-haired African American gentleman wearing a light-blue tie and gray suit who spoke calmly, never breaking eye contact with the board members.

> Mr. Chairman, my name is Julius Chambers and I am an attorney, and I've been practicing civil rights litigation now for about 50 years. I spent a lot of time litigating the Charlotte-Mecklenburg school case and a number of other cases in North Carolina. In fact, I started years ago with the Raleigh school case and I dreamed that we had made progress here in Raleigh and had merged Raleigh and Wake County. . . . We are now reopening a lot of issues and a lot of problems. I hope you pause a moment and ask yourself about the problems you might be creating for the children you are serving and the parents. . . . For the children, they have gotten used to going to school with a diverse population. They have gotten used to other children, of different races and nationalities, and you may be depriving them of that opportunity now. Second, with respect to the parents, I don't know if you have asked yourself what your actions last week, this week are doing to the county and the city. . . . I trust that you will think more carefully about the plan that you will likely take and not approve this plan. It is not in the best interest of Raleigh. Thank you.[3]

He finished his remarks before the beeps cut him off, turned, and walked back to his seat as the sizable audience applauded. This was Julius LeVonne Chambers, the man who had argued *Swann v. Charlotte-Mecklenburg Board of Education* before the U.S. Supreme Court, resulting in the landmark 1971 decision that allowed busing for integration. It was astonishing that someone of his stature had felt compelled to offer his remarks at this local school board meeting, waiting for his turn to speak along with the rest of the public. This was three short years before his death in 2013. And yet the school board members seemed to have no idea who Mr. Chambers was. According to one of my interviewees who was present for the meeting, "I remember that day [March 23, 2010]. I did not speak, but I remember the incredible ignorance of the board members in terms of recognizing Julius Chambers and many of the other people who came to speak."[4]

Indeed, many of the speakers that night seemed to anticipate that there would be a gap in understanding Wake County's and North Carolina's history. Benita Jones, who immediately followed Julius Chambers and underscored that he was a "*legend* in North Carolina educational legal history," explained that the state had waged a "hard-fought battle to achieve diverse and high-quality schools." An attorney for the UNC Center for Civil Rights at the time and herself a product of the Wake County Public School System, Jones attempted to explain how moving away from community-based or "neighborhood schools" had actually represented a significant step forward because it purposefully disrupted racial inequity: "I urge you all to learn and understand the historical context of terms such as 'neighborhood schools' and 'busing.' School resegregation and the re-emergence of racially identifiable schools and the often intentional creation of high-poverty schools is a statewide issue, and Wake County is merely the bellwether for what will be acceptable for the rest of the state. . . . Where a child goes to school *does* impact the resources and the influences available to that child."[5]

Brenda Miller, a white retired WCPSS teacher, used the metaphor of a garden "which took a long time to cultivate" to convey the complexity and interdependence of a system that was the product of a great many people's efforts.[6] She implored the board to fix rather than "dig up" the whole thing. Chris Aycock, also a product of WCPSS, spoke of Wake County as a single community, saying "we will rise and fall as one."[7] Lifelong Raleigh resident and Enloe High graduate Annette Exum, who was one of only seven Black women in her class at North Carolina State University—a class with only a hundred women total—described her grief at the board's decision: "One of the things that died today was the principle of reducing the effects of racial isolation."[8] Exum was one of the people who had stayed late into the evening to have her chance to speak. More than forty speakers were postponed until after the board had conducted its business; less than half lasted until the bitter end to be heard.

Of the small number of individuals who spoke in support of the board's directive for community-based schools, most framed their comments in terms of complaints about the current system. Jennifer Mansfield argued that the diversity policy (Policy 6200) could not be effectively implemented across the entire county, impugning the shortcomings of the policy as it had played out rather than its intentions.[9] Sarah Redpath, making space for herself amidst what she called a "lion's den of political gladiators," accused "entrenched business interests" of using the schools as a recruitment tool to attract employees without caring for the children: "As long as the schools looked good, the children didn't matter."[10] Debbie Overby, who described herself as a graduate of Wake County schools, objected to "forced busing, forced year-round schools—forced anything," emphatically concluding her remarks with this statement: "This is the United States of America! People should not be forced here in Wake County to do anything they don't want to do!"[11] The only nonwhite person to speak in favor of the community-based schools directive and against the diversity policy was Bill Randall. He began by saying that economic and racial diversity impose "an unfair burden on the citizens of this county." He then praised a neighborhood-based charter school in New York City: "All of the students—the Black students—graduated from high school and one hundred percent of them went on to college," which he said was "*not* the result of racial diversity and economic diversity." Claiming that diversity programs treat symptoms rather than the "root of the problem," he argued that "the number one problem contributing to blighted conditions and impoverished conditions, low graduation rate, poor economic success, [and] juvenile delinquency is the absence of a father in the home—baby daddy needs to stop!"[12]

Occasional voices called for a third way, preserving diversity while also creating more stability in assignments and proximity to home, but in that moment, these comments passed without gaining traction.

When the board began their deliberations in earnest, their exchanges were contentious and unproductive. Several amendments intended to lessen the chances of resegregation were defeated by 5–4 votes. Chair Margiotta provided the tiebreaking vote each time, eliciting shouts of disapproval from the audience. The only debate that was even tentatively substantive concerned an important, difficult issue: whether taking account of students' socioeconomic status in a student assignment policy is justified at all. As we saw in chapter 2, this debate pertains to the issue of equality of treatment and how schools should account for differences in background. Keith Sutton, the board's only African American member at the time, argued that attention to poverty was warranted. John Tedesco, by contrast, defended the view that schools should be class- and race-blind, educating whoever happened to be in proximity to the school. He argued that taking poverty into account was a type of "profiling" that underestimated students' abilities, a view that echoed George W. Bush's criticism in 2000 of the "soft bigotry of low expectations."[13] With diplomatic skill and restraint, Sutton pushed Tedesco to consider examples of interventions for "at risk" children, such as the Big Brothers Big Sisters program where Tedesco himself worked at the time. Wasn't the existence of such programs evidence of the fact that some children need extra attention? But Tedesco sharply disagreed and seemed to take offense at the personal example, drawing a distinction between voluntary interventions and mandatory ones. "Profiling" was what schools were doing when they factored in the socioeconomic status of students, families, or neighborhoods in any way. Everyone should be treated the same, he insisted.[14]

Notably, "profiling" has been a catchword used to discredit race-conscious policies that try to remedy past racial discrimination. The highly charged term incriminates the good intentions of, say, affirmative action, by associating it with racial bias. "Profiling" used in this way draws a false equivalency between a policy like affirmative action and something like the racial animus of a police officer who disproportionately suspects people of color of shoplifting. In contrast to profiling, "color blindness" is used to describe the ideal for a post-racial society that treats everyone the same. Chief Justice John Roberts famously articulated this ideal of equality in the *Parents Involved* case: "The way to stop discrimination on the basis of race is to stop discriminating on the basis of race."[15] However, philosopher Elizabeth Anderson has argued that color blindness is "conceptually confused, empirically misguided, and lacking a morally coherent rationale."[16] Although desirable in an ideal world, color blindness is counterproductive in a nonideal world such as the one we inhabit because it pretends that centuries of discrimination can be remedied with the power of positive thinking. In subverting substantive justice, the call for color blindness is often made in bad faith. Color blindness sounds good, neutral, and fair, but on the national level, there is evidence that supposedly race-neutral policies feed separate and unequal.[17] What is needed is recognition that race-based harms can only be remedied by race-conscious repairs.[18] As Anderson explains, *Brown v. Board of Education* "held that ending racial segregation was a constitutional imperative and a requirement of justice, and its successor cases, notably *Swann v. Charlotte-Mecklenburg Board of Education* . . . held that race-conscious assignment of students to schools may be necessary to achieve this goal."[19] In Wake County, the diversity policy had been the latest iteration of a longstanding effort to foster the racial and socioeconomic integration of its public schools.

Unfortunately, even though the school board's debate that March evening touched on a fundamental issue and might have proven productive if given enough time—should any aspect of a student's background or identity be factored into a student assignment policy?—Margiotta grew impatient with the back-and-forth and cut it off after a few minutes. "Enough," he said.[20] One of the late-night public speakers, Matthew Booker, specifically noted that the exchange between Sutton and Tedesco was the kind of conversation that the board should be having "for months, not for minutes."[21] But sustained attention to difficult problems and civil deliberation never materialized. Instead, rancor and dysfunction marked the board majority's governance for the rest of 2010 and well into 2011. The board majority was accused of meeting in secret (in violation of open meetings law), curtailing public participation in meetings, and making rushed and ill-informed decisions. They engaged in name calling, infighting, and even an alleged affair between two members. As a board member reflected in her interview with me:

> To be honest with you, I think it was about governance. I think it was about the two years of the Margiotta board that were so chaotic and lacking transparency, impulsive decisions, and I won't say scandal, but just poor decision making and a vilification of public input that I think was part of it. The community expected its public school board to behave better. I think that was a recurrent theme that resonated when I was on the campaign trail. They did not want a return, the voters I spoke with . . . the people I spoke with did not push for a return to the diversity policy as much as they wanted grown-ups on the school board. They wanted open government and civil government.[22]

Adding to the polarization that gripped the board in those years was a narrative of insiders and outsiders—something that was mentioned in numerous opinion articles in the *N&O* and by several of my interviewees. Even the mayor of Raleigh at the time, Charles Meeker, came under fire when he partly blamed the missteps of the board majority on the fact that they were "not from this area."[23] "Insiders" were understood to be longer-term residents of Wake County who understood and appreciated the decades of effort that went into creating an integrated school system. "Outsiders" were understood to be newer arrivals from other parts of the country who felt no particular investment in or curiosity about the history of Wake County or North Carolina, and no particular responsibility for maintaining its gains. Their concerns lay elsewhere; for example, in gaining needed stability for their children and tightening the connection between home ownership and school assignment. Although ultimately the deepest divides in this debate were not based on the number of years one had been a resident of Wake County, a recounting of this story would be incomplete without describing how people situated themselves in relation to the county's history.

How Important Is It to Understand (Local) History?

The incredible irony of northern transplants seeking to disrupt the gains of an integrated southern school system was not lost on local observers at the time. The surprising role reversal was reminiscent of President Reagan's famous gaffe in 1984 when he misread his Charlotte-based audience and complained about busing at a campaign stop in the Mecklenburg suburbs. Reagan hit the familiar conservative talking points, claiming that busing makes children "pawns in a social experiment that nobody wants." But unfortunately for him, Charlotte-Mecklenburg residents at the time were extremely proud of their successfully integrated school system, and his remarks were met with stony silence. The lead editorial the next day in the *Charlotte Observer* headlined, "You were wrong, Mr. President," and minced no words that the city's proudest achievement was its fully integrated school system.[24]

In Wake County during the years of the Margiotta board, there were similar expressions of pride in an integrated system and exasperation with those who took it for granted:

> Some on the Wake County school board were offended by Raleigh Mayor Charles Meeker's remarks at a community meeting. This board needs to realize that it's not about how they feel. It's not about where you come from or when you came. It's about collectively confronting our segregationist history, learning from that, and so not dooming ourselves to repeat it.
>
> I was born in Raleigh. I attended my neighborhood school, A. B. Combs, where the first-through-sixth-grade student body included one African American. I was bused to Carnage Junior High in 1973. My parents were wringing their hands. But guess what? As a community we came together and made it work, well, for a very long time.
>
> I've lived since graduating from Broughton High School and UNC in four other states and overseas, including a stint in New Jersey where my kids attended neighborhood schools, with the requisite exorbitant taxes. Returning to Wake County after almost three decades away, I appreciate even more what we did here in the South, in the '70s. We don't want to go back. We value diversity, equality and excellence in our schools. Get over yourselves, school board. This is bigger than you.[25]

On the same day this letter to the editor was published, July 4, 2010, Jason Morgan Ward, a young history professor teaching at Mississippi State University at the time, also weighed in on the direction of the Wake County school board. Ward, a Raleigh native who had attended school in Granville County where his father worked, proudly described Wake County: "Whatever its flaws, my hometown has refused to resegregate its schools behind code words and catchphrases. School leaders in Wake took the 'public' in public education seriously." He also contrasted Wake schools with the schools of the Mississippi Delta and New Haven, Connecticut, both of which he had observed firsthand early in his career. "Deep South or way up North, disinvestment and disillusionment ravage public education. Living in the nation's poorest state and then in the richest, I looked at the schools through Raleigh eyes and wondered: Who would have let such a thing happen?"[26]

His "Raleigh eyes" also looked skeptically at what the Wake County school board was promoting as progress: "What none of us could foresee was a school board majority that views educational balkanization as the wave of the future. Public-school antagonists who sell resegregation as entrepreneurial, anti-establishment innovation, with schools such as Enloe and Southeast Raleigh—my sister's alma mater—in the crosshairs. An ideological coup that seeks to impose a sink-or-swim mandate on low-income, minority students to bolster cynical and timeworn talking points." Without holding up Wake County schools as perfect, Ward recognized that something of value had been achieved and was at risk of being lost: "Don't let a bad situation go south—or north—on you, courtesy of those who promote racially isolated, high-poverty schools as if this were school reform."[27]

The history of public education in Wake County, North Carolina, and the South in general is obviously more complicated than can be conveyed in a single letter to the editor or op-ed. Yet many of the published opinions from this period (2009–2011), read together, tell a compelling, coherent story with a consistent message: recognize the imperfect, fragile, significant gains that were accomplished. People spoke from their personal experiences and memories, connecting with history in small ways. For example, in 2010, N&O editorial writer Jim Jenkins commemorated the fiftieth anniversary of the first Black child to integrate a white school in Raleigh in the fall of 1960, second grader Bill Campbell:

> Campbell, who'd go on to be mayor of Atlanta, was the first black child to go to a white Raleigh public school, Murphey School. He was the only minority student there for five years. Even after the 1954 *Brown v. Board* decision by the U.S. Supreme Court, public schools in the South continued to resist integration, throwing various roadblocks in the paths of black families or playing games of intimidation. And yes, this was going on in a state about to elect the relatively progressive Terry Sanford as governor and vote in majority for John F. Kennedy for president in November of that same year.[28]

Jenkins did not mention that Campbell's acceptance into the Murphey elementary school followed immediately in the wake of another Black family's thwarted efforts to enroll their teenage son in all-white Raleigh schools. The parents of Joe Holt Jr. waged a legal battle from 1956 to 1960 to enroll him in Josephus Daniels Junior High School and then Broughton High School, and endured threats, hate mail, and job loss for their persistence. Repeatedly told by the school board that his enrollment was "denied in best interest of the boy," Joe Holt finished his education in segregated schools, graduating from J. W. Ligon High School in June 1960.[29] Joe Holt's story was just one part of the larger context of the Campbell family's courage. Both families bravely "dragged too many of the white power structure in Raleigh by their heels into school integration." With a long memory and the personal experience of having attended all-white Raleigh public schools himself, Jenkins expressed his exasperation in regard to those in 2010 who showed no interest in this complex history: "Today's debate over school assignments, playing out in the rhetoric of a Wake County school board majority that is either unfamiliar with or uninterested in history, oblivious to the damning consequences of segregation . . . ought to scare everybody with a memory of what it was like 50 years ago, or 50 years ago and then some."[30]

Another compelling example came from Margaret Newbold, the granddaughter of Nathan Carter Newbold, who had served as North Carolina's first director of the Division of Negro Education for the North Carolina State Department of Instruction from 1913 to 1950. In her op-ed, Newbold expressed pride in her grandfather's efforts to "rectify the inequities" between Black and white schools throughout the state. Nathan Carter Newbold had worked within the confines of Jim Crow's "separate but equal" to try to improve Black education. For example, he coordinated with northern philanthropic organizations like the Julius Rosenwald Fund to build new schools for Blacks in the 1920s, and with the Anna T. Jeanes Fund to train and pay Black teachers.[31] He also left behind a record of his observations and judgments in periodic reports. According to his granddaughter: "In the 1912–1914 State Department of Education Biennial Report, he wrote that, 'The average Negro rural schoolhouse is really a disgrace to an independent, civilized people. To one who does not know our history, these schoolhouses, though mute, would tell in unmistaken terms a story of injustice, inhumanity, and neglect on the part of white people. Such a condition would appear to an observer as intolerable, indefensible, unbusinesslike and, above all, un-Christian.'"[32]

Margaret Newbold was herself a 1972 graduate of Broughton High School and experienced some of Raleigh's first attempts at desegregation: "I was lucky to be in one of the first classes at Broughton High School when it was merged with Ligon, the former Black high school. That experience was one of the best of my life. It exposed me to new people and new friends. It was a challenging time for our community and extremely stressful for many of the Black students who had to go to Broughton, but they showed great courage, and we all learned and grew. We worked together to make Broughton a more inclusive community and us more well-rounded individuals."[33] Informed by the legacy of her grandfather's work and her own experiences with integration, Newbold challenged the school board in 2010 not to discard hard-won progress: "History teaches us that separate is never equal. We cannot start that slide to separate and unequal again."[34]

Significantly, the story these "insiders" told was not a triumphant narrative. For every element of progress that was a source of pride, there were at least as many setbacks and losses. Integration brought educational gains for Black students, but it also meant many Black teachers and principals lost their jobs in favor of their white counterparts when schools and their staff combined.[35] It also meant that curriculum taught in Black schools was not necessarily honored or incorporated into integrated schools, as there was little sense of reciprocity or sharing of school cultures, just one-way efforts at assimilation.[36] Even fierce proponents of integration acknowledged that it came with costs for Black communities.[37] Cases like the one referenced in chapter 3, of the man who described how integration had ruined his life, were not rare.[38] Philosopher Elizabeth Anderson refers to these costs and stresses, borne disproportionately by people of color, as the "ordeal of integration."

Moreover, even a cursory look at North Carolina's history reveals that integration has always been a decidedly mixed affair, with cases of moderation or exceptionalism in point-counterpoint with repression and violence. North Carolina's 1868 constitution, the product of a "fusion coalition" of freed Blacks with local and northern whites, guaranteed every child an access to sound basic education, but fulfilling this commitment statewide has remained out of reach to this day.[39] Indeed, the Radical Reconstructionists set out to spend equal amounts for each school-age child regardless of race, but were quickly repressed by a Klan-led revolt of conservatives in 1870–1871 who "impeached Radical governor William Woods Holden, forced [Massachusetts native Rev. Samuel Stanford] Ashley to resign as superintendent of public instruction, gerrymandered legislative districts to prevent a successful counterrevolution, and rewrote the law apportioning educational funds."[40] Fusion rule between 1896 and 1900 increased spending on Black education, but these gains, too, were reversed through disenfranchisement of Blacks after 1900.[41] The Raleigh *News & Observer*—although eventually a more balanced regional newspaper and important outlet for community debate—was an explicit vehicle of the statewide white supremacy campaign in the late 1800s and early 1900s, when it was under the direction of Josephus Daniels. In fact, as a propaganda arm of white Democrats at the time, it helped facilitate the violent 1898 insurrection in Wilmington, the country's only successful coup of a legitimately elected government.[42] Governor Charles Aycock (1901–1905), often lauded as the "education governor" in history textbooks for his contributions to public education, building an average of one school a day at a time when North Carolina was largely rural and poor, in reality prioritized disenfranchising Black voters and institutionalized inequities in funding for Black schools.[43] Legally segregated schools were maintained for decades during the Jim Crow era, and yet there were people like Nathan Carter Newbold, who worked for thirty-seven years to mitigate rank inequities.

After the *Brown* decision in 1954, North Carolina avoided the worst extremes of the campaign of Massive Resistance to integration.[44] It did not shut down its schools in defiance, as happened in Virginia, but its Pearsall Plan effectively stalled integration statewide for the better part of a decade. The Pearsall committee claimed to be speaking for all North Carolinians when it wrote the following in its report: "We believe that members of each race prefer to associate with other members of their race and that they will do so naturally unless they are prodded and inflamed and controlled by outside pressure. We think it is also true that children do best when in school with children of their own race."[45] The report also candidly noted who held power statewide: "If the white people do not support a public school system in North Carolina, there will be no public education. To gain that support we believe it will be necessary to provide an available escape from a possibly unacceptable situation."[46] White parents were thus placated with the promise of private school vouchers and school closure, if needed. Local school districts were given the authority to assign students to schools according to "what is best for the child."[47] Eerily prescient, Pearsall's committee anticipated the logic of the *Milliken* and *Parents Involved* U.S. Supreme Court decisions, drawing—or rather, inventing—a distinction between de jure and de facto segregation and unabashedly saying the quiet part out loud: "A color bar by law is one thing. A factual local condition bar, even if color is one of the causes of the condition, is a different thing."[48] In other words, North Carolina could comply with the letter of the law as dictated by *Brown* while still allowing for de facto segregation in its schools to carry on as before.

As the Civil Rights Movement of the 1960s gained momentum and federal legislation eventually brought full citizenship rights to Black Americans, North Carolinians in some respects parted company with staunch segregationists like Alabama Governor George Wallace, who in 1963 famously called for "segregation now, segregation tomorrow, segregation forever." North Carolina elected governors like Terry Sanford (governor 1961–1965) and Jim Hunt (governor 1977–1985 and again 1993–2001), each of whom made major advancements for public education in both K-12 and higher education. After he was inaugurated, Governor Sanford and his wife sent their two children to the Murphey School, the same public school that had been integrated by young Bill Campbell in the previous fall. Their decision carried enormous symbolic significance at the time.[49] Sanford prioritized improving North Carolina's public schools and convinced the legislature to raise taxes to accomplish it. Per pupil spending increased, teacher pay increased, library and other resources increased—for all children. Governor Hunt, serving an unprecedented four terms that spanned from the late 1970s to the beginning of the new millennium, truly earned the title of "education governor." He directed significant increases in education spending and enforced the norm of equitable distribution of education resources.[50] The investments of this era fueled growth and prosperity. However, by 2010, when Republicans gained control of the state legislature for the first time in over a century, priorities shifted away from full funding for public education. The Republican-controlled state legislature also enacted some of the most egregious gerrymandering in the nation and a "monster" voter suppression law in 2013 that was ultimately struck down by a federal appeals court for discriminating against and targeting African Americans "with almost surgical precision."[51] Thus, the successful pushback that had taken place in Wake County in 2011 against a Republican-controlled school board, though significant, ran counter to where the state as a whole seemed to be headed. After voting for Obama in 2008, North Carolina has supported Republican presidential candidates from 2012 through the 2020 election.

Wherever one looks in the history of public education in North Carolina, the struggle to overcome centuries of racial oppression was ongoing, victories were at best partial. Those with living memories of Terry Sanford or Jim Hunt, or the 1976 merger of the Raleigh City and Wake County schools, understood that progress was fragile and not fully redemptive of past sins. Racism is still with us. Inequity is still with us. Perhaps disregard for a complicated past is what made the push to create neighborhood schools in Wake County so objectionable: "outsiders" who felt the history of segregation was not their problem to deal with were found to be as galling as anyone who actively embraced segregation or racist ideologies. This exasperation came through clearly in letters and op-eds published in 2009–2011. Yet, as I have suggested, so did appreciation for past leaders like Dudley Flood, Gene Causby, John Murphy, and Vernon Malone who, along with many others, worked hard to make integration succeed. Flood, who is Black, and Causby, who was white, traveled together throughout North Carolina to help various communities desegregate their schools: "Seven days a week, from 1969 to 1973, they met with all stakeholders to work through local issues and racial tensions that were threatening to tear communities apart."[52] After John Murphy died in 2011, the N&O ran an editorial praising his work as the first superintendent (1976–1981) of the merged Wake County system, leading the community through resentments about the merger and standing by racial integration.[53]

A 2006 video commemorating the thirtieth anniversary of the merger speaks to the depth of the community's pride in that accomplishment. "A Community United: Celebrating 30 Years of Courageous Leadership" brought together eleven community leaders to discuss their memories of the merger of Raleigh City and Wake County schools: Bob Bridges, Peggy Churn, Frank Daniels Jr., Aaron Fussell, J. T. Knott, Vernon Malone, Marvin Musselwhite, Walt Sherlin, Roy Tilley, Wesley Williams, and Smedes York.[54] They explained how the state legislature moved ahead with the merger despite the public's decisive rejection (2–1 defeat) in a nonbinding referendum, noting the intense lobbying efforts of the business community and bold leadership of the Wake

County legislative delegation: "I think it represents leadership at its finest. The leaders in the community not liking the direction they see the community headed, believing as a community we can do better, and we can make some hard decisions now that will benefit our community in the future."[55] They also acknowledged the opposition to merger from both whites and Blacks. Some in the Black community had not wanted merger because they feared they would lose control of their schools. However, Vernon Malone, first chair of the board of education of the merged system and African American, explained, "There were people who were vehemently opposed to merger, vehemently opposed, but once they made up their minds that this is where we ought to go, they worked more diligently to make it work than some of those who had been on the front end of saying it should be done. It was amazing to see that evolution in mind and emotion." He said Wake County "never lost one school day because of disruption in schools." Malone also described a shared commitment to educational excellence for all children and specifically praised John Murphy on this point: "He was one of the first educators I heard in my lifetime who would publicly say minority kids can learn and we're going to see that that happens." Peggy Churn, Principal of York Elementary at the time of the merger, shared her thoughts on the community's mindset in 2006: "I think that if there is a disappointment, it is that there are people who take all of this for granted now. And they don't understand the courage, the boldness, the work, the commitment that occurred for us to be what we are today. I think that's really important for us all to keep in mind." The video was filmed just three short years before the 2009 election.

"Please Respect Our History": Disagreements over Past and Present in Wake County

Like the members of the public who implored the opponents of the diversity policy to study North Carolina's and Wake County's history, many of the leaders I interviewed in 2018–2019, especially if they had themselves lived through the merger of Raleigh and Wake County schools, described a community that had survived a difficult reckoning—not unscathed, not triumphantly but better off for the effort. In the words of one of my interviewees who was a teenager at the time of the merger, "I think a lot of people wanted to do what was right in reference to our past history."[56] The Margiotta board's lack of interest in this difficult history was thus astounding to her: "I remember the first time I spoke [at a board meeting] and the main things I felt was I just felt offended because I felt like we had it right here, not perfect, but we were on the right track and I remember saying something in the first speech about, 'Please respect our history.'"[57]

Another one of my interviewees expressed some sympathy with people who were new to the area: "I mean there's so many people here that come from other parts of the country where the way we do things here is just absolutely mind-boggling to them. And I understand that. So, I don't blame parents for moving here and just being completely overwhelmed and frustrated with how we do things. I really, I sympathize with them. But, that keeps our taxes low, and people like low taxes."[58] And from a less sympathetic interviewee: "Because these people are moving from, I'm sorry, I'm a southerner, I don't know where you're from, so please don't take this . . . They come from these little small municipalities in New York, New Jersey, Connecticut, where you have, 'My school, my money. My school, my money.' Okay? And, they're small. . . . It's not spread out like we are in Wake County. . . . From an economies of scale stand-point, it makes more sense to have a consolidated school system."[59]

I had discussed this issue of "insiders-outsiders" at length with former super-intendent Bill McNeal, who understood both the point of view of the new-comers and that of local politicians who profited from parents' discontent; for example, politicians reasoned, "I can assure my reelection if I sit with this group."[60] Speaking about the early 2000s, he explained,

> Well, you have to understand we were a growing county, okay? And as people
> moved to Wake County, many of them came from small independent school
> districts in the Northeast. And the small independent school districts ran
> things the way they wanted to. They had their own tax base, the whole nine
> yards. They come to Wake County and they look around and they say, "Wait a
> minute. What do you mean I live here, and I can almost see the school, and my
> child can't go to that school?" Because their expectation was that when I come
> to the county, and I move into this home [then I get a particular school
> assignment]. . . . And by the way, the Realtors didn't help us a great deal. . . .
> They would never tell the parent that's not your base school, 'cause a lot of
> times, they would put erroneous base schools down if you buy the home.[61]

However, from the point of view of an activist within the Republican party and a native southerner, the bigger problem was the frequency of the reassign-ments and the instability that it caused in the lead-up to the 2009 election, in addition to thwarted expectations:

> It was the mandatory reassignments. And the reason that the school system
> did it was to achieve socioeconomic balance in the school system, and people
> saw their child[ren] being used as pawns. Every year they were reassigning, and
> then you'd go to three schools in five years or something like that, you didn't
> have that stability. There wasn't an ability to create culture and community in
> the schools, things like that. And parents, it was just infuriating to their lives to
> have to deal with this. And one, they had a school as the crow flies about a mile

away, and they couldn't go to that school, but they were having to go to a school 30 minutes away, and it infuriated them that they couldn't [get] in that school.[62]

Even a strong supporter of the diversity policy conceded the possibility that divisions in the community were not necessarily unbridgeable. She suggested that there should have been "some logistical fixes to not have those parents be so upset. Like I felt like it wasn't so much that they didn't want their kids to go to school with low-income people, it wasn't that for the people. It was just that they, it was just so super inconvenient in some cases."[63]

Notwithstanding some reasonable complaints about instability and inconvenience, an examination of the public debate in 2009–2011 suggests that echoes of past ideologies could still be heard. Perhaps the most notable were echoes of the Pearsall committee's statement in 1956 that the "separateness of the races is natural and best."[64] Even in the twenty-first century, this reasoning has had surprising staying power. Take, for example, these excerpts from letters to the *N&O* published in 2010: "Perhaps minority families who actually live in Wake County, like most of us, prefer that their children attend schools in their communities."[65] And: "Having lived in North Carolina less than four years, I have yet to understand the segregation debate. . . . I live in a community that is probably equally Black and white. We are not a well-integrated community. People gravitate toward those with whom they feel comfortable. On my morning walks, I see students awaiting the school bus, invariably separated into discussion groups identifiable by the color of their skin. Forcing students to go to class with other races is not going to integrate them."[66] These letters seem to agree that separateness of the races is natural and best, especially if this separation is freely chosen and preferred by the people themselves. Indeed, the preferences of individuals seem most determinative, and more important than chasing the difficult dream of integration.

Echoes of separate and equal also reappeared as ostensibly "race neutral" or post-racial color blindness. This letter asserted that integration efforts were no longer necessary: "While it's lovely that Wake County has been awarded from afar for its diversity efforts, the reality is many of the families actually experiencing the system are far less impressed with the results. Finding a loophole (socioeconomics) to ignore the fact that busing for race has been struck down by the Supreme Court of the United States (and deemed unnecessary by most of the country) is somehow considered 'progressive' when really we need to move ahead with the times."[67]

Clearly there were differences of opinion about what constituted progress and how the community should understand itself in relation to its segregationist past. For some, embracing community-based schools—"neighborhood schools"—appeared to be an act of willful ignorance that turned a blind eye to the history of segregation and discarded what had been built without much concern for the costs. For others, moving forward required leaving old policies behind, following people's preferences, and trying a different way. Since there was a strong sense at the time that a portion of the community was uninterested in seeking greater understanding of the past, it is legitimate to ask, What happens when a community is not particularly aware of its local, regional, or national history? For one, ideas like "separate but equal" may reemerge without critical examination, or they may emerge in a new guise. For another, as expressed by one of my interviewees, a longtime Raleigh business leader, there is the feeling of a lot of wasted effort: "There are a bunch of us that've been around a long damn time and have seen things really improve. So at our age, this is really disappointing to see all of that work unraveled. . . . And we were really rolling. I mean, we were good. Everybody worked really hard. Politics aside, this is just really sad for a lot of us. Because it's been a lot of work."[68]

As Wake County moves further into the twenty-first century, it becomes clearer that ideological commitments matter more than simply where one grew up or whether one is an "insider" or "outsider" to a particular region of the country. One of the most influential is the ideology of school choice, which has grown in prominence nationally as overt desegregation efforts have receded.

The Unraveling of School Desegregation Efforts across the United States

On the national level, it has been observed that "desegregation was like an unreliable car: it took forever to warm up, ran well for a brief period, and then sputtered and eventually died."[69] Spurred by efforts to finally enforce the legal requirements of *Brown*, school desegregation gained momentum through the 1970s, especially in the South, peaking nationwide in 1988. However, *Milliken* (1974) stunted cross-district integration and arguably incentivized white flight to suburban schools. *Parents Involved* (2007) further constricted desegregation by ending race-based student assignments. Even where desegregation efforts had been relatively successful, they unraveled as districts were released from court orders and voluntary efforts to integrate by using race as a factor in student assignment were deemed unconstitutional.[70]

The legal challenges that led to the unraveling of desegregation emanated from various and sometimes surprising quarters. For example, Black families from Louisville, Kentucky, initiated a lawsuit that, when combined with a lawsuit from Seattle, resulted in the *Parents Involved* decision that would end race-based student assignment efforts. Sarah Garland tells their story in *Divided We Fail: The Story of an African American Community That Ended the Era of*

School Desegregation, explaining how the protection of a beloved African American high school, Central High, led to the original lawsuit. Central High was in danger of being closed because it could not attract enough white students. Louisville's desegregation plan had required every school to maintain a white majority, and crucially, school district officials had prioritized following this rule ahead of listening to the voices and preferences of Black parents. In response, a group of African American plaintiffs sued in a district court "to end racial quotas at the school and keep it open."[71] They won. Garland writes, "For the most part, it was not that Black activists opposed racial integration. . . . What they opposed was how desegregation had so often worked as a one-way exchange, and the lack of concern about how the loss of their schools and their voice might affect their community."[72] In addition to equal educational outcomes, Black parents wanted "equal power over the schools and over the content and trajectory of their children's education—something they argued that racial integration in the schools never produced. Desegregation had been framed as a way to make up for what Black people lacked. They wanted recognition that . . . their culture had strengths."[73] *Parents Involved* caused a sea change in how school districts could pursue integration; less commonly acknowledged is the fact that it also contained a painful lesson about the consequences of not listening to Black communities and what they felt they had to give up with integration.

The lawsuit that ended the busing program in Charlotte, North Carolina, also contributed to the unraveling of desegregation efforts, but for more predictable reasons: white parents wanting access to desirable schools and disregarding historical efforts at desegregation. Five of the six white plaintiffs in *Capacchione v. Charlotte-Mecklenburg Schools* (1999), the district court case that challenged the use of race in student assignments in the Charlotte-Mecklenburg school system, were newcomers to the Charlotte area. According to Roslyn Mickelson and her coauthors, white newcomers "were accustomed to predominantly white, suburban school districts; and, not having lived through CMS's desegregation battles, they lacked the pride of more established Charlotteans in the busing plan."[74] Recognizing that support for the busing plan was waning, John Murphy (the same superintendent who had served Wake) had introduced a system of magnet schools in the early 1990s to maintain desegregation: "The plan sought to hitch CMS's wagon to the rising star of school choice."[75] Angered when unable to access a desired magnet school for his daughter and believing she had been denied because she was white, William Capacchione sued.

These are by now familiar storylines: Black voices and Black contributions are ignored or undervalued while white voices leverage power to gain access to desired spaces. School integration efforts then succumb to other priorities. As various legal cases played out in the early part of the new century, desegregation efforts have been eclipsed by what is broadly known as the school choice movement.

"Everybody Wants to Choose Their School": The Pull toward Privatization

For better or worse, school choice is part of the landscape of public education in the United States. Whether it is the choice of where to buy a home to gain access to desirable public schools, the choice of a magnet school, the choice of a charter school, or the choice to use a private school voucher to exit the public system altogether, American parents are expected to put some effort into selecting a school for their child.[76] They are expected to do their homework and be savvy consumers, not simply count on the local public school to be of good quality with excellent teachers and a robust curriculum. In fact, to speak of the government's responsibility to provide an adequate public education is almost taboo in a culture that prizes choice and individual agency.[77] Choosing a school is treated as the parents' responsibility, one that expresses their competence as parents, their values, and their commitment to their child. It is both a form of expressive individualism and an expectation of intensive parenting.[78] According to one of my interviewees, a school board member, "Everybody wants to choose their school. . . . I think it's the only way [parents] feel like they do something right for their child."[79]

School choice, like other important choices, rests on the freedom to discern and pursue individual preferences, a foundational value of any free society. In the American context, school choice also operates within a framework of consumerism that treats education as a private good. Alongside a consumerist mindset, school choice often operates with the assumption that competition among schools yields better results, greater variety, higher quality. In other words, school choice carries with it an inherent faith in the mechanisms of a free market. The accumulation of individual choices can and does impact the common good, including the nature of the options available to all children. But school choice, insofar as it is a part of a broader ideology of individualism, is not constrained by these concerns. Nor does it worry about the zero-sum game mentality that it fosters. Making choices involves exercising power, such as the power to exclude. But the ideology of choice prioritizes individual freedom over the value of equality or community. Despite this morally problematic tradeoff, "school choice" endures in the United States.

"School choice" is also a term with a history, like the term "neighborhood schools." Reviewing this history illuminates how school choice has intersected in different ways with the cause of school integration, sometimes encouraging it, oftentimes thwarting it. Erika Wilson describes this history in her article "The New White Flight," documenting the ways in which school choice has been and continues to be used "as a vehicle to allow whites as a collective to satisfy their aggregate preference for predominantly white schools."[80] In the years following *Brown*, "school choice" and "freedom of choice" were euphemisms for resisting school desegregation in the South. White families left the public system for private schools, called "segregation academies," often with the help of government vouchers. Black students were given the "free" choice to select a public school in an environment openly and violently hostile to integration. Unsurprisingly, very few Black students attempted to attend white schools, and white students saw no reason to leave what they had. Later, as white flight dramatically altered the racial composition of urban and suburban schools around the country, school choice was harnessed to *facilitate* desegregation, usually by attracting white students to specialized magnet schools placed in urban centers. In more recent years, school choice has been sold as a way to provide better options to low-income students whose neighborhood schools are deemed to be "failing." Wilson focuses her specific analysis on "white charter school enclaves," which she defines as charter schools that "enroll a student body that is greater than 50 percent white, although white student enrollment in the school district in which the charter schools are located is less than thirty percent."[81] Ultimately, she argues that this kind of parental choice—the kind that leads regularly and predictably to increased segregation—should be better regulated. In this case, freedom of choice should have some limits.

School choice remains a difficult concept, both nationally and within Wake County. People generally value choice. But they also worry about its effects. Indeed, some of the most common themes from the interviews I conducted with community leaders related to school choice.[82] Those who were worried about the effects of school choice often connected these concerns explicitly with broader concerns about privatization, a process of restructuring how education is delivered that relies on choice. It was clear from these discussions that privatization represents a major point of contention in the fight over the future of public education.[83]

Privatization is a process of moving to the private sector what has previously been provided by the government. Milton Friedman advocated for the privatization of public education in 1955, the year after *Brown* was decided. He was the first to refer to public schools as "government schools"—a term of disparagement meant to imply an inefficient and ineffective monopoly. Friedman argued that the private sector would strengthen the quality of schools through competition in a free market. Just as FedEx and UPS could do a better job than the U.S. Post Office, Friedman claimed, so too would private schools innovate and offer more attractive options, thereby pressuring traditional public schools to either improve their product or lose their "clientele."[84] The end game, however, was a fully privatized system with a plethora of choices to satisfy a variety of consumer preferences, not necessarily a strengthened set of public schools.

Thus, hastening the demise of "government schools" was an inherent goal of the privatization movement from the beginning. The Reagan administration in the 1980s implemented a strategy of starving the public sector and redirecting energy and resources to private solutions, from airlines to education and beyond.[85] Proponents of privatization have continued that work for the last forty years.

On the national level, underinvestment in public education has been stark. The COVID-19 pandemic of 2020–2021 has shined a light on the problem of deferred maintenance, deteriorating facilities, and unsafe air circulation: "[In the summer of 2020], the U.S. Government Accountability Office released its first report since 1996 on the physical condition of the nation's public schools. It found that a majority cannot make needed major building repairs because of the expense. Among the most common problems encountered were those involving expensive H.V.A.C. systems, which deal with heating, cooling and ventilation. The study found that forty-one percent of schools needed to repair or replace their antiquated heating and ventilation systems."[86] Notably, according to the GAO survey, about half of districts nationwide use local sources such as local property taxes to fund school facilities. High-poverty districts more commonly rely on state funding and lack the ability to supplement with local funds.[87]

Since the 2010 election when the Republicans gained a majority in the state legislature, North Carolina's underinvestment in public education has also been stark. North Carolina cut per pupil funding sharply at the start of the 2008 recession and never restored that funding as the economy recovered. North Carolina now ranks forty-second in per pupil funding among the states. Compared to fiscal year 2008–2009, North Carolina is providing schools with 800 fewer teachers, 500 fewer instructional support personnel (e.g., school nurses, who are now shared between schools), and 7,730 fewer teacher assistants, and it also imposed a 40 percent cut to spending on textbooks, classroom supplies, and school technology.[88] Funding effort (the percentage of school spending as a proportion of the state's GDP) has also declined: North Carolina's ranking fell from an already poor forty-second in 2008 to forty-ninth in 2018.[89] At the same time, the North Carolina legislature has redirected resources to alternative educational options, including private school vouchers.[90] The amount being spent on private school vouchers has steadily increased from $15 million when the program was first introduced in 2013 to over $60 million in 2021.[91] Eligibility for access to vouchers has also expanded beyond the originally intended low-income households.[92]

As has been mentioned, North Carolina legislators lifted the cap on charter schools in 2011. Previously limited to one hundred statewide, the number of charters has more than doubled in a decade. State funding for charters exceeded $734 million for the 2019–2020 school year.[93] Although charter schools are still public schools in the sense of receiving public funding, they are often privately managed by for-profit, out-of-state companies and are not governed by elected officials. Charters also play by a different set of rules than traditional public schools in North Carolina and are arguably advantaged in the competition for students. Charters have no curriculum requirements and are free to modify their academic calendar. By not being required to provide transportation to students or free and reduced-price lunches, charters are also free to shape their student body to favor those who can afford to provide these things for themselves, and to exclude those who cannot.

The people I interviewed had varying opinions about the inherent value of school choice and privatization. Most agreed that privatization, by definition, undermines public options. Whether that process was deemed helpful or harmful depended on the value attached to traditional public schools. Advocates for traditional public schools clearly saw privatization as a major threat. However, school choice by itself was not necessarily seen as problematic if there was a "level playing field" between the different types of schools, like charters and traditional public schools. As one activist noted, "If we leveled that playing field, I know the last man or woman standing would be the [traditional] public schools."[94] However, most agreed there was not a level playing field between traditional public schools and other educational options.[95]

Several conversations centered on charter schools and the role they are playing in reshaping the educational landscape statewide and nationally. For example, charters can pose a threat to traditional public schools in rural communities with fewer resources. They are also harmful when they facilitate secession from a larger integrated school district, as the North Carolina General Assembly made possible by allowing four predominantly white Charlotte suburbs to form their own charter districts apart from the CMS system.[96] But even in Wake County, which has managed to remain a single district, charter schools are creating significant challenges. Put starkly by one school board member, "Charter schools are killing the health of our schools."[97] According to another: "Our charter schools in Wake County and in North Carolina are statistically more segregated than our public schools, and they are not, in my opinion, providing any innovative work. . . . They were intended to be innovators [but] now they are just escape valves for parents who want some control or don't get what they want from the public school system."[98] Indeed, research supports the contention that charter schools aggravate segregation. In addition to Erika Wilson's work on "white charter school enclaves," Helen Ladd and Mavzuna Turaeva have demonstrated that the movement of white, but not minority, students from traditional public schools to charter schools increases segregation between schools.[99] Charters in North Carolina are allowing white parents to exercise their power to bend the system to their preferences.

However, notably, charters are also popular with some Black families, raising the questions about whether charters facilitate self-segregation more generally and whether self-segregation is to some extent desirable. Wilson notes
that, compared to white parents, "parents of color also prefer schools in which
their children are in the racial majority, but their preference is not as strong."
Nor is their preference equivalent in impact: "Given the historical significance
of all-white spaces, the result of their preference is not exclusionary."[100] In addition, it is important to remember how unevenly school choice is experienced.
Sociologist Mary Patillo's qualitative study of poor and working-class Black
parents in Chicago demonstrates that real choice is largely the domain of
privileged people who enjoy empowerment, agency, and control. For the
low-income parents in her study trying to select a high school for their child,
numerous barriers obstructed access to school options, such as lacking the
transportation or the time to visit schools. Parents "expressed experiential
knowledge of being chosen, rather than choosing... and highlighted the
opacity, uncertainty, and burden of choice, even while they participated in it
quite heartily."[101]

The Question at the Heart of School Choice: Private Consumption or Collective Character?

One interview I conducted with a strong proponent of school choice illus-
trated how difficult it is to honor the choices of individuals while making sure
the accumulation of individual choices does not erode the common good. I
spoke with Terry Stoops, the director of the Center for Effective Education at
the conservative John Locke Foundation, who had published an opinion
piece in the *New York Times* in 2012 in favor of school choice.[102] He had
argued that Charlotte-Mecklenburg's system of neighborhood schools
combined with parental choice produced better outcomes for low-income
students than Wake County's diversity policy. He also thought "choice" was
more durable than "forced busing." I had never met Stoops before our interview but found him surprisingly open to criticizing aspects of the school
choice movement, despite his strongly worded op-ed and unwavering commitment to choice itself.

Stoops expressed support for school integration, but he was clear in his view
that academic achievement was the core purpose of education. When these
goals might conflict, he was willing to subordinate integration to the primary
goal of academic achievement.

> I think [diversity is] important, but whether that is our overriding goal, and
> whether that dictates how all other policies should be managed, I think is

where I might draw the line. As I said, student achievement is my number one focus. That doesn't mean that we can't have other foci [like] having integrated schools. And I think to do that, honestly, I think that the best way to do that is through school choice rather than forced assignment of students. Where a child in any neighborhood has a chance to go to a school in any other neighborhood. I think that if we're ever going to achieve any sort of integration of the schools with parents on the side of that effort, and not feeling that they're disadvantaged by it, it'll be through a system of school choice. Initiated by a school, fair to all kids, with access to schools being available to students broadly.[103]

In truth, his reasoning resonated with Bill McNeal's understanding that schools had to be in the business of education and anything other than a focus on academic achievement would ultimately be torn down by parents. Both McNeal and Stoops seemed to agree on the importance of voluntary buy-in.

It was also clear that Stoops had a strong respect for individual choices, regardless of whether they promoted integration or not.

I mean, it's hard for me to think about, and it's impossible to know, what criteria parents use to make that choice. So I'm not assuming that they are making a choice actively looking to segregate their child. There's any number of factors that are involved. Plus, you have this strange situation where you have all African-American schools, African-American charter schools. . . .
I remember a few years, reading a dissertation of a researcher that asked the parents, does it bother you that this school is segregated? This is an all-Black school. And overwhelmingly, the parents said, it doesn't bother us at all.[104]

People have different reasons for holding the preferences they do. Black parents might prefer an all-Black school for their child because they perceive it to be a superior academic and social environment, or for any number of reasons. They might also prioritize the quality of education irrespective of a school's demographics.[105] As is well known, W.E.B. Du Bois argued in 1935 that "theoretically the Negro needs neither segregated schools nor mixed schools. What he needs is an education."[106] Although Stoops called it a "strange situation," he respected that all-Black schools were sometimes the result of parental preference.

Stoops told me he and his wife had recently started a charter school, Carolina Charter Academy, which was an enormous investment of time and energy. An obvious supporter of charters, Stoops nevertheless conceded that they eat away at traditional public schools' "market share." The solution, in his view, was for traditional public schools to embrace more choice: "When you start to restrict parents' choices, they start to seek them out in other ways, and I think in Wake County and Mecklenburg County, they seek them out with charter schools. So, I think in a way that a district providing more choice is actually the foil for charter schools. I think that's the secret sauce."[107]

Traditional public schools thus should join the fray and try to distinguish themselves with niche programming, unique missions, and memorable branding. And yet, despite his unequivocal commitment to choice as an expression of individual freedom, Stoops recognized that the school choice movement has neglected concerns about equity.

> But one part of the school choice movement that's disappointing is not taking the other side seriously about the desire for equity. . . . It's their inability to see it beyond a means, an individualistic means, rather than a communitarian mean[s]. That's an unfortunate outgrowth of some of the thought that's happening in school choice. And I think that's because it's being led by Libertarian groups that don't really want to think about what some of the communitarian goals are. They want to think about what individualistic goals are and try to fulfill those. So there's a balance there somewhere, but I have yet to really discover it in the school choice circles that I'm in.[108]

He is not alone in seeking that balance between individual choice and equity. The fact that he was willing to criticize the focus on individualism in the school choice movement suggested an openness to conceiving of education as both an individual and social good. In short, there seemed to be an opportunity to find some common ground.

Likewise, Rob Schofield, director of the liberal-leaning NC Policy Watch, was willing to criticize progressive groups for embracing an unfettered "what's in it for me" consumerism at the expense of the common good: "I think it's not just with the schools, I think it's a kind of value that we need to espouse in all relationships between people and their government. People relate to their government like they do unfortunately too often, like they relate to Home Depot. . . . I want the best thing I can get for my kids at the cheapest possible price. I feel like progressives have kind of fallen for that to a certain extent, we're all, what's in it for me. It's this transactional kind of relationship, rather than ownership and common good."[109] That he was willing to see the decline in the general commitment to the common good as a problem that transcends political party affiliation was also a sign that constructive public debate might be possible in the future.

Clearly, the freedom to choose a school for one's child has enormous appeal in the United States for a host of reasons. It resonates deeply with our individualism and desire for self-expression. It can reinforce a sense of identity, and garners loyalty and buy-in. It also feeds our consumerism and satisfies the perceived requirements of proactive or intensive parenting. However, as legal scholar Martha Minow has argued, the "frame of consumerism" is inadequate to the task of envisioning what public education should look like. She writes, "The very framework of choice pushes the character of emerging schools off the screen of public discussion and treats the question as one of private consumption rather than collective character."[110]

Moreover, because school choice is experienced through the racist structures that are deeply embedded in our national history, choices are not neutral in their impact but often exacerbate inequality. Parents nowadays may tell themselves that their choices are "acts of consumerism rather than segregationist tactics," especially if they do not know their local or national history, but their school choices are having significant consequences, including exacerbating segregation and undermining the health of the nation's public educational system.[111]

Fusion Coalitions and Fighting for the Future

As we have seen, school integration is a fragile and imperfect endeavor. The story of Wake County shows that progress in school integration was incremental and mixed with setbacks and losses. Yet the early multiracial leadership of the merged Wake County school system in the 1970s and 1980s made important, historic gains. Similarly, the groundswell that resisted the Margiotta board and ultimately elected a new school board in 2011 was historic and noteworthy. It was an example of what is possible when a multiracial coalition—or fusion coalition, as Rev. William Barber often calls it—unites around a common cause. Fusion coalitions are stronger because they build on a variety of perspectives. To confront the issue of school integration, different racial and political perspectives are crucially important. Our knowledge of the past is incomplete without them. Effective policy making for the future is impossible without them.

The story of Great Schools in Wake, the group of local activists largely credited with leading the fight to successfully oust the Republican majority in 2011, exemplifies the power of a fusion coalition. It was Great Schools in Wake that made sure people knew what was going on during school board meetings, encouraged people to attend and speak at those meetings, and did the research to find out the facts about things like the lengths of bus rides and the frequency of school reassignments. According to community leader Yevonne Brannon, who would later create a statewide nonprofit organization called Public Schools First NC, the people who were energized to speak up were a diverse group.

> So we got caught not listening carefully or not understanding some of the unrest and some of the concerns that were going on in the community. So we got caught in the headlights, right? But the community responded, and it

responded quickly and immediately. . . . You saw a lot of people step up and say we're sorry we've been so quiet. . . . We want to get more involved and we want to stand up and protect this. I think it was really good and we had people in that room that were diverse age-wise and from different communities. Wake Forest, Knightdale, Apex, Cary. People who had kids in the school system, some who did not. Some educators. People of color. Republicans and Democrats. Can't tell you how many times people said to me, "I'm a Republican, but can I come to your meeting?" I would go, "Yes! You can come to the meeting."[112]

She described what felt like a strong and unique moment of solidarity.

What we saw and maybe won't ever see it again, I don't know, because growth overwhelms everything after a while. The sense of community gets harder and harder to feel. But I felt like there was such a sense of community in those years from 2009, 2011, 2013. That four years was probably one of the most remarkable periods of time that I'll ever have as a community member. I felt like the community was really working together. People from lots of different walks of life, from Wake Medical Center director, to people who were real estate agents, to police officers and teachers and people at the gas station. Everybody kind of knew what was going on, was very excited and we did turn that school board around.[113]

Brannon explained how the sustained commitment eventually had an impact: "It was something remarkable to do by a bunch of people. Predominantly women. Who had never really been engaged in civic disobedience, civil protest. Look how we packed those boardrooms, look how we showed up, we stayed there at meetings that went to 10, 11 and 12:00 at night. For five years straight we were packing those board meetings. . . . That was a tremendous amount of commitment. And the community responded, the community answered the call. This is a very proud time in our history."[114]

It is only in hindsight that I have come to fully appreciate the larger context of this history and how Great Schools in Wake's activism fit into it. As a transplant myself to the area, I had a lot to learn about the history of segregation and desegregation efforts in Wake County. What stands out to me now is the coalition's determination not to go backward but to preserve and improve upon imperfect gains. In addition, the ownership of the problem of segregation was a revelation—a stark departure from the cultural mindset of my youth growing up in the Northeast, where school segregation was often quietly assumed to be a southern problem, despite manifest evidence to the contrary.

The years since the 2011 election have seen tremendous changes in Wake County, statewide, and nationally. Pandemic exhaustion, political polarization, teacher shortages, and the relentless push toward privatization all shape the current moment. The fight for the future is now in many ways the fight to preserve public education itself. But we still need public education. As Reverend Barber has remarked, "Fully funded public education is a bedrock of multicultural democracy."[115] In chapter 5, we will look back at the public debate in Wake County and ask two key questions: What are the moral logics that might make the case for true integration? What are the moral arguments that might save public schools?

5

Moral Logics and the
Case for True Integration

Nice white parents shape public schools even in our absence because public schools are maniacally loyal to white families even when that loyalty is rarely returned back to the public schools. Just the very idea of us, the threat of our displeasure, warps the whole system. So separate is still not equal because the power sits with white parents no matter where we are in the system. I think the only way you equalize schools is by recognizing this fact and trying wherever possible to suppress the power of white parents. Since no one's forcing us to give up power, we white parents are going to have to do it voluntarily. Which, yeah, how's that going to happen?

—*Nice White Parents*, Episode Three: "This Is Our School, How Dare You?"

If there were an answer to the question of how to rein in the power of white parents in any episode of *Nice White Parents*, the podcast series by reporter Chana Joffe-Walt that first aired in the summer of 2020, it was perhaps implied in the following observation: "In order to address inequality in our public schools, we are going to need a shared sense of reality."[1] We need to be looking at the same facts, aware of the same history, cognizant of the consequences of our own actions, and willing to see our interconnectedness as individuals. However, illuminating a shared sense of reality, as important a task as that may be, is still only the first step in solving inequality. Whether we are examining a single public school in Brooklyn, New York, or a large countywide district in

North Carolina, inequality and school segregation are tenacious, American problems. In fact, many would argue that American public schools are operating exactly as they were intended: as a linchpin of a racial caste system that perpetuates advantages and disadvantages.[2] They might further claim that the self-interest of white parents is immovable and that recognizing a shared reality—learning the facts, learning the history, recognizing responsibility, and appreciating a common destiny—is not enough to change hearts and minds or to alter a system that entrenches privilege. These claims are reasonable, but I am not prepared to render a final judgment on the moral capacities or limitations of my fellow Americans. I believe people are generally capable of self-reflection and change, especially when they are reminded of the benefits of the common good, or what author and economic policy advocate Heather McGhee calls "solidarity dividends."[3] I believe people can be persuaded to do better if given reasons to do better. Thus, I agree with Joffe-Walt that trying to illuminate a shared sense of reality is a good place to start.

I studied Wake County's perspectives on school integration during an intense period of public debate about the district's diversity policy. The policy was dismantled in early 2010, and the groundswell of support to save or reinstate it lasted at least until the next election cycle in 2011. I focused on the public debate because I heard moral arguments being made in school board meetings and read them in the pages of the newspaper. As an ethicist, I take moral arguments seriously. I also believe more generally that values and ideas matter: they motivate people to act, undergird major policy decisions, and infuse our institutions with meaning. Yet we rarely focus on an explicit examination of values, perhaps because they are generally viewed as private, unchangeable, or beyond the scope of a civil public debate. We know that people have opinions about a range of issues—we are awash in national polling data—but often resist a deeper analysis of where those views came from or how they can be shaped. I set out to learn something about one community's values by listening to and doing a close reading of words—published opinions, delivered speeches, and interviews where I asked people directly about their values. I endeavored to pinpoint the most salient themes and to capture enough detail to represent the general scope of the public debate in Wake County for a brief window of time. Because I was also personally immersed in the debate as a parent-activist myself, I brought years of observations to this project.

Having spent time listening and reflecting in previous chapters, in this chapter I respond to what I found. First, I will distill the main values in the debate and major points of contention. In brief, I found the greatest number of themes coalescing around competing conceptions of equality and freedom. I will summarize these conceptions, drawing on a range of examples. Then I will describe the moral logics that emerged in my analysis of how people expressed their views. "Moral logics" are interpretive frameworks that help make sense of and bring logical coherence to moral judgments or moral reasoning. In my evaluation, the moral logics of individualism and pragmatism were two prominent frameworks for understanding the issues surrounding school integration. A third framework, what could be called "civic idealism," will also be considered.

Throughout this chapter, I compare this public debate in Wake County to the most persuasive arguments I have found that promote "true" integration. I draw especially upon the work of Elizabeth Anderson, including her book *The Imperative of Integration* (2010); Michael Sandel's *The Tyranny of Merit: What's Become of the Common Good?* (2020); and Heather McGhee's *The Sum of Us: What Racism Costs Everyone and How We Can Prosper Together* (2021), among other resources, for analyzing the moral logics that circulated in the community conversation.

I also take a closer look at who typically holds power and what that means, what is now referred to in education circles as "the problem of nice white parents." Ultimately, I argue that the moral logics of individualism and pragmatism are inadequate by themselves for a multiracial democracy. This chapter contends that a multiracial sharing of power is the only sustainable and defensible path forward. It also offers the following prescriptive conclusions: privileged parents must take more responsibility for the damage wrought by unchecked individualism; integration should be framed not only as equalizing resources but as a corrective for the moral, cultural, and cognitive deficiencies resulting from unearned privilege; integrated schools are better schools; and true integration and true inclusion rests on solidarity rather than striving. In sum, I write in this chapter as an ethicist, analyzing arguments and making one of my own.

Competing Conceptions of Equality, Revisited

At the heart of the debate about integration versus segregation is really the question of how human beings within a polity ought to relate to one another across differences, regardless of whether those differences are real or perceived, innate or constructed. Differences of race, ethnicity, socioeconomic status, health, ability, gender, sexuality, and more press the questions of what it means to treat people equally or how to know when equal treatment has been achieved. That we struggle to define equality in the face of so many differences speaks to our human desire for fairness and our shared membership in a human community. Although we may never agree on a universal ideal of equality, we hold on to the concept as valuable and argue over its meaning. Despite disappointments and failures, especially in the United States, we hold on to the idea of equality because to abandon it as naïve, illusory, or unworkable seems tantamount to abandoning democracy itself. We also recognize, at base, that equal treatment under the law is preferable to the chaos of "might makes right"—the idea that the powerful determine the rules and declare what is right to suit their own interests. Even if societies past and present offer ample evidence of power abuse, most people generally aspire to do better, or suspect there are good reasons to try.

Communities like Wake County that erupt in conflict about their public schools are often a window into our country's larger wrestling with equality and freedom.[4] Such conflicts reveal aspects of our current thinking, suggesting which ideas are ascendant and which are in decline. Take, for example, the angry pushback by parents who did not want to see gifted and talented programming removed from their children's elementary schools in New York City, or who did not want to see entrance exams removed from the application process for NYC's elite public high schools.[5] Or consider the way public schools became highly politicized in the 2021 Virginia governor's race, where the Republican candidate exploited parents' fears that their children were being indoctrinated by critical race theory.[6] The New York parents wanted to ensure access for their own children to the highest quality instruction and most elite schools. The Virginia parents wanted more control over what their children were taught about race, history, and personal responsibility. These examples suggest that public education is viewed not as a community exercise in inculcating democratic values but as an extension of the parents' preferences for their children and as a private good that cements advantage and ensures success.

What made the example of Wake County in 2009–2011 different was not that Wake parents lacked strong feelings and preferences but that all sides of the debate largely framed their preferences in terms of what they believed was good for the community. Did the student assignment policy benefit all students? Were socioeconomically integrated schools better schools? Was the diversity policy worth the costs and inconveniences? Was the goal of equality or equal treatment truly being served? The conflict was thus not merely a battle of competing individual demands but a larger conversation about values. Also, there were no public threats of violence, as has happened more recently at school board meetings.

One conception of equality alive in the debate about the diversity policy in Wake County was that people should be treated "the same." We saw this idea in chapter 2, in numerous letters to the editor and op-eds. Some argued that taking differences like socioeconomic status, academic achievement, or race into account when assigning students to schools was both unnecessary and unfair. They argued that schools should be composed of students who live nearby, whoever they happened to be, and that tinkering with the existing landscape of individual families constituted "social engineering." This view of equality relies on the formal rule of justice: equals should be treated equally. Fairness here is found in formal structures, universally applied. Differences between people, background, context are irrelevant.

This view, descended from Kantian ethics, has its strengths. Universal moral rules that resist making exceptions out of self-serving convenience provide a backbone for morality. To take an extreme example, if torture is considered morally wrong, then torturing someone would be wrong regardless of who is doing the torture, regardless of who is being tortured, and regardless of how useful the information potentially obtained. The ends do not justify the means. But in the arena of school assignments, we are in the realm of distributive justice and the premise that everyone is equally situated is flawed. Systemic racism has warped the starting line from which each individual child begins. All neighborhoods are not equally situated and did not come into being purely through the free choices of individuals. All students are not equally prepared, as they carry with them inherited advantages and disadvantages. The wealth gap alone between white and Black families speaks to generations of unfairness, including unfair housing practices and redlining practices that directly helped white families accumulate wealth at the expense of Black families. A view of equality that disregards differences between people, background, and context would be inadequate when what is being considered is fair access to the basic good of education. Distributive justice calls for the fair distribution of benefits and burdens in a society, but not necessarily for treating everyone the same.

Another view of equality circulating in the debate was more attuned to differences between people, background, and context. This view is better characterized as equity: to each according to need rather than to each exactly the same. Equity acknowledges the existence of systemic disadvantages and tries to compensate for them by changing the distribution of benefits and burdens. Attending a high-poverty school with few resources, high teacher turnover, an anemic PTA, and students who come to school hungry and distracted by their hunger or homelessness are realities that reinforce and perpetuate systemic disadvantage. Disrupting the creation of high-poverty schools is a way of compensating for the disadvantage in the short term and leveling the playing field in the longer term. As we saw in published opinions and public speeches, many people believed it was the school system's responsibility, especially the democratically elected school board members' responsibility, to disrupt the creation of high-poverty schools rather than simply letting the chips fall. Members of the public who felt this goal was important marshaled a significant body of social-scientific evidence to support the claim that high-poverty schools perpetuate disadvantage. They also drew on ample evidence supporting the claim that integrated schools confer academic and social benefits. However, not everyone agreed the diversity policy was the best strategy to achieve equity, and there were intense disagreements about whether the policy had truly benefited the least well-off.

Interviews with community leaders discussed in chapter 3 went deeper, revealing an additional conception of equality that helped to explain some of the motivation behind the fierce protection of the diversity policy and the gains accomplished during the "golden era" of Wake County schools. This view is best characterized as a belief or faith in the radical equality of human worth. Several of the people I interviewed saw public education not as a positional or private good in a competitive society but as something more akin to a basic human right to which everyone is entitled. Education is a necessary building block to human flourishing and therefore exists in a separate category from things that might enhance one's quality of life but are essentially optional, like a big house. According to this view, a just society that values each human being as equally worthy would not subject something as fundamental as education to a zero-sum game with winners and losers. My interview with a former superintendent also underscored the radical equality between parents, who share a common desire to see their children grow and flourish. This common desire can be a source of social solidarity and, when harnessed productively, can build community support for public education.

Chapter 4, which went deeper still into the additional dimension of history, described the enduring appeal of separate and equal as another conception of equality, despite its repudiation by *Brown v. Board of Education*. The energy behind embracing separate and equal yet again seems to be coming from at least two different places: (1) the United States Supreme Court's more recent endorsement of "color blindness" as the best incarnation of the ideal of equality, and (2) the desire of some families—including both white and nonwhite families—to self-segregate into homogeneous enclaves. Sharp divisions within the Supreme Court reflect the polarization in American society on this subject. Chief Justice John Roberts's famous pronouncement, "The way to stop discrimination on the basis of race is to stop discriminating on the basis of race," seems to will into being by wishful thinking an ideal world of free and equal people. By contrast, Justice Sonia Sotomayor's view, "The way to stop discrimination on the basis of race is to speak openly and candidly on the subject of race, and to apply the Constitution with eyes open to the unfortunate effects of centuries of racial discrimination," seems to recognize the reality of unequal treatment.[7] In Sotomayor's view, ostensibly race-neutral policies are likely to recreate inequality by ignoring the effects of racial discrimination. They give a green light, again, to separate and unequal. To block racial discrimination and truly bring forth a world of free and equal people, sometimes it is necessary to implement policies that explicitly factor in race, socioeconomic status, or other differences. The debate in Wake County over the diversity policy encapsulated the disagreement about the best way to respect differences while also honoring equal treatment; for example, whether factoring in socioeconomic differences in a student assignment plan was a form of "profiling" or a justified means to a more equitable end. Divergent opinions were especially apparent on the night the school board majority voted to abandon the diversity policy.

As for families choosing more segregated environments for their children, some of the people I interviewed were unbothered by this phenomenon and willing to defer to diverse parental preferences even if those preferences implicitly embraced separate and equal. Others, especially supporters of traditional public schools, were concerned about the evidence from North Carolina that charter schools exacerbate school segregation. They were more willing to interrogate parental preferences and more bothered by the outcome of segregation. Research in this area does suggest that the choices of white families and of nonwhite families have different impacts: a white family choosing a majority white charter school because of perceived superior quality or for any other reason is not equivalent to a Black family choosing a majority Black charter inside a society that has historically discriminated against Black people. The former perpetuates a type of opportunity hoarding among an advantaged group; the latter provides nurture and support for an historically disadvantaged group. One of my interviewees emphasized the long history of Black Americans building parallel institutions when not welcomed into white ones, noting the ways in which this strategy is ongoing, even in ostensibly diverse spaces. Another interviewee described the benefits of attending an HBCU (historically Black college or university) and the challenges of attending a predominantly white institution (PWI) as a person of color, whether at the college or K-12 level. History certainly illuminates why integrated schools might not be desirable to some; integration triggered real losses for Black communities in addition to demonstrable benefits.

Separate and un/equal was also fiercely debated in letters to the editor and op-eds, as described in chapter 2, often through comparisons of Wake County to Charlotte-Mecklenburg schools. Those who felt that Charlotte-Mecklenburg was doing a better job serving its low-income students by giving more resources to high-poverty schools were implicitly endorsing separate and equal, even if they did not name it as such. Others disagreed both about the facts on the ground—how the two systems compared according to relevant metrics—and on principle. To them, separate was by definition unequal.

Nikole Hannah-Jones has written about the enduring appeal of separate and equal, but also its inadequacy: "This sense of helplessness in the face of such entrenched segregation is what makes so alluring the notion, embraced by liberals and conservatives, that we can address school inequality not with integration but by giving poor, segregated schools more resources and demanding of them more accountability. True integration, true equality, requires a surrendering of advantage, and when it comes to our own children, that can feel almost unnatural."[8] Hannah-Jones's quote suggests that integration is clearly the harder path, but it is arguably the only path to true equality. As will be discussed later in this chapter, the ideal of radical equality of human worth and the conception of equity both support pursuing integration. Fundamentally at issue is how we both define and enact justice.

Competing Conceptions of Freedom

Different conceptions of freedom likewise circulated in the public debate in Wake County, although there was perhaps a smaller range of views here. Americans generally cherish their freedom and are comfortable articulating an understanding of freedom that is highly individualistic: freedom is the pursuit of rational self-interest, overriding most other interests most of the time. The COVID-19 pandemic has sharpened this individualistic conception of freedom in the early 2020s. For example, even when COVID-19 infection rates were at their highest, some people vehemently refused to wear a face mask, even though evidence indicated that masks help reduce the spread of the virus.[9] Some have also defended their freedom to refuse a vaccine, even though vaccines have proven to be effective in reducing the severity of the illness. A quarter of Americans were unwilling to get the COVID-19 vaccine, according to polls in 2021.[10] Others insisted on their right to congregate despite the public health risk and defied stay-at-home orders.[11] However, few sites of COVID controversy have been more acrimonious than school board meetings across the country where parents pleaded, sometimes in tears, often in anger, to allow their children to attend school without wearing a mask.[12] These ardent defenders of freedom rejected the proposition that reasonable constraints on individual freedom could ultimately expand everyone's freedom and safety in the long run.[13] John Stuart Mill and his descendants in the liberal tradition might wonder how freedom has come to be so narrowly and superficially understood. But our sense of solidarity has become so weak in the United States that the benefits of working in concert with others toward a common goal, even during a once-in-a-century global pandemic, have proven unpersuasive to many Americans.

Looking back at the debate in Wake County over a decade ago, one of its more remarkable features in light of this American tendency to define freedom individualistically was the effort by some to articulate a communitarian vision for the schools. By communitarian vision, I mean the idea that everyone's well-being was interconnected, and that everyone's options could be enhanced if the good of the whole system was taken into account in a way that reflected the community's shared values. The "healthy schools" index was part of this shared vision in the 1990s and 2000s, as was the goal after the merger of Wake County and Raleigh City schools to stabilize minority enrollment at 15–45 percent across all schools in the district. The early leaders of the merged school system in the 1970s and 1980s clearly believed that a strong overall school system redounded to everyone's individual benefit. They conveyed a sense that individual freedom was not in conflict with caring about the good of the whole.

But this community consensus proved to be fragile. Discontent grew as the population of Wake County exploded and more people moved to the area from other parts of the country. Chapter 4 looked at the role of history in a community's self-understanding. Did it matter if people were aware of Wake County's and North Carolina's segregationist past? Did it matter if they were newcomers to the area and lacked a sense of investment in the community's efforts to integrate? Those with firsthand experience of the system when it was working well were more likely to defend its benefits than those who experienced the strains of population growth, which triggered the reassignment of students to fill new schools and the need for year-round schools to expand existing capacity.

In general, strong conceptions of individual freedom went hand in hand with strong endorsements of school choice and viewing education as an individual good. There was a deep divide between people who viewed public education as an institution that reflects the community's collective aspirations and people who viewed education as primarily a private good in a free market. Those who viewed education primarily as a private good tended to see themselves as rational actors whose relationship with their child's school was transactional; they could "walk with their feet" if they were dissatisfied.[14] They also tended to see competition between schools for customers as the most efficient mechanism for ensuring and improving school quality. Many people who wrote or spoke to defend school choice did not necessarily adopt Milton Friedman's agenda to replace all public schools with private ones, but they accepted a market mindset as natural and legitimate. Parents and students are the "customer base" that needs to be kept happy; schools must provide a desirable product or be forced out of business.

By contrast, those who were skeptical of the school choice movement tended to orient themselves toward public education as citizens rather than consumers. By this I mean they were more likely to see public education as an institution in which they played some small part in creating rather than a ready-made product existing to be consumed. They embraced the idea that government has a role to play in the provision of public services and did not view "the government" as an oppositional actor. Although they made choices like any other parent about their children's education, these skeptics of the school choice movement did not see their relationship with their child's school as primarily transactional. It was more like a community or even religious affiliation— something into which time and energy were invested, perhaps through participation in the PTA or through service as an elected official, and to which they committed their loyalty. In addition, as was discussed in chapter 3, some of my interviewees brought an intense idealism to the purpose of public schools, especially the idea that they must be open to everyone (e.g., the "blueberry story"). This vision of education was incompatible with a market mindset;

education, like health care, is so fundamental to human flourishing that it should be provided to everyone. To encourage a model where some schools fail, or spend years deteriorating on their way to failing, would mean consigning some unlucky children to a substandard education. Through no fault of their own, children whose parents are unable or unwilling to be savvy consumers in the pursuit of a good education would be seriously disadvantaged.

Those who were critical of the rhetoric of school choice did not necessarily value individual freedom any less than school choice proponents, but they often better understood the history of how "choice" has been used to stall or thwart integration. In the immediate aftermath of *Brown*, "freedom of choice" typically functioned to reinforce de facto segregation. Whether he intended to or not, Milton Friedman offered opponents of integration a facially neutral "nonracial defense of segregation" by elevating freedom of choice in his argument for privatization.[15] Similarly, *Parents Involved* also reinforced de facto segregation by prioritizing freedom of choice, reasoning that the harm to an individual denied his choice of school is weightier than the goal of achieving racial integration. As was discussed in chapter 4, the ideology of school choice and privatization are exacerbating segregation in the twenty-first century. In North Carolina, charter schools and private school vouchers draw students, teachers, and funding away from what might otherwise be a strong traditional public school system. Charter schools have been compared to twentieth-century "segregation academies" in that they give motivated white parents an exit strategy from traditional public schools. Put more bluntly: "Charter schools are killing the health of our schools."[16] Some of my interviewees expressed concern that, especially given all the current pressures, it would be tempting in Wake County to embrace the ideology of school choice, surrender to the script of separate and equal, and be relieved of the hard work of integration.

Despite divergent views about school choice and the school choice movement, appreciation for the benefits of "choice" in less stridently ideological terms was widely shared by my interviewees.[17] With the right circumstances—that is, a level playing field and adequate funding—healthy competition between schools could be beneficial.[18] For example, when first introduced, the competition between magnet and base schools was thought to be manageable and productive. There was also wide appreciation for the idea that education need not be one-size-fits-all, that students benefit from a variety of approaches and programs, and that the original aspirations of charter schools—that is, that they could be incubators of innovative ideas in pedagogy—were sound. To be strongly skeptical of the school choice movement did not mean embracing the so-called monopoly of "government schools" but rather meant seeing the benefits of a dynamic, creative, and unified public system. Notably, there was an appreciation, even among school-choice skeptics, that voluntary choice garners "buy-in" and loyalty. It seems widely acknowledged now in Wake County and beyond that desegregation achieved through voluntary choice is more durable and politically sustainable than nonvoluntary assignments.[19]

In fact, I would note as an aside that an interesting and ongoing evolution of beliefs about "choice" has emerged in the United States over the last few decades. This development is perhaps most obvious in the realm of childbearing and reproductive choice, but it is also clearly apparent in how Americans approach their children's education. I see similar appreciation for choice for similar reasons, largely tracking the ascendancy of neoliberalism in American culture. Whereas in the past, people might have been more likely to accept parenthood or motherhood as their default role in life, much as they were likely to accept their default school assignment, now they recognize that voluntarily chosen childbearing makes for better parents and happier kids, and deliberately chosen schools make for greater investment and excitement about a child's education.[20] There is more energy and positive feeling toward choice compared to a predetermined school assignment, and a greater sense of ownership. According to some, being assigned to a school rather than choosing it generates a "helpless feeling" for parents.[21]

Given this backdrop, the stunning overturning of *Roe v. Wade* in 2022 by the U.S. Supreme Court represents a powerful movement against individual freedom, or at least against the individual freedom of women or persons who can become pregnant. Indeed, the helpless feeling of parents who are unable to choose their child's school pales in comparison to the helpless feeling of women who will be unable to obtain a safe and legal abortion. Once again, as in the days before *Roe*, women have been forced to be Good Samaritans where nowhere else in American law is anyone else required to put the life of another person above their own.[22] Why is so much asked of women and so little of others? In the case of school choice, (white and privileged) parents have been free to be oblivious to the cumulative impact of individual choices. No national policy or messaging encourages them to consider that their own pursuit of "good schools" could be inclusive of, even dependent upon, a healthy community of learners and a wider community of interconnected families.

In the twenty-first century, politicians and parents alike struggle to conceptualize the social goods of education in a way that keeps them on equal footing with individual benefits, never mind explaining how social and individual goods might be mutually reinforcing. Dewey's use of the term "socialism" would trigger panic among many Americans, as that term has become a right-wing dog whistle. But what he intended to convey was the expansive possibilities of an inclusive, generous, forward-looking investment in the community: "What the best and wisest parent wants for his own child, that must the community want for all of its children. Any other ideal for our schools is narrow and unlovely; acted upon, it destroys our democracy. All that society has accomplished for itself is put, through the agency of the school, at the disposal of its future members. All its better thoughts of itself it hopes to realize through the new possibilities thus opened to its future self. Here individualism and socialism are at one."[23] Even if we replaced "socialism" with a less triggering word to modernize the quote, it would still be a challenge to overcome the fear that what is good for the individual and what is good for society are naturally opposed, or at least independent of each other. Caring about one side of the equation is assumed to be costly for the other.

As we saw in chapter 2, the debate in Wake County focused directly on this point: how to hold together education as both an individual and social good. Richer notions of freedom—that freedom consists not merely of individual actors pursuing their rational self-interest but also of people choosing to work toward a purpose that redounds to the good of the whole—were articulated by a few, but not with a vocabulary that caught hold. "Taking one for the team" in matters of school assignment did not inspire serious, long-lasting support for the diversity policy.[24] Talking about how a family could contribute to what the school system needs was rare—and usually resisted if framed in terms of a sacrifice. Being able to articulate how individual freedom is enhanced by supporting the common good was even rarer. Philosopher Michael Sandel has argued that our ability to recognize the value of the common good by any available terminology or framework has seriously atrophied. But we need a renewed appreciation for the common good if we are going to strengthen public education for everyone.

Different Underlying Conceptions of the Good

Although it is certainly fair to describe the debate in Wake County as a showdown between the competing values of "diversity" and "stability," there was a great deal more to the story, as I have endeavored to show.[25] Inside tightly crafted speeches and letters, people brought their heartfelt convictions to the question of how schools should be organized, revealing greater complexity and depth than a simple either-or between two preferences. Different conceptions of equality and freedom were often woven into arguments. And underlying these conceptions were different ideas of "the good"—substantive ideas about what it means to live a good life, be a good person, create a good community.

In his reflections on justice, political philosopher John Rawls argued that individuals' "comprehensive doctrines" are best left out of the fray of political debate as people work to define an "overlapping consensus" that will define just laws.[26] He thought a core overlapping consensus could be built on publicly accessible reasons that people coming from a variety of backgrounds would be able to understand and endorse. Critics of Rawls have countered that the public sphere does not need to be so sanitized of deep moral or religious convictions, and in any event, comprehensive doctrines have a way of making themselves apparent when the thing being debated is perceived to be deeply significant. At its most intense, the battle over the diversity policy was perceived by those who participated in it as deeply significant. To the participants, it was a debate rich in moral meanings.

Perhaps one of the most important moral questions was the following: How much responsibility should we take for past wrongs, like segregation? More broadly, what do we owe one another? Different people answer that question differently depending on their interpretation of the facts—for example, were neighborhoods segregated by the free choices of individuals, by prejudice, by government policies? But even if people can manage to agree on the facts, they answer the question of what we owe one another differently, depending on their vision of a good person, a good community. Their reasons run deep and are often assumed to be off-limits as "private." While tolerance, forbearance, and mutual respect are important virtues in a liberal democracy, they are also fully compatible with civic engagement and disagreement. This is the work of democracy—to discuss, debate, and reason together in search of a shared vision.

Dewey's view of democracy, and especially the moral anthropology upon which it rests, is instructive here: "Men are not isolated non-social atoms, but are men only when in intrinsic relations to men."[27] Likewise, democracy is not the unstable aggregation of isolated atoms but an organic whole. Political philosopher Matthew Festenstein describes Dewey's understanding of democracy as follows: "Democracy is a form of moral and spiritual association that recognizes the contribution that each member can make in his or her particular way to this ethical community. And each of us can contribute to this community since we each only become the individuals we are through our engagement in the institutions and practices of our society."[28] Thus, democratic government represents the people only "so far as they have become organically related to one another, or are possessed of unity of purpose and interest."[29]

The public debate that transpired in Wake County tapped into deep values. It was a moment of heightened engagement, emotion, contestation, and reasoned argument. Without claiming to understand individuals' deepest moral convictions or comprehensive doctrines, which would be impossible merely based on a short letter or speech, we can still gain an appreciation for the moral logics discernible in people's arguments. Moral logics bring coherence to moral judgments. They give insight into underlying values. They are not as complete as a comprehensive doctrine or worldview, but they provide a common vocabulary for describing the contours of a fundamentally normative debate.

What Were the Core Moral Logics?

Out of many voices, what were the core moral logics that were operating in this debate? Looking across all the data I collected for this project, and looking specifically at the question of this community's commitment to integration and how or whether it is valued, a few moral logics stand out as prevalent. First, individualism and pragmatism were common and easily recognizable.

Individualism is perhaps the most familiar and quintessentially American moral logic. To be clear, individualism should be distinguished from individual freedom. A free society permits individuals to pursue their own vision of the good without undue constraint. This respect for individual freedom is a core tenet of the liberal tradition, enshrined in our Declaration of Independence as respect for the inalienable rights of "life, liberty, and the pursuit of happiness." However, individualism goes further. It takes the satisfaction of individual preferences as the defining locus of value and the essential barometer for the rightness of a moral decision. It downplays the extent to which individuals are formed in relation with one another, in communities, and instead tends to assume individuals come fully formed with the preferences they seek to satisfy in a public context or contest. Individualism thus undervalues the capacity for individuals to develop together a vision of the good that could be shared. School choice in a free market of choices makes sense according to the moral logic of individualism, where each family is vying for the best opportunity for their child.

The elevation of individual property rights over other rights also flows from an embrace of individualism. For many, being able to buy and secure access to education through the purchase of a home is arguably one of the most revered transactions in American culture. Suggesting any other way to conceptualize access to public education can seem absurd. And yet Wake County tried to loosen the connection between property ownership and school access, prioritizing (for a time) a more collective vision for how its public schools should be organized in order to produce a result that aligned with the community's values. Because individualism is such a dominant framework in our society, determining many of our priorities, it can be hard to notice unless it is brought to our attention through a contrast. The communitarian or community-oriented vision expressed by many defenders of the old diversity policy provided such a contrast.

Unfortunately, individualism takes no stand against inequality, nor does it necessarily take issue with racism. Individualism also gives little weight to the value of school integration per se, unless school integration happens to coincide with and serve (white) parents' interests—what critical legal theorists have labeled "interest convergence."[30] Writers and scholars like Nikole Hannah-Jones and Jonathan Kozol have studied the issue of school segregation across the United States for many years and have seen firsthand the savage inequalities this country permits for its children of color. They have concluded with clear-eyed bitterness that white parents will not be denied their preferences.[31] White parents will protect their interests at any cost, whether that is through departure or secession from the traditional public school system (e.g., charter schools, charter districts, private schools, or old-fashioned white flight), or through the policing of municipal boundaries to protect access to quality public schools, or through the use of the courts to secure access or alter policies according to white preferences. Realistic appraisals by those who have studied this topic across the United States deserve respect and consideration. How did Wake County compare?

Examples of individualism in my data were plentiful. The parent who wanted her child to have access to the resources of a downtown magnet school without having to send her child to the "ghetto" was only the most obvious. Most people were usually not that forthright in staking their claim to the school system's benefits while rejecting perceived burdens. More commonly, people simply disparaged having any collective goal by labeling it "social engineering," "forced busing," "socialism," and the like. Or they framed their arguments positively in terms of the reasonable benefits of neighborhood schools; for example, enabling more frequent parent involvement in the school building and a more proximate network of school friends.

Another moral logic recognizable in my data was pragmatism. What is best is simply what works, what takes care of necessities, and what responds most adequately to a problem. Pragmatism strives for tangible benefits rather than displays of idealism and accepts imperfection so long as some good can be gained. For example, pragmatism values school integration when it works to provide a good education. In this sense, school integration is instrumentally valuable. It is the thing that enables what is truly valued for its own sake. This logic recapitulates the reasoning of W.E.B. Du Bois.

> Theoretically the Negro needs neither segregated schools nor mixed schools. What he needs is Education. What he must remember is that there is no magic, either in mixed schools or in segregated schools. A mixed school with poor and unsympathetic teachers, with hostile public opinion, and no teaching of truth concerning black folk, is bad. A segregated school with ignorant placeholders, inadequate equipment, poor salaries, and wretched housing, is equally bad. Other things being equal, the mixed school is the broader, more natural basis for the education of all youth. It gives wider contacts; it inspires greater self-confidence; and suppresses the inferiority complex. But other things seldom are equal, and in that case, Sympathy, Knowledge, and the Truth, outweigh all that the mixed school can offer.[32]

More than eighty years after Du Bois published these words, Black parents are still making the same shrewd calculation: which school will provide the safest, most beneficial path for my child in a society that is inherently unequal.

In general, the Black parents and community leaders I interviewed had a sophisticated understanding of the lay of the land, relevant history, and people's motivations. They appreciated the academic and social opportunities provided by Wake County's schools, particularly the magnet schools, but generally valued the quality of the education provided in these integrated environments, not merely the fact that student populations were diverse. In this their priorities mirrored the priorities of Black parents in Boston who allowed their children to be bused to the Boston suburbs beginning in 1966: "While black parents who volunteered for the METCO [Metropolitan Council for Educational Opportunity] experiment valued diversity, they ranked the suburban schools' academic excellence as the most important reason for participating."[33] Some of the opinion writers published in the *N&O* who identified as Black or Hispanic likewise tended to state their priorities plainly in favor of a good education: diversity was less important than graduating from high school, either college ready or with employable skills.

As I studied my interview transcriptions and pored over published opinions, I saw individualism and pragmatism as two primary moral logics that provided coherence to people's arguments about integration. With the pragmatic orientation, people valued integration primarily as an instrumental good that makes other goods possible, like student achievement, community well-being, and economic prosperity; that is, integration is useful if it facilitates the equalization of resources, but if it fails to facilitate that goal, or if the goal can be reached another way, nothing of significant value is necessarily lost by abandoning integration. With the individualistic orientation, people valued the freedom to choose one's school, even if that freedom of choice undermines integration—that is, student populations need not be mixed so long as resources are provided to meet needs. Separate can be made (theoretically) equal again. In the pragmatic orientation, integration is important, but still only instrumentally valuable. In the individualistic orientation, integration is entirely incidental—valued, if at all, as a cosmetic good—and secondary to freedom of choice.

One key premise of both orientations is the assumption that academic achievement can be separated out from social and civic functions of education (raising citizens in a democracy) and treated as an individual good. Understandably, most parents value the individual benefits of an education: academic achievement, preparation for the real world, social mobility. No one would dispute that education is at a minimum an individual good. To recall Dewey: "We are apt to look at the school from an individualistic standpoint, as something between teacher and pupil, or between teacher and parent. That which interests us most is naturally the progress made by the individual child of our acquaintance, his normal physical development, his advance in ability to read, write, and figure, his growth in the knowledge of geography and history, improvement in manners, habits of promptness, order, and industry—it is from such standards as these that we judge the work of the school. And rightly so."[34] But Dewey, significantly, asked for more: "Yet the range of the outlook needs to be enlarged." Evidence for the need of an enlarged outlook is very much apparent in the Wake County debate.

A third moral logic operating in the debate could be called civic idealism, a framework that recognizes the inherent value of true integration, understood here to mean a multiracial sharing of power that is more than just a balancing of interests but something that becomes creative, collaborative, and unifying.

In my interviews, civic idealism could be seen in the openness to genuine change demonstrated by some parents, especially to the prospect that their children's experience with integrated public education would be better than their own. It could be seen in the belief that education "goes beyond the books" in forging new kinds of relationships and consequently different kinds of worldviews. In public speeches, civic idealism could be seen in comments like that of Julius Chambers, who observed that children had "gotten used to other children of different races and nationalities," suggesting that this experience was transformative. Following up on Chambers, Benita Jones quoted Justice Thurgood Marshall in the close of her speech: "Unless our children begin to learn together, there is little hope that our people will ever learn to live together."[35] And within published opinion pieces, there were memorable examples of people who were eager to attest to the inherent value of integration: "We all learned and grew. We worked together to make Broughton a more inclusive community and us more well-rounded individuals."[36] In other words, there was evidence in the debate that some people believed in the ideal of integration as described by philosopher Elizabeth Anderson: "The ideal of integration envisions a restructuring of intergroup relations, from alienation, anxiety, awkwardness, and hostility to relaxed, competent civil association and even intimacy; from domination and subordination to cooperation as equals."[37]

Civic idealism could also be seen in multiracial coalitions of leaders that emerged at key moments in Wake's history. The state legislators, school leaders, and business leaders who pushed for the 1976 merger of city and county schools are the most obvious example. They had the foresight to envision something beyond what the citizens of Wake County were willing to support on their own. Equally important were the early leaders of the merged district, like Vernon Malone, and subsequent school boards and visionary superintendents, like Bill McNeal. They knew that things like academic quality, teacher preparation, and efficient utilization of resources were essential, but they succeeded because their visionary leadership sold the public on an idea: integrated schools can be excellent schools. Both their pragmatism and their idealism were necessary to make integration work. The key underlying premise seemed to be that true integration produces something that is greater than the sum of its parts. As McNeal explained: "I thought we were different in this sense. . . . We didn't come at integration or desegregation from the lens of just putting the children together, and children getting to know each other. We came at it from the lens of how do we improve the academics of all our children, and I think that to me was a different lens than some other places."[38] McNeal also intuitively understood the power of putting parents on equal footing with one another. All parents want their children to flourish. Working to create schools that are "excellent for all children" respects that fundamental equality and forges solidarity.

A multiracial coalition of leadership also emerged in the aftermath of the 2009 school board election, as a conglomeration of groups challenged the dismantling of the diversity policy and worked to elect a new slate of candidates in 2011. The NAACP, Great Schools in Wake, churches, youth activists like NC HEAT, and others came together around a common cause. Their strength was in their "all-hands-on-deck" approach to civic engagement and in their shared belief that the community could shape its own future. Multiracial sharing of power can also be seen to this day in Wake County schools led by principals of color who work to hire more teachers of color; develop equity plans built on input from students, teachers, and parents; push the validity of "de-tracking"; and reform their school discipline practices.

Civic idealism that recognizes the inherent value of true integration was expressed by parents, community leaders, activists, faith leaders, and students themselves. Beyond merely acknowledging the preferences of individuals (individualism) or the tangible benefits of integration (pragmatism), this moral logic recognizes that multiracial sharing of power made possible by true integration opens up new pathways. The resulting collaboration will be different from and greater than the sum of individual benefits. It also recognizes that neither individualism nor pragmatism are adequate by themselves for a multiracial democracy.

What Can Be Said about Wake County's Commitment to Integration?

Wake County may not be unique—it was as slow to adopt policies to advance school integration as many other American communities, not making significant strides until the historic 1976 merger. But Wake is significant, notable for the successes of its socioeconomic diversity policy and longstanding magnet program and for continuing the struggle to deliver high-quality, equitable public education, despite the unrelenting pressures of privatization and the ideology of school choice.

Having studied the history of school segregation around the United States, I can say that the arc of the typical American story has become all too familiar:

integration worked well in some places for a time, sometimes even better than the naysayers had anticipated. Students themselves often did the heavy lifting to make it work, as they saw the benefits firsthand.[39] Then things began unraveling, perhaps because the investment in integrated schools was not strong enough to begin with. Sometimes it was "outsiders" coming in who inadvertently unraveled what was built; for example, people from the Northeast moving to the South looking for lower property taxes, a big house, and good schools, who believed school segregation was not their problem to solve, despite (ironically) often coming from segregated school districts themselves. Often it was white families resolutely preferring white spaces and leveraging their power to ensure access to them. Sometimes it was Black families or families of color who had grown weary of chasing acceptance in white spaces that did not serve them well. In any event, conservative courts washed their hands of integration efforts in the early 2000s, cementing an ideological shift that commodifies education—seeing it exclusively as an individual, private good. Population growth, transportation challenges, and even climate change make people averse to the burdens of busing and attracted to the nostalgic appeal of neighborhood schools. Nationwide, many people have grown comfortable with a two-tiered system of "have" and "have-not" schools. And a multitude of empirical measures indicate that our schools are as segregated as they were before *Brown* and in many ways worse off—poorer, understaffed, underresourced, unhealthy.[40]

Despite the bleak national picture, I still believe there are reasons for hope, based on Wake County's example. Having lived through the struggles in Wake County for the last twenty years, I see evidence that the dream of integration has not died here—especially in the magnet schools. However, my fear is that school integration is now a small-scale, boutique experience for liberal parents who want their children to be exposed to it. By no means is it a community-wide commitment backed by those in power, particularly in the state legislature. North Carolina is intensely gerrymandered to be dominated by conservative rural interests at the expense of metropolitan counties like Wake. What could change that? What is missing is a recognition from white parents that it is (past) time for them to question the impact of their individual choices on both the present and future and to leverage their power for the common good.

I return now to the questions that opened this chapter: How do we rein in the power of white parents, or at least direct that power toward the cause of racial equality? Is illuminating a shared sense of reality enough of a catalyst to enable that change? How do we sustain the energy and hopefulness needed to solve inequality in the face of cynicism and despair, including the belief that racism is a permanent feature of American society? One school board member I interviewed characterized the problem thus:

Some people have talked about [how] we need to educate folks and, you know, I don't know that that's it. What . . . are you going to talk folks to death about the benefits and values of diversity and that sort of thing? . . . I don't know that they're going to get it, and all of a sudden be converted to, "Oh, okay. I get it. I'm cool with my child riding past two middle schools to get to the third one down the street, for the benefit of all the students in the county. I get it, I'm cool with that." That's not going to happen. That's not going to happen.[41]

Maybe he is right. Or maybe our current social disintegration makes change inevitable, for the simple reason that savage inequalities are inherently unstable.

Making the Case for True Integration

In closing, I would like to offer the following prescriptive conclusions: (1) White parents in every school district where integration is at stake need to take more responsibility for the damage wrought by unchecked individualism; (2) integration should be framed not only as equalizing resources but as a corrective for the moral, cultural, and cognitive deficiencies resulting from unearned privilege; (3) integrated schools are better schools; and (4) true integration and true inclusion rests on solidarity rather than on striving. These assertions are part of making the case for true integration. They build on the logic of civic idealism that I heard in the public debate in Wake County and affirm that a multiracial sharing of power is the only path forward—or at least the most morally defensible path and the most likely to succeed. They are influenced by what I have learned from a close reading of the public debate along with a close reading of the scholarly debate about integration and who I believe has the most persuasive arguments.

(1) White Parents Need to Take More Responsibility

I am not pessimistic enough about human nature to believe that all white people will cling indefinitely to their power and privilege in the United States until it is wrested away from them by force. This position may fly in the face of common sense. But I believe it is possible to change minds and behavior through better information and better arguments, and I have seen evidence in Wake County that there can be openness to change where one might least expect it. As mentioned above, the goal of the *Nice White Parents* series was to make white parents more aware of how they have used their power in harmful, self-serving ways. Similarly, Amanda Lewis and John Diamond, authors of *Despite the Best Intentions: How Racial Inequity Thrives in Good Schools*, try to enlighten white parents about how their actions cause harm, even when not consciously intended. The title of one chapter, "Opportunity Hoarding: Creating and Maintaining Racial Advantage," pinpoints the source of the problem. Privilege perpetuates privilege: "White parents are not just passive recipients of structural advantages. Individually and collectively they still participate, working to ensure the rules, policies, and arrangements that are serving their children well do not change. Likely they do this not out of animosity toward others but out of a fierce interest in advocating for their own children."[42]

Lewis and Diamond recognize that not all parents have the resources to translate their love and care into greater material advantages for their children. They conclude, "The answer is not for all parents to do what these white parents do—the whole point is not everyone can."[43] However, the problem is not just finite resources, unevenly distributed. The problem is that a hierarchy needs someone to be on the bottom. And white parents do not want it to be them: "These parents start planning and optimizing for kids in second grade, like it's war, preparing for battle."[44]

Elizabeth Anderson pointedly identifies the conscious and unconscious work of privileged parents in maintaining their advantages through policies like academic tracking: "Notwithstanding powerful evidence from schools that reject tracking that doing so improves the education of poor students and students of color at no academic cost to white middle class students, privileged parents demand schools that reproduce hierarchy and undermine democracy."[45]

Would it make any difference if privileged parents understood the ways in which their opportunity hoarding reproduced hierarchy and undermined democracy? Maybe in some cases it would, but not in all. Some white parents might welcome the opportunity to take responsibility and leave behind their "innocence" in perpetuating structural racism. Others would lean further into individualism, committing to integrated schools only as long as they served their interests or leveraging their power to get what they wanted at any cost.

Perhaps what is needed for white parents to take greater responsibility is better leadership—from our elected leaders, from the courts, from the business community. No one (still living) has been able fully to explain how the people of Wake County went from decisively rejecting a referendum on merger to accepting the merger that was imposed by the state legislature in 1976, other than to say that courageous leadership sold the idea to a reluctant public and worked hard to make it succeed. Most people embraced the new merged school system, igniting what would become the "golden era" of Wake County schools. Likewise, after the *Swann v. Charlotte-Mecklenburg Board of Education* (1971) decision, the people of Charlotte-Mecklenburg embraced the busing program that was imposed and worked hard to make their integrated schools succeed. Positive experiences with integration seemed to reinforce positive feelings about integration. As Anderson has astutely noted, "Opposition to integration is based more on anticipatory fear than on evidence. The whites who are most opposed to integration are those with the least experience of it."[46]

Unfortunately, in more recent years we have seen a weak commitment to integrated schools at every level. According to Anderson, "Overwhelming white resistance to school integration" has eroded our convictions and our courage.[47] She describes five key U.S. Supreme Court cases that have dramatically undermined integration over the last fifty years: *Milliken v. Bradley* (1974), *San Antonio Independent School District v. Rodriguez* (1973), *Board of Education v. Dowell* (1991), *Freeman v. Pitts* (1992), and *Parents Involved v. Seattle School District* (2007), incisively summarizing their impact as follows:

> These decisions amount to a recipe for accommodating white opportunity hoarding: let white flight reproduce segregation across district lines; turn a blind eye to massive violations of the Fair Housing Act and state collusion in neighborhood segregation; permit segregated suburbs to hoard school revenues; let school districts transmit white preferences for racial segregation from neighborhoods to schools by allowing them to revert to neighborhood school assignments; and entitle whites to lock in the results of this segregation by blocking schools' race-conscious efforts to avoid spreading the effects of whites' private acts of social closure. Call this outcome "color-blind" and declare it a triumph of equal protection.[48]

Viewing these cases together, it certainly is understandable why some would see calculation and collusion in the entrenchment of white supremacy. To these court decisions could be added the more recent phenomenon of state legislatures, such as in North Carolina, enabling privatization through school voucher programs and charter schools, arguably encouraging segregation.

So, what is left to convince white parents to take more responsibility for the impact of their choices if leadership is lacking, the memory of positive experiences with integration is inconsistent, and the compulsion of opportunity hoarding is irresistible? I would suggest that a country of atomistic individuals striving and competing in a zero-sum game for superior position in a hierarchy cannot long endure. A fundamentally unequal segregated school system leads to a fundamentally unequal and unstable society. White parents need to recognize what white supremacist policies are costing them: not merely material costs in our consumeristic culture but moral costs, costs to integrity, and costs to democracy.

To knowingly support this unequal system is both immoral and self-defeating. As Heather McGhee has explained, draining the public pool to avoid integrating it meant that no one who couldn't afford a private pool had a place to swim in the summer.[49] Parents need to be reminded to care about the common good and to have a loyalty that extends beyond their own children. Call it enlightened self-interest, call it civic idealism, call it necessity. Or consider it a requirement of justice: "In a country built on racial caste, equality means those who have had unearned advantage have to give some of that up," argued Nikole Hannah-Jones in a 2018 speech at Duke University.[50] An observation of hers noted earlier in this book bears repeating: "True integration, true equality, requires a surrendering of advantage, and when it comes to our own children, that can feel almost unnatural."[51] The stresses of the pandemic have intensified and highlighted this "natural" desire to protect and promote one's own. As I read about parents who buy air purifiers for their child's classroom—never mind that not every classroom in their child's school has access to an air purifier—and want to take that purifier with them as their child ages up to the next grade, I am reminded of how common it is for parents to advocate for their own children, especially during a time of heightened fear.[52] At the same time, the utter obliviousness of some parents to the disadvantages of others and to an unequal system suggests it is past time for privileged parents to question the impact of their choices. "People's refusal to do what morality requires does not generate a valid claim on their part to be let off the moral hook."[53]

(2) Integration Should Be Framed Correctly

Integration is often framed as helping students of color while only marginally benefiting or at least not harming white students. This framing appears frequently in academic discussions of integration, and it was brought into the debate in Wake County by supporters of the diversity policy. It is true, substantial evidence supports the many benefits of integration for racial minorities: "A number of studies have estimated the effect of racial desegregation on a wide array of different outcomes. . . . This line of work has found desegregation to increase Black educational achievement and attainment. These studies also find desegregation to increase the later-life earnings of Black males, improve Blacks' later-life health status, reduce the possibility of criminal behavior and victimization, and limit the likelihood of living in poverty as an adult. Most of this work finds desegregation to have either no effects or small positive effects on White students' outcomes."[54]

Substantial evidence also demonstrates the harms of high-poverty schools and racial isolation for poor and minority students. However, this framing of integration as significantly helping one group of students (poor and minority) while having no or minimal effect on another group of students (privileged and white) is incomplete and can be misleading.[55] It silences the ways that integration was and is costly to Black communities, for example, and it grossly underestimates the ways white children are harmed by being educated in segregated white spaces where they are allowed to remain ignorant and develop attitudes of entitlement and unearned privilege. It also reinforces the erroneous assumption that the benefits of integration flow in one direction: from the more privileged to the less privileged. One group is assumed to possess things of value; another group is assumed to be at a disadvantage. Putting the groups together equalizes resources, but not in a way that takes anything away from the privileged group. In this way the framing of integration as "not harming" white students appears crafted so as to not alarm white parents and to reassure them that integration will not disrupt their children's benefits.

I agree with Elizabeth Anderson that we need to change how integration is framed and bring to it a contrary perspective: "Far too much has been written about cognitive and cultural deficiencies of disadvantaged groups, and not nearly enough about the cognitive and cultural deficiencies of groups that are privileged by segregation. Segregation makes the privileged insular, clubby, smug, and filled with an excessive sense of their own entitlement. It makes them ignorant of the less advantaged and their lives, neglectful of the often disastrous consequences their decisions wreak on them, uncomfortable interacting with them, and consequently unaccountable and irresponsible."[56] Framed in this way, integration looks less like doing disadvantaged groups a favor and more like an absolute imperative if white parents want their children to grow up to be responsible, functioning adults.

My research in Wake County shows that there are indeed people who understand this imperative, including Jackson Foster, the young Wakefield High School student who stayed late into the evening at the March 2010 school board meeting to express how much he needed exposure to difference, how the diversity policy benefited him and white students like him, not only the Black students who were bused to his school.[57] Similarly, Rev. Nancy Petty understood that white families were deluding themselves, living in an enclave of whiteness— "gated whatever-ville"—ultimately setting their children up for failure: "I don't think those parents realize what a detriment that is to that child. You know, all at the expense of thinking, I want my child to have the best. And the best means only being with people like us."[58]

Or in the words of school board member Christine Kushner, who served on the board for eleven years (2011–2022):

> You teach your child that you deserve something better than other kids. You deserve something apart from other kids and I think that's a corrosive value. It sounds so self-righteous, saying that out loud. But, I do think it's something dangerous to teach a child, but it's one of my greatest frustrations as a school board member, is watching parents so fervently advocate for their own child, that they can't see how that single-focused advocacy not only harms other children but in the long run is gonna harm their child, because they're not building community for their child. They're not building an inclusive society going forward.[59]

Learning from multiple perspectives helps to broaden one's horizons and increase one's competencies.[60] It reduces prejudice.[61] It specifically helps to relativize white-centric notions of quality and success, including the assumption that predominantly white schools are superior. It also helps to temper a blind faith in meritocracy by bringing greater awareness of structural injustices and systemic racism. In short, integration should be framed not only as equalizing resources but as a corrective for the moral, cultural, and cognitive deficiencies resulting from unearned privilege.

(3) Integrated Schools Are Better Schools

In 1955, Milton Friedman, the father of the school choice movement, offered up the following advice: "The appropriate activity for those who oppose segregation and racial prejudice is to try to persuade others of their views; if and as they succeed, the mixed schools will grow at the expense of the non-mixed, and a gradual transition will take place."[62] Loath to encourage "forced" anything, Friedman essentially issued a challenge: sell the idea of integrated schools as better schools and people will come. Perhaps the time has come to take him up on that challenge using the evidence that exists.

I believe integrated schools are better schools because they provide superior academic benefits as well as better preparation for students to become competent citizens in a multiracial society who meet each other as equals. By contrast, segregated education provides a lesser education for everyone, both white students and students of color. According to Erika Wilson, "For white students, integrated education provides them with tangible social-psychological benefits that make them better citizens. For students of color, integrated education increases their access to both intangible and tangible educational inputs."[63] White students gain tangible educational benefits as well: "Diverse schools are linked to a host of positive learning outcomes for white students. These include more robust classroom discussions, the promotion of critical thinking and problem-solving and higher academic achievement."[64]

A relatively new national organization seems to have taken up the promotion of integrated schools in earnest. Integrated Schools: Families Choosing Integration lists the following vision statement on its website: "Integrated Schools envisions a racially/socioeconomically integrated public school system in which resources are shared equitably, power is created equally, and humanity is valued unconditionally. Core to a more cohesive and inclusive society will be three main drivers: (1) with new narratives around parenting, race and education, enough white and/or privileged families will prioritize antiracist integration to support policy, (2) all communities will reap the benefits of integrated schools, and (3) constituencies will demand that all policies be grounded in equity."[65]

This group recognizes that the benefits of integration go beyond individual measures of success. They also recognize that the justification for integrated schools goes well beyond mere interest convergence, where people pursuing their rational self-interest happen to overlap in wanting the same thing. (Accurate though interest convergence may be, it is ultimately a dead end: when interests diverge, so too will the efforts at integration.) Instead, the goal of creating a more cohesive and inclusive society is the primary justification, and the benefits of integrated schools will be widely shared.

In Wake County, the magnet schools provide a great example of the strength of integrated schools—not merely for the educational "goodies" that they are perceived to contain but for the relationships they enable. "I think the school is the place where it begins," said one of my interviewees, "I really do." Speaking specifically of Enloe High School, this African American mom described her daughter's interactions with students of different backgrounds. Familiarity bred civility, collaboration, and friendship, demonstrating the basic claims of social contact theory—that social contact with people who are "different" reduces prejudice and builds trust. Groups of students would periodically come to her house to work on a school project and she would marvel at their camaraderie and productivity: "I go up to my bonus room and it looks like [the] United Nations. I'm serious. It looks like the United Nations, and I said, 'This is the way it's supposed to be.'"[66] Rather than reproducing the hierarchy of the outside world, the world of the school created something different. Diverse magnet schools in Wake County are thus what Elizabeth Anderson would call sites of democratic education.[67]

If parents realized that integrated schools are better schools, they might give them the loyalty they deserve. If parents experienced relations of equality with other parents in integrated schools, and saw their children experiencing relationships in equality and friendship in integrated schools, they might give those schools the loyalty they deserve.

(4) True Integration Rests on Solidarity Rather Than Striving

True integration rests on a radical commitment to the equality of all human beings. It requires shared decision-making of coequal stakeholders. It envisions a multiracial sharing of power that is creative and collaborative. It does not merely bring people together into the same shared space or endorse a balance of power between different groups who may or may not have converging interests. According to Anderson, "Integration is the negation of segregation: it consists in comprehensive intergroup association on terms of equality."[68]

True integration is also built on solidarity rather than an ethic of striving in a zero-sum game. In his recent book *The Tyranny of Merit*, Michael Sandel explains how Americans' faith in meritocracy has distorted self-perceptions: the well-off believe they have earned every bit of their good fortune; the least well-off internalize blame and responsibility for their own disadvantages. He refers to this as the "politics of hubris and humiliation."[69] Throughout *The*

Tyranny of Merit, Sandel criticizes America's "meritocratic arms race" and the dangerous consequences of conflating human worth with achievement or meritocratic prestige. These criticisms serve his larger argument to remind Americans of the meaning of the common good and the solidarity required to care about its value. He writes: "What if the real problem with meritocracy is not that we have failed to achieve it but that the ideal is flawed? What if the rhetoric of rising no longer inspires, not simply because social mobility has stalled but, more fundamentally, because helping people scramble up the ladder of success in a competitive meritocracy is a hollow political project that reflects an impoverished conception of citizenship and freedom?"[70]

What would be a richer conception of citizenship and freedom? One that allows people to live lives of decency and dignity, according to Sandel, and to "deliberate with their fellow citizens about public affairs."[71] He does not advocate for a "common result" where everyone achieves the same thing, but he proposes a version of the American dream that would support a broad equality of condition. He ends the book with the image of a library—the Library of Congress in particular—as emblematic of this version of the American dream: something truly great that our democracy built that everyone from all walks of life can use and enjoy.

Could caring about the common good—the things that can be shared, the foundation of our social bonds, the things we can build together for everyone's use and enjoyment—be the key to civic idealism? Could caring about the common good or "communitarian solidarity" partly explain Wake County's success? We need leaders who initiate conversations about the common good, at every level: the school, the neighborhood, the state, the nation.

There are many pressures reinforcing Americans' tendency to see themselves as embattled in a constant struggle of competitive striving and to seek out and prefer separate enclaves. Enclaves can serve as a refuge, after all, not only sites of exclusion. But there are also good reasons to resist those pressures and to see integration as not optional but imperative. In responding to the *Nice White Parents* podcast series, Michelle Burris and Stefan Lallinger of the Century Foundation offered this reminder about the value of true integration: "We are presenting this commentary to push back against certain themes in the narrative that award-winning producer Chana Joffe-Walt weaves for *Nice White Parents* listeners, and to remind Americans of the promise that heroes like Dr. Martin Luther King, Jr., saw in integration, and explain why there is cause for hope in 2021. As author Vanessa Siddle Walker eloquently stated in her recent book, Dr. King dreamed of a 'genuine integration,' one that 'must lead us to a point where we share in the power that all our society will produce.' We believe in that goal."[72]

Integration has tremendous creative potential; there is greater strength in the appreciation of differences. Integration is not the same as assimilation or homogenization. Rather, "it is a constant generator of new cultural diversities and epistemic perspectives."[73] As observed by a Wake County school board member: "I think today, people tend to knock that idea of assimilation and not wanting to see race, and we're actually getting away from that, but I think it's in a good way. Because there's not this idea of seeing one race or one color or not seeing color, but it's appreciating the differences that each person, be it color, gender, culture, what they bring and appreciating that, not just tolerating or respecting the fact that you're different, but I appreciate the fact that you're different and what you bring."[74]

What then happens, substantively, through "solidarity" rather than competitive striving? Friendships, yes, but more than that. From the former Mayor of Charlotte, North Carolina, and former U.S. Secretary of Transportation, Anthony Foxx, who experienced firsthand a successfully integrated school: "We learned through experience to live together. We learned through experience to share in each other's successes and setbacks. We learned through experience to believe that we're part of the same family, not just as West Charlotte alumni, but also as Charlotteans, as North Carolinians and as Americans. When Martin Luther King, Jr. delivered his 'I Have a Dream' speech, our experiences were exactly what he imagined."[75]

For both students and parents, integrated schooling affects their lives well beyond the classroom. Rather than reproducing the hierarchy of society, integrated schools are sites of democratic renewal and cultural transformation.

Appendix A

News & Observer
Search Process

NewsBank Inc.'s America's News archival software was used to search for and download *News & Observer* articles. We accessed this software through the Park Library at the University of North Carolina at Chapel Hill. Articles were identified in two phases. Inclusion criteria for phase one were articles that contained the designated search terms (see below), were published by the *News & Observer* on or between January 1, 2009, and December 31, 2011, and were classified in NewsBank as "opinion" or "editorial." Exclusion criteria for phase one were articles that did not include mention of the composition of a school's population, student achievement as a function of school demographics, the relationship between school demographics and the larger community, or actions of the school board related to any of the above. Inclusion criteria for phase two were articles specifically referenced in phase one articles (but not already captured in our initial searches). Exclusion criteria for phase two were articles already included in phase one.

In phase one, three searches were conducted. The first search was for articles that included the search terms "Wake County Board of Education" or "Wake County Public Schools," yielding 122 articles. The second search was for articles that included the term "WCPSS," yielding 70 additional articles. The third search was for articles including the terms "wake county school board" or "wake school board," yielding 485 articles. To reduce this yield to a manageable size, we ran that search with additional limiting terms ("divers*," "segregat*," "neighborhood schools," "integrat*," "school choice," "busing," "magnets," or "year-round schools"), which pared 485 articles down to 232. Duplicate articles were removed from the sample, yielding a phase one sample of 419 articles. In phase two, each article specifically referenced by articles in phase one that were not already included in the phase one sample were located using available title, author, and the date of publication information. Phase two yielded a sample of 24 articles. Both phases were combined, yielding a final sample of 443 articles. During coding, 32 articles that met exclusion criteria were removed from the sample. The final sample size was 411 articles.

105 articles from 2009, removed 14 irrelevant articles → 91
229 articles from 2010, removed 9 irrelevant articles → 220
109 articles from 2011, removed 9 irrelevant articles → 100

Appendix B

Interviewees and Questions

Total number of interviews: 22
Number of women: 14
Number of men: 8
White: 17
Black: 5
Activists/Community Leaders: 15
School District Leaders/Elected Officials: 5

Political Party Affiliation

Registered Democrat: 15
Registered Republican: 4
Unaffiliated: 1
Unknown affiliation: 2

Date of Voter Registration in Wake County

Registered after 2010: 1
Registered 2000–2009: 2
Registered 1990–1999: 10
Registered 1980–1989: 3
Registered 1970–1979: 2

Registered 1960–1969: 2
Unknown date: 2

Sample Interview Questions

1 Please tell me about your interest in or involvement in the Wake County public schools.
   a. Do you have or have you had a child attending the Wake County public schools?
   b. Do you or have you ever volunteered in the Wake County public schools?
   c. Do you or have you ever served as a teacher or administrator in the Wake County public schools?
   d. Do you or have you ever served on the Wake County Board of Education?
   e. Have you ever spoken at a public meeting (e.g., Wake County Commissioners or Board of Education) with regard to an issue involving the Wake County public schools? Please tell me more about what this was about.
   f. Have you ever published an opinion (e.g., in a local newspaper or online blog) with regard to an issue involving the Wake County public schools? Please tell me more about what this was about.
2 What are some of the qualities of public schools that are most important to you? Please tell me why these are important to you.
3 If you chose to send your child(ren) to Wake County public schools (as opposed to another alternative, such as private school or home school), what are some of the reasons why you made this choice?
4 How important to you is the makeup of a school's student population? What is your view of the ideal relationship between a public school's student population and the population of its surrounding community?
5 How important is it in 2018/2019 to have schools that are racially or socioeconomically diverse? What are some of your reasons?
6 What in your view would make public schools better, both in Wake County and thinking about American public schools more generally?
7 What in your view is the role of public schools in the 21st century United States?

Appendix C

Key Participants

Wake County School Board Members after 2009 Election (Republicans Won 4/4 Seats)

District 1—Chris Malone, Republican, elected 2009
District 2—John Tedesco, Republican, elected 2009
District 3—Kevin Hill, Democrat
District 4—Keith Sutton, Democrat
District 5—Ann McLaurin, Democrat
District 6—Carolyn Morrison, Democrat
District 7—Deborah Prickett, Republican, elected 2009
District 8—Ron Margiotta, Republican
District 9—Debra Goldman, Republican, elected 2009

Wake County School Board Members after 2011 Election (Democrats Won 5/5 Seats)

District 1—Chris Malone, Republican
District 2—John Tedesco, Republican
District 3—Kevin Hill, Democrat, reelected 2011
District 4—Keith Sutton, Democrat, reelected 2011
District 5—Jim Martin, Democrat, elected 2011
District 6—Christine Kushner, Democrat, elected 2011
District 7—Deborah Prickett, Republican
District 8—Susan Evans, Democrat, elected 2011
District 9—Debra Goldman, Republican

WCPSS Superintendents

Dr. William "Bill" McNeal, served 2000–2006, National Superintendent of the Year in 2004

Dr. Del Burns, served 2006–2010, resigned in February 2010 in conflict with the 2009 board

Dr. Donna Hargens, served in 2010, interim superintendent between Burns and Tata

Retired Brigadier General Anthony "Tony" Tata, hired in January 2011 by the 2009 board, fired in September 2012 by the 2011 board

Local Journalists

Steve Ford, columnist for the *News & Observer*

T. Keung Hui, education reporter for the *News & Observer*

Rick Martinez, columnist for the *News & Observer*

Cash Michaels, reporter for *The Carolinian*

Bob Geary, reporter for *The Indy*

Activists

Great Schools in Wake, pro-diversity parent activist group

Wake Schools Community Alliance, pro-neighborhood schools parent activist group

NC HEAT, pro-diversity youth-led activist group

Rev. Dr. William Barber, president of NC chapter of the NAACP

Yevonne Brannon, founding member of Great Schools in Wake

Rev. Nancy Petty, senior pastor, Pullen Memorial Baptist Church

Tim Tyson, arrested in June 2010 protesting the Wake County School Board

Mary Williams, arrested in June 2010 protesting the Wake County School Board

Community Leaders

Charles Meeker, mayor of Raleigh

Tom Oxholm, former school board member

Claude Pope Jr., chairman of the Wake County Republican Party

Attorneys

Julius Chambers, attorney, argued *Swann v. Charlotte-Mecklenburg Board of Education*

Benita Jones, attorney for UNC Center for Civil Rights

Ann Majestic, WCPSS board attorney

Judge Howard E. Manning Jr., presided over the *Leandro* school funding case

Thought Leaders

Bob Luebke, policy analyst at Civitas Institute

Rob Schofield, *NC Policy Watch*

Terry Stoops, John Locke Foundation

Acknowledgments

To have the opportunity to put words to some of what I observed during a remarkable period of Wake County's history is a great privilege. However, there are as many different ways to tell the story of what happened here as there are people who participated in or witnessed the debate in real time.

The idea for this book has been a part of my consciousness for many years. I am grateful for the Faculty Research and Professional Development grant that allowed me to finally bring the book to life. The College of Humanities and Social Sciences Research Office and the Office of Research, Innovation, and Economic Development at NC State University made the work possible.

I could not have conducted a content analysis of over four hundred articles without the help of my research assistant, Kati Scruggs. Kati is a brilliant, diligent, and clear-eyed researcher, and our analysis benefited greatly from her insights. Access to the archive we needed to conduct our research was facilitated by the Park Library at the UNC Hussman School of Journalism and Media in Chapel Hill and the assistance of its generous library staff.

My interviewees, named and unnamed, are the heart of this book. I am grateful for the time they spent talking with me, their honesty, and the trust they placed in me to represent their piece of the story accurately. I am also grateful to different branches of the Wake County Public Libraries for allowing me to use their study rooms to conduct interviews and for their own efforts in sustaining community conversations about integration, such as the panel discussion in February 2020 with Joe Holt Jr., the first person who tried to integrate Raleigh's public schools.

I want to thank Dr. Michael Pendlebury, head of the Department of Philosophy and Religious Studies at NC State University, and Dr. Blair Kelley, assistant dean of Interdisciplinary Studies and International Programs, for supporting my scholarly leave during the spring 2021 semester. The book could not have been written without time away from teaching and administrative duties. I am also very grateful to Ann Rives, then the business services coordinator for the Department of Philosophy and Religious Studies, for facilitating every logistical aspect of life as an academic researcher.

My dear colleagues at NC State gave me valuable feedback on my writing, including Jason Bivins, Mary Kath Cunningham, Levi McLaughlin, Bill Adler, Kathleen Foody, Xavier Pickett, Veljko Dubljevic, Amy Glaser, and Michael Pendlebury. I deeply appreciate their perspectives and knowledge. My son, James Wood, helped to create the charts and graphs in chapter 1. Ashley Mason helped with proofreading, although any remaining mistakes are my own.

It has been a pleasure working with Peter Mickulas, my editor at Rutgers University Press. I am grateful to him and Lisa Nunn, series editor for Critical Issues in American Education at Rutgers University Press, for believing in this book.

The principals and teachers of the Wake County Public School System, particularly Hunter Elementary, Ligon Middle School, and Enloe High School, taught me a great deal about the world of public education. They have inspired my lasting admiration and loyalty. Likewise, my own parents serve as constant inspiration. My mother, a revered public school teacher in New Jersey for over twenty-five years, showed me how a public school education can be an excellent education. My father, a minister in the United Methodist Church in New Jersey for over forty years, showed me the irreplaceable value of community.

Finally, and most importantly, I want to thank my husband, Swain Wood, my first and best reader, a sharp editor, and my most brilliant conversation partner. Thank you for walking alongside me every step of the way.

Notes

Chapter 1   Wake County's Example

1   Wake County Board of Education Meeting, Part 2 of 4, December 1, 2009, *WRAL News*, 01:54:35 (01:17:03 minute mark), https://www.wral.com/news/education/video/6591678/.

2   Rucker Johnson, *Children of the Dream: Why School Integration Works* (New York: Basic Books, 2019), 218–219.

3   "Strategic Plan: Core Beliefs," Wake County Public School System, accessed February 25, 2021, https://www.wcpss.net/Page/4775.

4   WakeEd Partnership, https://www.wakeed.org/about; and Public School Forum of North Carolina, https://www.ncforum.org.

5   Public Schools First NC: https://www.publicschoolsfirstnc.org; Great Schools in Wake: https://www.publicschoolsfirstnc.org/great-schools-in-wake/; Dudley Flood Center for Educational Equity and Opportunity: https://www.ncforum.org/floodcenter/; EdNC: https://www.ednc.org; Center for Racial Equity in Education (CREED): https://www.creed-nc.org; Every Child NC: https://everychildnc.org.

6   Specifically, in 1997, the North Carolina Supreme Court held in *Leandro v. State* that the state constitution's right to education "is a right to a sound basic education. An education that does not serve the purpose of preparing students to participate and compete in the society in which they live and work is devoid of substance and is constitutionally inadequate." Education Law Center, accessed August 26, 2022, https://edlawcenter.org/litigation/states/northcarolina.html.

7   "District Facts," Wake County Public School System, accessed February 25, 2021, https://www.wcpss.net/domain/100.

8   The Equity in Opportunity Act aimed to increase voucher value and loosen eligibility requirements. North Carolina General Assembly, House Bill 32, 2021–2022 Session, https://www.ncleg.gov/BillLookup/2021/H32. The state budget bill eventually signed into law in the summer of 2022 included a significant increase for private school vouchers: "From $120.54 million to $176.54 million for the 2023–2024 school year." See Greg Childress, "Budget Bill Sent to Cooper Puts NC's Controversial School Voucher Program on Path to Dramatic Expansion,"

NC Policy Watch, July 7, 2022, https://ncpolicywatch.com/2022/07/07/budget
-bill-sent-to-cooper-puts-ncs-controversial-school-voucher-program-on-path-to
-dramatic-expansion/.

9 "Wake County, Cities & Towns: Twelve Municipalities in Wake County,"
accessed October 22, 2021, https://www.wakegov.com/living-visiting/cities
-towns.

10 Author's calculations, based on publicly available data. "District Facts Reports by
Year," Wake County Public School System, accessed August 26, 2022, https://
www.wcpss.net/domain/100.

11 Wake County, "District Facts."

12 Wake County, "District Facts."

13 "Table 215.30. Enrollment, Poverty, and Federal Funds for the 120 Largest School
Districts, by Enrollment Size in 2017: 2016–17 and Fiscal Year 2019," National
Center for Education Statistics (NCES), accessed November 7, 2023, https://nces
.ed.gov/programs/digest/d19/tables/dt19_215.30.asp. Additional information
about NCES: "The National Center for Education Statistics (NCES) is the
primary federal entity for collecting and analyzing data related to education in
the U.S. and other nations. NCES is located within the U.S. Department of
Education and the Institute of Education Sciences. NCES fulfills a Congressional
mandate to collect, collate, analyze, and report complete statistics on the condition of American education; conduct and publish reports; and review and report
on education activities internationally." "About NCES," National Center for
Education Statistics (NCES), accessed November 7, 2023, https://nces.ed.gov
/about/.

14 Gary Orfield et al., "Harming Our Common Future: America's Segregated
Schools 65 Years after *Brown*," Civil Rights Project, May 10, 2019, www.civilrights
project.ucla.edu. (See Table 5: "Percentage of Black Students in 90–100% Non-
White Schools" and Table 8: "Percentage of Latino Students in 90–100%
Non-White Schools.")

15 Nikole Hannah-Jones, "It Was Never about Busing," *New York Times*, July 12,
2019, https://www.nytimes.com/2019/07/12/opinion/sunday/it-was-never-about
-busing.html. Her source: Gary Orfield and Erica Frankenberg, "*Brown* at 60:
Great Progress, a Long Retreat and an Uncertain Future," University of California Civil Rights Project, May 2014, https://civilrightsproject.ucla.edu/research/k
-12-education/integration-and-diversity/brown-at-60-great-progress-a-long-retreat
-and-an-uncertain-future.

16 See, for example, Elizabeth A. Harris and Kristin Hussey, "In Connecticut, a
Wealth Gap Divides Neighboring Schools," *New York Times*, September 11, 2016,
https://www.nytimes.com/2016/09/12/nyregion/in-connecticut-a-wealth-gap
-divides-neighboring-schools.html.

17 All statistics for Westfield and Plainfield, NJ, come from the National Center for
Education Statistics, "District Directory Information," accessed February 25, 2021,
https://nces.ed.gov/ccd/districtsearch/.

18 "2020–21 District Facts Reports by Year," Wake County Public School System,
accessed February 25, 2021, https://www.wcpss.net/domain/100. Compare with
"District Demographic Dashboard 2015–19 for Wake County Schools, NC: 60%
white, 20% Black, 10% Latino, and 7% Asian," National Center for Education
Statistics, accessed February 25, 2021, https://nces.ed.gov/Programs/Edge
/ACSDashboard/3704720.

19 "District Facts: Our Budget," Wake County Public School System, accessed February 25, 2021, https://www.wcpss.net/domain/100; NCES, "District Directory."

20 "2020–21 District Facts Reports by Year," Wake County Public School System, https://www.wcpss.net/domain/100. The average free and reduced-price lunch rate across all schools in 2020–2021 was 27.7%.

21 "Growth and Population Trends," data from U.S. Census Bureau, Wake County, accessed August 26, 2022, https://www.wakegov.com/departments-government /planning-development-inspections/planning/demographics; "County-to-County Migration Flows: 2015–2019 ACS," U.S. Census Bureau, accessed September 2, 2022, https://www.census.gov/data/tables/2019/demo/geographic-mobility /county-to-county-migration-2015-2019.html.

22 Todd Silberman, "Wake County Schools: A Question of Balance," in *Divided We Fail: Coming Together through Public School Choice* (New York: Century Foundation Press, 2002), 141–166.

23 Gerald Grant, *Hope and Despair in the American City: Why There Are No Bad Schools in Raleigh* (Cambridge, MA: Harvard University Press, 2009), 104.

24 Grant, *Hope*, 91.

25 Grant, *Hope*, 131.

26 Grant, *Hope*, 188.

27 Toby Parcel and Andrew Taylor, *The End of Consensus: Diversity, Neighborhoods, and the Politics of Public School Assignments* (Chapel Hill: University of North Carolina Press, 2015), 4–12.

28 According to a more recent study, some nodes were reassigned multiple times during the 2000s, while others were never touched. See Deven Carlson et al., "Socioeconomic-Based School Assignment Policy and Racial Segregation Levels: Evidence from the Wake County School System," *American Educational Research Journal* 57, no. 1 (2020): 272, https://doi.org/10.3102/0002831219851729.

29 Parcel and Taylor, *End of Consensus*, 112–113.

30 Parcel and Taylor, *End of Consensus*, 113.

31 Parcel and Taylor, *End of Consensus*, 116.

32 Parcel and Taylor, *End of Consensus*, 106

33 Parcel and Taylor, *End of Consensus*, 108, 92–93, 126. The authors also use the term "civic capacity."

34 Sheneka Williams, "The Politics of Maintaining Balanced Schools: An Examination of Three Districts," in *The Future of School Integration: Socioeconomic Diversity as an Education Reform Strategy*, ed. Richard Kahlenberg (New York: Century Foundation Press, 2012), 278.

35 See, for example: Sean Reardon and Lori Rhodes, "The Effects of Socioeconomic School Integration Policies on Racial School Desegregation," in *Integrating Schools in a Changing Society: New Policies and Legal Options for a Multiracial Generation*, ed. Erica Frankenberg and Elizabeth DeBray (Chapel Hill: University of North Carolina Press, 2011), under "Part III: Student Assignment Policy Choices and Evidence," https://doi.org/10.5149/9780807869208 _frankenberg.

36 M. Monique McMillan et al., "Can Class-Based Substitute for Race-Based Student Assignment Plans? Evidence from Wake County, North Carolina," *Urban Education* 53, no.7 (2018): 843–874, https://doi.org/10.1177 /0042085915613554.

37 Carlson et al., "Socioeconomic-Based School Assignment," 258–304.

38 Carlson et al., "Socioeconomic-Based School Assignment," 28, 29, 35, 41.

39 Carlson et al., "Socioeconomic-Based School Assignment," 41.

40 From several interviews with current and former board members, the authors identified the following factors: The downturn in the economy in the mid to late 2000s; population growth; the advent of year-round schools (and lawsuit filed in 2007 by Wake CARES); frequent student reassignment; formation of parent advocacy groups; national, partisan support of school board candidates; a coalition between some groups of parents and conservative Republicans. Jenni Owen and Megan Kauffmann, "The End of a Diversity Policy? Wake County Public Schools and Student Assignment Case," E-PARCC Collaborative Governance Initiative, PARCC, Syracuse University (2014): 21, https://www .maxwell.syr.edu/research/program-for-the-advancement-research-on-conflict -collaboration/e-parcc/cases-simulations-syllabi/cases/the-end-of-diversity -policy-wake-county-public-schools-and-student-assignment.

41 Owen and Kauffmann, "Diversity Policy," 12.

42 Key stakeholders were listed as follows: The John Locke Foundation, NAACP, Wake County BOE, Wake County Parents, Wake Ed Partnership, Wake Schools Community Alliance, and WakeUP Wake County. Owen and Kauffmann, "Diversity Policy," Appendix 7; Great Schools in Wake Coalition partners, a multiracial/multiethnic list of 43 groups, included five PTAs from area schools, three local chapters of the NAACP, nine faith/church groups, the Coalition of Concerned Citizens for African American Children, 100 Black Men of Triangle East, YWCA of the Greater Triangle, WakeUP Wake County, League of Women Voters of Wake County, NC Justice Center, BiggerPicture4Wake, and many more. Owen and Kauffmann, "Diversity Policy," Appendix 6; Owen and Kauffmann, "Diversity Policy," 30–33.

43 See, for example, Stephanie McCrummen, "Republican School Board in NC Backed by Tea Party Abolishes Integration Policy," *Washington Post*, February 26, 2011, https://www.washingtonpost.com/education/republican-school-board-in-nc -backed-by-tea-party-abolishes-integration-policy/2011/01/03/ABXQIkD_story .html; Richard Kahlenberg, "What Tea Party Defeat in Wake County Means for Schools," *Washington Post*, October 20, 2011, https://www.washingtonpost.com /blogs/answer-sheet/post/what-tea-party-defeat-in-wake-county-means-for -schools/2011/10/19/gIQAaxh4yL_blog.html; Michael Winerip, "Seeking Integration, Whatever the Path," *New York Times*, February 27, 2011, https://www .nytimes.com/2011/02/28/education/28winerip.html.

44 *The Colbert Report*, season 7, episode 10, "The Word—Disintegration," performed by Stephen Colbert, aired January 18, 2011, on Comedy Central, https://www.cc .com/video/1zj4bl/the-colbert-report-the-word-disintegration.

45 Toby L. Parcel and Roslyn A. Mickelson, "School Desegregation and Resegrega-tion in the Upper South: An Introduction and Overview," *American Behavioral Scientist* 66, no. 6 (2022): 671–677, https://doi.org/10.1177/00027642211033282.

46 White students are no longer a majority in American public schools: "In 2016, the public school enrollment across the United States was 48.4% white, 26.3% Latino, 15.25 black, 5.5% Asian, and 1.0% American Indian." Orfield et al., "Harming Our Common Future," 15. Lower birth rates and immigration are greater factors than white departure for private schools, according to the authors. See also Gary Orfield et al., *"Brown* at 62: School Segregation by Race, Poverty, and State," Civil Rights Project, May 16, 2016, https://www.civilrightsproject.ucla.edu/research/k

-12-education/integration-and-diversity/brown-at-62-school-segregation-by-race
-poverty-and-state/Brown-at-62-final-corrected-2.pdf.

47 Martha Minow, *In Brown's Wake: Legacies of America's Educational Landmark*
(New York: Oxford University Press, 2010); James Ryan, *Five Miles Away, a
World Apart: One City, Two Schools, and the Story of Educational Opportunity in
Modern America* (New York: Oxford University Press, 2010).

48 Roslyn Mickelson, Stephen Smith, and Amy Hawn Nelson, eds., *Yesterday, Today,
and Tomorrow: School Desegregation and Resegregation in Charlotte* (Cambridge,
MA: Harvard Education Press, 2015); Sarah Garland, *Divided We Fail: The Story
of an African American Community That Ended the Era of School Desegregation*
(Boston, MA: Beacon Press, 2013); Sarah Caroline Thuesen, *Greater Than Equal:
African American Struggles for Schools and Citizenship in North Carolina,
1919–1965* (Chapel Hill: University of North Carolina Press, 2013); Kris Nordstrom, "Stymied by Segregation: How Integration Can Transform North
Carolina Schools and the Lives of Its Students," Education and Law Project of the
North Carolina Justice Center, March 1, 2018, https://www.ncjustice.org
/publications/stymied-by-segregation-how-integration-can-transform-nc-schools/;
Ethan Roy and James Ford, "Deep Rooted: A Brief History of Race and Education in North Carolina," August 11, 2019, https://www.ednc.org/deep-rooted-a
-brief-history-of-race-and-education-in-north-carolina/; Vanessa Siddle Walker,
*The Lost Education of Horace Tate: Uncovering the Hidden Heroes Who Fought for
Justice in Schools* (New York: New Press, 2018).

49 Richard Rothstein, *The Color of Law: A Forgotten History of How Our Government Segregated America* (New York: W. W. Norton & Company, 2017); Elizabeth McRae, *Mothers of Massive Resistance: White Women and the Politics of
White Supremacy* (New York: Oxford University Press, 2018).

50 Claude S. Fischer et al., *Inequality by Design: Cracking the Bell Curve Myth*
(Princeton, NJ: Princeton University Press, 1996); Annette Lareau, *Unequal
Childhoods: Class, Race, and Family Life* (Berkeley: University of California Press,
2011); Margaret Hagerman, *White Kids: Growing Up with Privilege in a Racially
Divided America* (New York: New York University Press, 2018).

51 Roslyn Mickelson, "The Cumulative Disadvantages of First- and Second-
Generation Segregation for Middle School Achievement," *American Educational
Research Journal* 52, no. 4 (August 2015): 657–692; Karolyn Tyson, *Integration
Interrupted: Tracking, Black Students, and Acting White after* Brown (New York:
Oxford University Press, 2011); Amanda Lewis and John Diamond, *Despite the
Best Intentions: How Racial Inequity Thrives in Good Schools* (New York: Oxford
University Press, 2015); Richard Kahlenberg, "From All Walks of Life: New Hope
for School Integration," *American Educator* (Winter 2012–2013).

52 Helen F. Ladd and Mavzuna Turaeva, "Parental Preferences for Charter Schools in
North Carolina: Implications for Racial Segregation and Isolation," (Working Paper
243, National Center for the Study of Privatization in Education, Teachers College,
Columbia University, New York, September 29, 2020); Helen F. Ladd, Charles T.
Clotfelter, and John B. Holbein, "The Growing Segmentation of the Charter School
Sector in North Carolina," *Education Finance and Policy* 12, no. 4 (2016): 536–563;
Erika Wilson, "The New White Flight," *Duke Journal of Constitutional Law &
Public Policy* 14 (2019): 233–284; Diane Ravitch, *The Death and Life of the Great
American School System* (New York: Basic Books, 2010); Noliwe Rooks, *Cutting
School: The Segrenomics of American Education* (New York: New Press, 2017).

53 Nikole Hannah-Jones, "Segregation Now," *The Atlantic*, May 2014, https://www
.theatlantic.com/magazine/archive/2014/05/segregation-now/359813/; "Choosing
a School for My Daughter in a Segregated City," *New York Times*, June 9, 2016,
https://www.nytimes.com/2016/06/12/magazine/choosing-a-school-for-my
-daughter-in-a-segregated-city.html; "The Resegregation of Jefferson County,"
New York Times, September 6, 2017, https://www.nytimes.com/2017/09/06
/magazine/the-resegregation-of-jefferson-county.html; "It Was Never about
Busing," *New York Times*, July 12, 2019. https://www.nytimes.com/2019/07/12
/opinion/sunday/it-was-never-about-busing.html.

54 An excellent example of this engagement with *Brown*: Roslyn A. Mickelson et al.,
"The Past, Present, and Future of *Brown's* Mandate: A View from North Carolina," *American Behavioral Scientist* 66, no. 6 (2022):770–803, https://doi.org/10
.1177/00027642211033296.

55 See, for example, the Harvard Graduate School of Education project called
RIDES: Reimagining Integration Diverse and Equitable Schools, https://rides.gse
.harvard.edu/about.

56 E. Torres and R. Weissbourd, "Do Parents Really Want School Integration?,"
report by the Making Caring Common Project, Harvard Graduate School of
Education (2020), 10, accessed February 5, 2021, https://mcc.gse.harvard.edu/.

57 Torres and Weissbourd, "Parents," 15.

58 Torres and Weissbourd, "Parents," 20.

59 Torres and Weissbourd, "Parents," 4.

60 Robert Bellah, "The Ethical Aims of Social Inquiry," in *Social Science as Moral
Inquiry*, ed. Norma Haan et al. (New York: Columbia University Press, 1983),
360–381.

61 My methodology was informed by the following: Carol A. B. Warren, "Qualita-
tive Interviewing," *Handbook of Interview Research*, ed. Jaber F. Gubrium and
James A. Holstein (Thousand Oaks, CA: SAGE Publications, 2001), 83–102;
Kathy Charmaz, "Qualitative Interviewing and Grounded Theory Analysis,"
Handbook of Interview Research, ed. Jaber F. Gubrium and James A. Holstein
(Thousand Oaks, CA: SAGE Publications, 2001), 675–694; Kathy Charmaz and
Linda Liska Belgrave, "Thinking about Data with Grounded Theory," *Qualitative
Inquiry* 25, no. 8 (2019): 743–753, https://doi-org/10.1177/1077800418809455.

62 Charmaz and Belgrave, "Thinking about Data," 750.

63 Robert Bellah et al., *The Good Society* (New York: Vintage Books, 1991), 254–286.

64 Bob Geary, "Great Schools in Wake Coalition," *Independent Weekly*, January 18,
2012, https://indyweek.com/guides/archives-guides/great-schools-wake-coalition/.
The full quote: "Brannon, a former county commissioner and longtime PTA
leader, says GSIW's success is due to the synergies of different groups and
individual talents. 'This group came together around a core value to lift up the
community. They came together to say that every child in Wake County,
regardless of economics or race or residence, deserves a fair shot at education.
That's what I love about it. I'm a child of the '60s, and I've had a lot of opportunities to be an activist, but this has really been, well, my word for it is remarkable.'"

Chapter 2   Contested Values in Wake's Debate

1 A remarkable example of disparate power and privilege can be found in James
Ryan, *Five Miles Away, a World Apart: One City, Two Schools, and the Story of*

Educational Opportunity in Modern America (New York: Oxford University Press, 2010).

2 In the 2021–2022 academic year, school board meetings have become sites of disagreement and threatened violence over mask mandates and COVID-19 vaccines, as well as the purported teaching of critical race theory. See, for example, Anya Kamenetz, "School Boards Are Asking for Federal Help as They Face Threats and Violence," NPR, September 30, 2021, https://www.npr.org/sections /back-to-school-live-updates/2021/09/30/1041870027/school-boards-federal-help -threats-violence.

3 Examples of angry parents filling auditoriums are portrayed in *This American Life*, episode 562, "The Problem We All Live With," Nikole Hannah-Jones and Ira Glass, aired July 31, 2015, on WBEZ Chicago, https://www.thisamericanlife.org /562/the-problem-we-all-live-with-part-one.

4 North Carolina's lieutenant governor objected to the social studies curriculum adopted in early 2021 because it addresses systemic racism. See Greg Childress, "Black Democrats Take Issue with Lt. Gov. Mark Robinson's Claim That There Is No 'Systemic Racism,'" *NC Policy Watch*, January 29, 2021, http://pulse .ncpolicywatch.org/2021/01/29/black-democrats-take-issue-with-lt-gov-mark -robinsons-claim-that-there-is-no-systemic-racism/#sthash.FvnZAL2t.dpbs.

5 Annette Lareau and Kimberly Goyette, eds., *Choosing Homes, Choosing Schools* (New York: Russell Sage Foundation, 2014).

6 A few of my interview subjects commented on this issue. Real estate agents in Wake County could not guarantee specific schools and lobbied against the assignment policy in the 2000s. See Sarah Ovaska, "Schools Shift May Reshape Raleigh," *News & Observer*, October 21, 2009. An excerpt from Ovaska's article: "'A switch to a neighborhood approach in the school system could bring much-desired stability to families living in the outlying areas of Raleigh where parents weren't sure what schools their children would go to when they bought their homes,' said Jill Flink, a Raleigh-based real-estate agent with York Simpson Underwood. 'It's been a problem for us,' said Flink, about the current system. She would tell clients, 'You're going to have to love your house, because your schools aren't fixed.'"

7 Jenny Anderson and Kristin Hussey, "Schools Look to Weed Out Nonresidents," *New York Times*, September 11, 2012, https://www.nytimes.com/2012/09/12 /education/standing-guard-against-education-thieves-at-coveted-schools.html.

8 Anderson and Hussey, "Nonresidents."

9 Nikole Hannah-Jones, "Choosing a School for My Daughter in a Segregated City," *New York Times Magazine*, June 9, 2016, https://www.nytimes.com/2016 /06/12/magazine/choosing-a-school-for-my-daughter-in-a-segregated-city.html.

10 Hannah-Jones, "Choosing a School."

11 Richard Rothstein describes the history of redlining and housing discrimination in *The Color of Law: A Forgotten History of How Our Government Segregated America* (New York: W. W. Norton & Company, 2017). Dorothy Brown explores the related topic of the Black-white wealth gap in *The Whiteness of Wealth: How the Tax System Impoverishes Black Americans—And How We Can Fix It* (New York: Crown, 2021).

12 James Ryan discusses the *Milliken* case and its impact in *Five Miles Away, a World Apart: One City, Two Schools, and the Story of Educational Opportunity in Modern America* (New York: Oxford University Press, 2010), 83. Ryan traces the buildup

to *Milliken* through a similar case in Virginia, *Bradley v. Richmond School Board*, which was presided over by U.S. District Court Judge Robert H. Merhige. Bucking popular views at the time, Merhige believed the government was responsible for so-called de facto segregation. According to Ryan, "This view of state responsibility . . . would blow up the distinction between de facto segregation and de jure segregation. The former was the term reserved for segregation that occurred because of private decisions and was generally thought to be beyond the reach of the Constitution; the latter referred to segregation by law and was the target of desegregation remedies. Merhige argued, in essence, that there was no such thing as de facto segregation. If accepted, and the de jure-de facto distinction dissolved, both North and South would have the same obligation to desegregate."

13 Positional goods derive their value from comparison to what others have. Positional goods are "scarce by definition." Competition for them is a zero-sum game. Lisa Herzog, "Markets," in *Stanford Encyclopedia of Philosophy*, August 30, 2021, https://plato.stanford.edu/entries/markets/. Original source: Fred Hirsch, *The Social Limits to Growth* (Cambridge, MA: Harvard University Press, 1976).

14 See, for example, Caitlin Flanagan, "Private Schools are Indefensible," *The Atlantic*, April 2021, https://www.theatlantic.com/magazine/archive/2021/04/private-schools-are-indefensible/618078/.

15 See previous discussion of the economies of scale made possible by the size and centralization of Wake's countywide district in chapter 1.

16 Stephen Samuel Smith, "Still Swimming against the Resegregation Tide—A Suburban Southern School District in the Aftermath of *Parents Involved*," *North Carolina Law Review* 88, no. 3 (March 1, 2010): 1152, https://scholarship.law.unc.edu/nclr/vol88/iss3/9.

17 Lisa and Michael Springle, letter to the editor, "The Damage Is Done," *News & Observer*, January 17, 2009.

18 Past Election Results, Wake County, North Carolina, https://www.wakegov.com/departments-government/board-elections/data-reports/past-election-results. For the 2009 Municipal Election, October 6, 2009, voter turnout was 11% (55,121 votes cast out of 482,580 registered voters) with the winning Board of Education candidates averaging about 4,500 votes apiece. Chris Malone (District 1)—3,931, John Tedesco (District 2)—3,255, Deborah Prickett (District 7)—6,630, and Debra Goldman (District 9)—4,450, https://s3.us-west-2.amazonaws.com/wakegov.com.if-us-west-2/prod/documents/2021-02/20091006.summary.pdf. For the 2011 Municipal Election, October 11, 2011, voter turnout was 21% (95,116 votes cast out of 449,478 registered votes) with winning Board of Education candidates averaging about 8,300 votes apiece. Kevin Hill (District 3)—8,116, Keith Sutton (District 4)—8,513, Jim Martin (District 5)—6,212, Christine Kushner (District 6)—11,810, Susan Evans (District 8)—7,129, https://s3.us-west-2.amazonaws.com/wakegov.com.if-us-west-2/prod/documents/2021-02/20111011.summary.pdf.

19 Anne Applebaum and Peter Pomerantsev, "The Internet Doesn't Have to Be Awful," *The Atlantic*, April 2021, https://www.theatlantic.com/magazine/archive/2021/04/the-internet-doesnt-have-to-be-awful/618079/.

20 "Submit a Letter," *News & Observer*, accessed November 3, 2023, https://www.newsobserver.com/opinion/letters-to-the-editor/submit-letter/.

21 Bob Geary, "Local Filmmaker Cash Michaels on Obama, Wake Schools and Race in N.C.," *Indy Week*, August 25, 2010, https://indyweek.com/news/local-filmmaker-cash-michaels-obama-wake-schools-race-n.c. Cash Michaels's film is

called *Obama in NC: The Path to History*, CashWorks HD Productions/Thunderball Films LLC.

22 "Our Impact: Markets," *News & Observer*, McClatchy, accessed March 23, 2021, https://www.mcclatchy.com/our-impact/markets/the-news-observer/. The *N&O* had a daily print circulation of 68,667 and a Sunday circulation of 84,995 in 2020. Digital traffic is much higher, with 25,393,000 average monthly page views in 2020.

23 Interview, September 20, 2018.

24 This parent's public comment was criticized in a letter to the editor by Jason Doll, "And 'Ghetto'?," *News & Observer*, December 20, 2009; Ellen McIntyre, letter to the editor, "Teachers for the Task," *News & Observer*, October 25, 2009. At the time, the writer was a professor and head of the Elementary Education department in the College of Education, NC State University.

25 Toby Parcel and Andrew Taylor, *The End of Consensus: Diversity, Neighborhoods, and the Politics of Public School Assignments* (Chapel Hill: University of North Carolina Press, 2015).

26 See, for example, Gene Nichol, "Falling Behind, Quietly," *News & Observer*, July 15, 2010. Nichol wrote about the Tea Party movement's grievances and the Wake County school board's "analogous war." At the time, Nichol was a professor at the UNC School of Law and director of UNC-Chapel Hill's Center on Poverty, Work & Opportunity; Jane Mayer, "State for Sale," *New Yorker*, October 3, 2011, https://www.newyorker.com/magazine/2011/10/10/state-for-sale. See also, Jane Mayer, *Dark Money: The Hidden History of the Billionaires behind the Rise of the Radical Right* (New York: Doubleday, 2016).

27 Ellen McIntyre, letter to the editor, *News & Observer*, October 25, 2009.

28 Cathy Kilburn, letter to the editor, "Parties, Show Respect," *News & Observer*, April 4, 2010.

29 Rick Martinez, "It's All about the System," *News & Observer*, April 14, 2010.

30 For a discussion of educational "theft," see Noliwe Rooks, *Cutting School: The Segrenomics of American Education* (New York: New Press, 2017).

31 Special thanks to my research assistant, Kati Scruggs, for her contributions to this analysis.

32 Claude E. Pope Jr., letter to the editor, "A School Mandate, Indeed," *News & Observer*, July 24, 2010.

33 Lisa Boneham, letter to the editor, "All-Inclusive," *News & Observer*, October 18, 2009.

34 Roger Joseph, letter to the editor, "It's on the Parents," *News & Observer*, January 19, 2010.

35 Susanne Robinson, letter to the editor, "If You Really Care, Get Involved," *News & Observer*, March 27, 2010.

36 See Martha Minow, "Confronting the Seduction of Choice: Law, Education, and American Pluralism," *Yale Law Journal* 120, no. 4 (January 2011): 814–848. "School system designers sought to harness the appeal of 'choice' in a kind of 'soft paternalism,' enticing white parents to choose public urban schools by endowing them with special programs" (825).

37 Winston T. Hooker Sr., letter to the editor, "The Actual Promises," *News & Observer*, March 13, 2010.

38 Jennifer Mansfield, letter to the editor, "About Appearances," *News & Observer*, October 4, 2009.

39 Dennis Jacobs, "School Choices," *News & Observer*, October 21, 2009. This person also noted in their letter that access to year-round schools was not equal. Year-round schools were introduced primarily to address overcrowding. Students were divided into "tracks," with each group taking turns being "tracked out" while the school operated year-round. When some students were given mandatory year-round assignments, with no choice of a traditional calendar assignment, some families fought that policy through a lawsuit and were successful. The case was decided just a few months before the 2009 election.

40 Capacchione v. Charlotte-Mecklenburg Schools, 57 F. Supp.2d 228 (W.D.N.C. 1999).

41 About Steve Ford:

> Steve Ford has lived in North Carolina since 1981, when he moved here to join *The News & Observer* of Raleigh. He retired in late 2012 as the paper's editorial page editor. In that job, he supervised the opinion pages, wrote editorials and wrote a weekly column. Steve grew up in Northern Virginia. He graduated from Yale University and served in the U.S. Army as a photographer, including a year in Vietnam. . . . He began volunteer work with the N.C. Council of Churches in the spring of 2013, helping to keep an eye on state government and writing about public policy issues.

"About: People," NC Council of Churches, accessed September 9, 2022, https://www.ncchurches.org/people/18376/.

42 Elizabeth Anderson, "What Is the Point of Equality?," *Ethics* 109, no. 2 (1999): 288–289.

43 Peter van Dorsten, letter to the editor, "Schools, Resources and Balance," *News & Observer*, October 8, 2010.

44 Steve Ford, "A Superintendent, outside the Box," *News & Observer*, June 20, 2010.

45 Steve Ford, "A Plunge toward Unequal Schools," *News & Observer*, May 23, 2010.

46 Ford, "Plunge."

47 Steve Ford, "Charter Champions Riding High," *News & Observer*, November 14, 2010.

48 See, for example, Roslyn Arlin Mickelson, Martha Cecelia Bottia, and Savannah Larrimore, "A Metaregression Analysis of the Effects of School Racial and Ethnic Composition on K-12 Reading, Language Arts, and English Outcomes," *Sociology of Race and Ethnicity* 7, no. 3 (2021): 401–419.

49 Nikole Hannah-Jones, keynote address, October 2, 2018, Public School Forum of North Carolina, Color of Education 2018, https://colorofeducation.org/events/color-of-education-an-evening-with-nikole-hannah-jones/. NAEP reading scores show white-Black score gap reduced by half from 1971 to 1988 (thirty-nine to eighteen points). These were the years the United States was most serious about integrating its public schools. Beyond academic outcomes, longitudinal data show that segregated schools lead to segregated lives. Excerpt from Nikole Hannah-Jones:

> Rucker Johnson, an economist out of Cal Berkeley, has studied 30 years of longitudinal data of Black children who in the 70s got access to desegregated schools, and what it shows is those schools changed the entire trajectory of their lives. . . . Those children were more likely to graduate high school, to go to college, they were less likely to live in poverty, they were less likely to go to jail, and more important than that, they passed that onto their own children. Those benefits went to the next generation. Children who attended segregated schools had the opposite effect, and they also passed along that to their next generation of children. (Minute mark 52:04)

50 Hannah-Jones, keynote address.

51 Marguerite LeBlanc criticized Rick Martinez for drawing this faulty correlation in her letter to the editor, "Corrupt Correlations," *News & Observer*, April 21, 2011. Le Blanc was responding to Martinez, "Diversity Gets an F," *News & Observer*, April 6, 2011.

52 Specifically:

> For their actions, now-Chairman Margiotta and the new majority have been called racists. The NAACP has spearheaded complaints that have fueled investigations by AdvancED, the high school accreditation agency, and the Civil Rights Office of the U.S. Department of Education. Drowned out in the racially charged din was the new majority's contention that the diversity policy was probably hurting poor and minority kids in the classroom. Their voices were largely ignored because of closed-mindedness that condemns social conservatives as incapable of caring about the future of poor and minority children. However, there's growing evidence that proves the opposite. In practice, Wake County's diversity policy benefited white and Asian students at the expense of poor and minority kids. That's a high price to pay to satisfy diversity supporters' outdated notion of social justice. (Rick Martinez, "Diversity Gets an F," *News & Observer*, April 6, 2011)

53 For example, one letter writer criticized the school board's claims about busing: "The March 23 response to the federal Department of Education's Office for Civil Rights uses selected data on student achievement in the Wake schools and falsely suggests that busing for diversity (5 percent of busing) is the root cause of poor achievement for the disadvantaged." Sharon Eckard, letter to the editor, "Achievement Factors," *News & Observer*, April 10, 2011. Similar criticisms were made by Linda Davis, letter to the editor, "Twisted Logic," *News & Observer*, April 8, 2011.

54 Rick Martinez, "Diverse Graduation Rates," *News & Observer*, December 23, 2009.

55 Rick Martinez, "Distraction from the Classroom," *News & Observer*, June 30, 2010.

56 Just a few examples: Beverley Clark, letter to the editor, "Sunday Forum," *News & Observer*, January 25, 2009 ("However, there is substantial research that at-risk students have a stronger academic experience in diverse schools than they do in high-poverty schools. The research also shows this benefit does not come at the expense of other students. If we returned to a segregated system, the costs, tangible and intangible, would be immense."); Stan Norwalk, letter to the editor, "Proof in Scores," *News & Observer*, July 17, 2010 ("The steady closing of the gap in the early part of the decade and enormous amounts of scientific data supported Burns' beliefs. Diversity as a means of improving educational quality was the focal point of his administration."); Harden Engelhardt, letter to the editor, "Helped by Diversity," *News & Observer*, October 19, 2010 ("I hope that the Wake County Board of Education will take note of a study released last week demonstrating that low-income students perform better academically in schools with low concentrations of poverty").

57 "Close to Home," editorial, *News & Observer*, March 4, 2010.

58 "Wake Students' Stake," editorial, *News & Observer*, March 23, 2010.

59 Robert Korstad and James Leloudis, both historians and senior fellows in the Kenan Institute for Ethics at Duke, "Poverty's Place in the School Debate," *News & Observer*, March 5, 2010. Authors of *To Right These Wrongs: The North Carolina Fund and the Battle to End Poverty and Inequality in 1960s America* (Chapel Hill: University of North Carolina Press, 2011).

60 Maria Mauriello, letter to the editor, "Policy Was Breached," *News & Observer*, July 15, 2010.

61 Nikole Hannah-Jones, keynote address. Referring to *Brown*.

62 T. Keung Hui, "Whose Schools Work Better?," *News & Observer*, February 8, 2009.

63 Bob Luebke, letter to the editor, "Edge to Charlotte," *News & Observer*, April 11, 2010.

64 Bob Luebke, letter to the editor, "Failure of a Policy," *News & Observer*, October 21, 2010.

65 Barry Saunders, quoting Rev. Dr. William Barber, in "Oppose Diversity? Not I," *News & Observer*, January 19, 2010.

66 National Association for the Advancement of Colored People, NC State Conference of Branches of the NAACP, Raleigh (Apex) Branch, South Central Wake Co. Branch, Wendell (Wake Co.) Branch, and NC HEAT, and Quinton White v. Wake County Board of Education and the Wake County Public School System, Complaint under Title VI of the Civil Rights Act of 1964, September 24, 2010, http://pulse.ncpolicywatch.org/wp-content/uploads/2010/09/Title-VI -Complaint-WCSB-9-24-2010-FINAL.pdf.

67 Kathleen Kennedy Manzo, "N.C. Judge Cites 'Academic Genocide' in Report on High Schools," *EdWeek*, June 07, 2005, https://www.edweek.org/leadership/n-c -judge-cites-academic-genocide-in-report-on-high-schools/2005/06.

68 "Protest, Promise," editorial, *News & Observer*, July 22, 2010.

69 Tammy Brunner, Executive Director, Wake County Democratic Party, "Wake Benefits from Balanced Schools," *News & Observer*, August 5, 2010.

70 Kristin Collins, "Black Voices Quiet," *News & Observer*, October 3, 2009.

71 Collins, "Black Voices Quiet."

72 Mary Williams, letter to the editor, "Proof of Devotion," *News & Observer*, July 3, 2010.

73 See, for example, Rick Martinez, "Diverse Graduation Rates," *News & Observer*, December 23, 2009. "As a Hispanic, I couldn't care less about the socioeconomic and racial makeup of the classroom where a Latino kid sits. The cultural experiences he or she may gain are meaningless if that child fails to graduate. That's why I tell minority parents no sacrifice is too great to get their kids into a private school. I urge them to ignore the minority leadership and to support policies that will allow our children to escape a public school system that fails roughly half of them."

74 Special thanks to my research assistant, Kati Scruggs, for formulating these observations. For an example of this pragmatic mindset, see Glenn Scott, letter to the editor, "Equality Must Matter," *News & Observer*, October 11, 2009. "As a black person, I do not wish for my children to go to school with white children—what I want for my son is a quality education, and under the rubric of 'neighborhood schools' I am not sure that will happen."

75 Allison Backhouse, letter to the editor, "Uncaring Crowd," *News & Observer*, November 27, 2011.

76 Sarah Redpath, letter to the editor, "Assuming Failure," *News & Observer*, October 4, 2009.

77 See, for example, Christopher Marsch, letter to the editor, "A System Trying to Hide Its Failures," *News & Observer*, September 29, 2009.

78 Robinson, letter to the editor, "Get Involved."

79 See Jennifer Mansfield, letter to the editor, "About Appearances," *News & Observer*, October 4, 2009.

80 Lisa Boneham, letter to the editor, "Tedesco's Fine Traits," *News & Observer*, March 28, 2010.

81 Tina Govan, letter to the editor, "Hiding How?," *News & Observer*, November 11, 2010.

82 Henry Frey, letter to the editor, "Paternalistic Party," *News & Observer*, May 8, 2010.

83 Andrea Gomez, letter to the editor, "A Ghetto-izing Proposal," *News & Observer*, December 5, 2010.

84 David Zavaleta, letter to the editor, "Housing Patterns," *News & Observer*, February 19, 2009.

85 Special thanks to my research assistant, Kati Scruggs, for formulating this initial observation. See, for example, Chris Evans, letter to the editor, "At Their Worst," *News & Observer*, December 3, 2009; Lincoln Hancock, letter to the editor, "When Money Drives," *News & Observer*, June 18, 2010; Henry Frey, letter to the editor, "Blundering Partisans," *News & Observer*, August 22, 2010; and "At Its Worst—A Flier Attacking a Group of Wake School Board Candidates Hits the Latest Low Point in Local Politics," editorial, *News & Observer*, September 16, 2011.

86 Tom Oxholm, "A Superior Plan for the Good of All," *News & Observer,* March 10, 2009. Oxholm served on the Wake County Board of Education from 1999 to 2003.

87 Oxholm, "A Superior Plan."

88 Collins, quoting Colethia Evans, in "Black Voices Quiet."

89 Allison Backhouse, letter to the editor, "Education First," *News & Observer*, May 24, 2009.

90 Allison Backhouse, letter to the editor, "The Changes Wake Schools Need," *News & Observer*, August 25, 2009.

91 Amelia Lumpkin, letter to the editor, "Failure Formula," *News & Observer*, April 10, 2011.

92 Anderson, "What is the point of equality?," 313.

93 Steve Ford, "Fighting the School Poverty Factor," *News & Observer*, June 27, 2010.

94 Michelle Burris and Stefan Lallinger, "Leaving Nice White Parents Behind in 2020: New Hopes for School Integration," Century Foundation, January 15, 2021, https://tcf.org/content/commentary/leaving-nice-white-parents-behind-2020 -new-hopes-school-integration/.

95 John Dewey, "Chapter 1: The School and Social Progress," in *The School and Society* (Chicago: University of Chicago Press, 1915), 19–20.

Chapter 3   Defenders of the Faith

1 "A Short History of Pullen," adapted from Roger H. Crook, *Our Heritage and Our Hope* and *An Inclusive Church in a Time of Conflict*, accessed April 16, 2021, https://pullen.org/history/.

2 Gerald Grant retells this story in *Hope and Despair in the American City: Why There Are No Bad Schools in Raleigh* (Cambridge, MA: Harvard University Press, 2009),82–83. A white University of North Carolina professor had joined some Black individuals for dinner after an event with James W. Ford, the Black

Communist Party candidate for U.S. vice president in 1936. Believing this private meal warranted his commentary, the *N&O* editorial writer called the professor's decision to socialize with Blacks as equals a "gratuitous gesture of defiance." Grant was drawing on the research of J. Michael McElreath, "The Cost of Opportunity: School Desegregation and Changing Racial Relations in the Triangle since WWII" (PhD diss., University of Pennsylvania, 2002). Original source: Raleigh *News & Observer*, November 1–2, 1936.

3 Memory F. Mitchell, "Edwin McNeill Poteat, Jr.," *Dictionary of North Carolina Biography*, ed. William S. Powell (Chapel Hill: University of North Carolina Press, 1994), https://www.ncpedia.org/biography/poteat-edwin-mcneill-jr.

4 G. McLeod Bryan, *Dissenter in the Baptist Southland: Fifty Years in the Career of William Wallace Finlator* (Macon, GA: Mercer University Press, 1985), 99.

5 The dissenting Baptist tradition speaks to the radical heritage of the dissenting Baptists of the English reformation of the seventeenth century. Notably, the Baptist tradition "honored radical dissent, independence of mind, and the private conscience," with the Bible as the sole rule of faith. John Bunyan's *Pilgrim's Progress* is the relevant touchstone. Bryan, *Dissenter*, 2–5.

6 "A Short History of Pullen."

7 "The Community of the Cross of Nails," Coventry Cathedral, accessed April 16, 2021, http://www.coventrycathedral.org.uk/ccn/about-us-2/.

8 Robert P. Jones has written about the decline of mainline Christianity as both a demographic group and a cultural force in the United States. He also writes about connections between evangelical Christianity and white supremacy, or Christian nationalism. See *The End of White Christian America* (New York: Simon & Schuster, 2016) and *White Too Long: The Legacy of White Supremacy in American Christianity* (New York: Simon & Schuster, 2020). See also Michael O. Emerson and Christian Smith, *Divided by Faith: Evangelical Religion and the Problem of Race in America* (New York: Oxford University Press, 2000).

9 Nancy Petty, interview with the author, February 25, 2019.

10 Rev. Dr. William J. Barber II, president, North Carolina NAACP, National Board NAACP, and pastor, Greenleaf Christian Church and Rev. Nancy E. Petty, pastor, Pullen Memorial Baptist Church, "An Open Letter to the Community, Clergy, and Civil Rights Leaders: Thoughts While We Were Being Handcuffed and Processed at the Wake County Jail on June 15 after Engaging in an Act of Nonviolent Civil Disobedience," 2010. Excerpt from letter:

Our actions are a call to the community. There is a tragedy unfolding in Wake County, but it is not confined to Wake County. What is happening in Wake County is a national issue. The shadow of re-segregation is falling across the state of North Carolina and the nation. And it represents a clear call to our community—Black, White, Latino, Asian—to employ all the moral, political, and legal means at our disposal to stop it before it's too late. Now is the time for us to stand together. Public education is for the people—all the people. This right established in our North Carolina Constitution in 1868 was created by an extraordinary coalition of whites and blacks—of lawyers and farmers—of those adept at politics and those who had only recently experienced freedom. This right—still a part of our constitution—ensures that every child in Wake County Schools will have an equal opportunity to a sound, basic education.

11 Rev. Dr. Barber describes the origins of the Moral Monday movement, including the first HKoJ (Historic Thousands on Jones Street) teach-in and march that took

place in February 2007, in *The Third Reconstruction: How a Moral Movement Is Overcoming the Politics of Division and Fear* (Boston, MA: Beacon Press, 2016) 50–53.

12 Nancy Petty, interview.

13 Email shared by Nancy Petty, February 25, 2019.

14 Nancy Petty, interview.

15 Some have argued that the United States offers a system of "apartheid education." See Jonathan Kozol, *Savage Inequalities: Children in America's Schools* (New York: Crown, 1991).

16 In response to litigation that has been ongoing since 1994 (the *Leandro* case), the WestEd Report makes specific recommendations to help North Carolina meet its constitutional duty. WestEd, *Sound Basic Education for All: An Action Plan for North Carolina*, 2019, https://www.wested.org/resources/leandro-north-carolina/.

17 Yevonne Brannon, interview with the author, January 11, 2019.

18 Interview, March 15, 2019.

19 Jamie Robert Vollmer, "The Blueberry Story," *Education Week*, March 6, 2002, https://www.edweek.org/education/opinion-the-blueberry-story/2002/03.

20 Interview, April 10, 2019.

21 Interview, March 27, 2019.

22 Interview, March 27, 2019.

23 Interview, December 18, 2018.

24 Interview, April 10, 2019.

25 Interview, March 15, 2019.

26 Nancy Petty, interview.

27 Christine Kushner, interview with the author, September 11, 2018; Interview, December 18, 2018.

28 Interview, April 10, 2019.

29 Interview, May 3, 2019.

30 Interview, May 10, 2019.

31 Rob Schofield, interview with the author, April 12, 2019.

32 Terry Stoops, interview with the author, May 14, 2019.

33 Interview, March 27, 2019.

34 Rob Schofield, interview.

35 Interview, March 13, 2019.

36 Interview, March 27, 2019.

37 In 2021, two years after my interview with Bill McNeal, Wake County dropped the name "Cameron" from the name of the library. The Cameron family were wealthy slaveholders in antebellum North Carolina. In 2022, the Wake County Board of Commissioners voted to change the library's name to the Oberlin Regional Library, in honor of Oberlin Village, the largest Reconstruction-era settlement of freed slaves in Wake County. See Cory Dinkel, "Wake County to Rename Library in Honor of Historic Black Community," *WRAL News*, April 4, 2022, https://www.wral.com/story/wake-county-to-rename-library-in-honor-of -historic-black-community/20220214/.

38 See Nikole Hannah-Jones, "Segregation Now," *The Atlantic*, May 2014. Segregated schools in the era before *Brown* tended to be socioeconomically mixed. By comparison, racially homogeneous schools in the twenty-first century are more likely to be high-poverty schools if they are populated by students of color. Successful schools need strong teachers and involved parents to hold schools' feet to the fire, according to McNeal.

39 Bill McNeal, interview with the author, March 29, 2019.

40 Bill McNeal and Tom Oxholm, *A School District's Journey to Excellence: Lessons from Business and Education* (Thousand Oaks, CA: Corwin Press, 2009), 2.

41 McNeal, interview.

42 McNeal and Oxholm, *A School District's Journey*, 11.

43 See Diane Ravitch, *The Death and Life of the Great American School System: How Testing and Choice Are Undermining Education* (New York: Basic Books, 2010).

44 McNeal, interview.

45 Incidentally, Nikole Hannah-Jones told a similar story in her Color of Education speech at Duke University about parents in New York City who without hesitation put their children on hour-long train rides to get to excellent schools. Referencing a saying from the 1970s, she quipped, "It's not the bus, it's us." Keynote address, October 2, 2018, Public School Forum of North Carolina, Color of Education 2018, https://colorofeducation.org/events/color-of-education-an-evening-with-nikole-hannah-jones/.

46 McNeal, interview.

47 McNeal, interview.

48 "Why can't we have nice things?" asks Heather McGhee in the opening of her book, *The Sum of Us: What Racism Costs Everyone and How We Can Prosper Together* (New York: One World, 2021). McGhee explores the American tendency to denigrate or eliminate public spaces and public institutions that must be shared, specifically with Black people.

49 McNeal, interview. All quotes in the remainder of this section are from this interview.

50 For background: Tony Tata was later nominated by then President Trump to be under secretary of defense for policy during a time when the White House was seeking "to install loyalists to key positions throughout the administration." Em Steck, et al., "Top Pentagon Nominee Pushed Conspiracy Theories That Former CIA Director Tried to Overthrow Trump and Even Have Him Assassinated," *CNN*, June 23, 2020, https://www.cnn.com/2020/06/23/politics/kfile-tata-conspiracy-theory/index.html. Tata's role is also discussed here: Susan B. Glasser and Peter Baker, "Inside the War Between Trump and His Generals," *New Yorker*, August 8, 2022, https://www.newyorker.com/magazine/2022/08/15/inside-the-war-between-trump-and-his-generals.

51 Amanda Lewis and John Diamond, *Despite the Best Intentions: How Racial Inequality Thrives in Good Schools* (New York: Oxford University Press, 2015). "Disciplinary routines communicate key messages to students about who is and is not a full citizen within the school context. They also have consequences for how students feel about school—do they feel valued, respected, and cared for?" (48)

52 Interview, May 10, 2019.

53 Interview, May 10, 2019.

54 Interview, April 10, 2019; Interview, December 18, 2018.

55 Interview, February 15, 2019.

56 Interview, February 15, 2019.

57 Interview, February 15, 2019.

58 Interview, February 10, 2019.

59 Interview, February 10, 2019.

60 Interview, February 15, 2019.

61 Interview, February 15, 2019.

62 Interview, December 18, 2018.

63 Interview, December 18, 2018.

64 Interview, April 10, 2019.

65 "About Us: History," The Youth Organizing Institute, accessed May 6, 2021, https://empoweryouthnc.org/about-youth-organizing-institute/history/. "The Youth Organizing Institute (YOI) formed in March 2010 to increase the representation of the voices of youth in the debate to dismantle the Wake County school system's diversity policy and its impact on the future of public schools. What became apparent was the absence of the voices of the low-wealth students and parents of color in the debate, those most affected by the achievement gap and by the school to prison pipeline."

66 National Association for the Advancement of Colored People, et al. v. Wake County Board of Education and the Wake County Public School System, Complaint Under Title VI of the Civil Rights Act of 1964, Submitted September 24, 2010, https://pulse.ncpolicywatch.org/wp-content/uploads/2010/09/Title-VI-Complaint-WCSB-9-24-2010-FINAL.pdf.

67 "OCR Resolution Agreement Summary," Communications Department, Wake County Public School System, undated, accessed November 4, 2023, https://www.wcpss.net/cms/lib/NC01911451/Centricity/Domain/4/wcpss-letterhead-OCR%20Resolution%20Agreement%20Summary%20.pdf.

68 Interview, February 15, 2019.

69 Interview, February 15, 2019.

70 Interview, February 15, 2021.

71 Interview, February 15, 2019.

72 Board members Margiotta, Tedesco, Goldman, and Malone were at the time relatively recent transplants to Wake County from the Northeast.

73 Interview, April 10, 2019.

74 "Student Experience in AP, IB, and Honors Courses," Enloe High School, February 19, 2021, YouTube video, https://www.youtube.com/watch?v=vdju-rho1TU.

75 Rob Schofield, interview.

76 Yevonne Brannon, interview with the author, January 11, 2019.

77 Interview, March 12, 2019.

78 Nancy Petty, interview.

79 Christine Kushner, interview.

80 Interview, February 6, 2019.

81 Christine Kushner, interview.

82 Interview, December 18, 2018.

Chapter 4 Arguing from the Past, Fighting for the Future

1 A video recording of the event supplemented my own recollection. Wake County Board of Education Meeting, March 23, 2010, WRAL News, accessed May 12, 2021, https://www.wral.com/news/education/asset_gallery/7282818/.

2 Wake County Board of Education Meeting, Part 6, March 23, 2010, WRAL News, minute mark 6:33–8:34 and 18:43–20:45, https://www.wral.com/news/education/video/7290295/.

3 Transcribed by the author. Wake County Board of Education Meeting, Part 6, 22:43–24:45.

4 Interview, March 15, 2019.

5 Wake County Board of Education Meeting, Part 6, 25–27.

6 Wake County Board of Education Meeting, Part 7, March 23, 2010, *WRAL News*, minute mark 3:41–5:31, https://www.wral.com/video/news/education/video /7290732/.

7 Wake County Board of Education Meeting, Part 6, 52:54–54:53.

8 Wake County Board of Education Meeting, Part 11, March 23, 2010, *WRAL News*, minute mark 34:20–36:05, https://www.wral.com/video/news/education /video/7291597/.

9 Wake County Board of Education Meeting, Part 7, 1:08–3:08.

10 Wake County Board of Education Meeting, Part 6, 37:08–39:07.

11 Wake County Board of Education Meeting, Part 6, 34:50–36:58.

12 Wake County Board of Education Meeting, Part 6, 16:43–18:34.

13 Transcript of George W. Bush's speech to NAACP, *Washington Post*, July 10, 2000, https://www.washingtonpost.com/wp-srv/onpolitics/elections /bushtext071000.htm.

14 Wake County Board of Education Meeting, Part 9, March 23, 2010, *WRAL News*, minute mark 58:00–1:10:25, https://www.wral.com/video/news/education/video /7291596/.

15 The quote is from *Parents Involved in Community Schools v. Seattle School District No. 1*, 551 U.S. 701 (2007), https://supreme.justia.com/cases/federal/us/551/701/.

16 Elizabeth Anderson, *The Imperative of Integration* (Princeton, NJ: Princeton University Press, 2010), 155.

17 See, for example, Rachel Reed, "*Plessy v. Ferguson* at 125," an interview with Lawrence D. Biele, Professor of Law at Harvard Law School, *Harvard Law Today*, May 19, 2021, https://today.law.harvard.edu/plessy-v-ferguson-at-125/.

18 Perhaps the most thorough argument for race-conscious repairs came from Justice Stephen Breyer in his lengthy dissent in the *Parents Involved* case. A short excerpt: Unless we believe that the Constitution enforces one legal standard for the South and another for the North, this Court should grant Seattle the permission it granted Clarke County, Georgia. See McDaniel, 402 U. S., at 41 ("[S]teps will almost invariably require that students be assigned 'differently because of their race.' . . . Any other approach would freeze the status quo that is the very target of all desegregation processes."). Courts are not alone in accepting as constitutionally valid the legal principle that Swann enunciated—-i.e., that the government may voluntarily adopt race-conscious measures to improve conditions of race even when it is not under a constitutional obligation to do so. That principle has been accepted by every branch of government and is rooted in the history of the Equal Protection Clause itself. Thus, Congress has enacted numerous race-conscious statutes that illustrate that principle or rely upon its validity. There is reason to believe that those who drafted an Amendment with this basic purpose in mind would have understood the legal and practical difference between the use of race-conscious criteria in defiance of that purpose, namely to keep the races apart, and the use of race-conscious criteria to further that purpose, namely to bring the races together. But I can find no case in which this Court has followed Justice Thomas' "colorblind" approach. And I have found no case that otherwise repudiated this constitutional asymmetry between that which seeks to exclude and that which seeks to include members of minority races.

Parents Involved in Community Schools v. Seattle School Dist. No. 1, 551 U.S. 701 (2007), https://supreme.justia.com/cases/federal/us/551/701/.

19 Anderson, *Imperative*, 166–167.

20 Wake County Board of Education Meeting, Part 9, 1:10:25.

21 Wake County Board of Education Meeting, Part 11, March 23, 2010, *WRAL News*, minute mark 26:36–28:46, https://www.wral.com/video/news/education /video/7291597/.

22 Interview, September 11, 2018.

23 Steve Ford, "Culture Clash Over Wake Schools," *News & Observer*, July 11, 2010. Charles Meeker, mayor of Raleigh for the last decade and a 35-year resident of the city, was merely stating the obvious. Several members of the Wake County school board's controlling bloc—four among the five members who want to remake the school system in the fond image of how they do things up North— are in fact, as Meeker observed, not from this area. Not originally, in any case. . . . Don't look for Charles Meeker to call anybody a carpetbagger. But there's no reason for him to back away from his premise that the school board's new direction is being set by folks whose values are out of kilter with those shared by a great many residents who have been around here long enough to understand why the Wake schools have been operated the way they have. Good Southerners understand that diversity is an important means to worthy ends.

24 This story is recounted in several sources, including James Ryan, *Five Miles Away, a World Apart: One City, Two Schools, and the Story of Educational Opportunity in Modern America* (New York: Oxford University Press, 2010), 113; Roslyn Arlin Mickelson, Stephen Samuel Smith, and Amy Hawn Nelson, eds., *Yesterday, Today and Tomorrow: School Desegregation and Resegregation in Charlotte* (Cambridge, MA: Harvard Education Press, 2015), 1–2; and Pamela Grundy, *Color and Character: West Charlotte High and the Struggle Over Educational Equality* (Chapel Hill: University of North Carolina Press, 2017), 112–114.

25 Celia Powell Liebl, letter to the editor, "Schools' Big Picture," *News & Observer*, July 4, 2010.

26 Jason Morgan Ward, letter to the editor, "Is This Where Wake Schools Are Headed?," *News & Observer*, July 4, 2010. Ward was a 1997 graduate of South Granville High School.

27 Ward, "Is This Where."

28 Jim Jenkins, "Anniversary for the 'First'," *News & Observer*, September 9, 2010. Jenkins retired from the *N&O* in 2018 after a 31-year career. He was the son of Jay Jenkins, who wrote and edited at the *N&O* before working for UNC President Bill Friday. See Ned Barnett, "You'll Be Missed, Jenkins," *News & Observer*, January 27, 2018, https://www.newsobserver.com/opinion/opn-columns-blogs /ned-barnett/article196890959.html#storylink=cpy.

29 From panel discussion featuring Joe Holt Jr., "Integrating Triangle Schools" (hosted by the Cameron Village Regional Library, February 1, 2020). Also, undated photocopied document compiled by Joe Holt Jr., "Local School Integration Sequence of Key Events," disseminated at the library event.

30 Jenkins, "Anniversary."

31 Ethan Roy and James Ford, "Deep Rooted: A Brief History of Race and Education in North Carolina," *EdNC*, August 11, 2019, https://www.ednc.org /deep-rooted-a-brief-history-of-race-and-education-in-north-carolina/. The authors are drawing on Thomas W. Hanchett, "The Rosenwald Schools and

Black Education in North Carolina," *North Carolina Historical Review* 65, no. 4 (1988): 387, 395. See also "Rosenwald Schools in North Carolina," NC Museum of History, https://www.ncmuseumofhistory.org/rosenwald-schools-north -carolina.

32 Margaret J. Newbold, op-ed, "We Can't Let Integration Slide," *News & Observer*, April 30, 2010. See also Nathan Carter Newbold family papers, 1848–1952 and undated, Duke University archives and manuscripts, https://archives.lib.duke.edu /catalog/newboldnc.

33 Newbold, "Integration." See also Ligon Magnet Middle School website, "About Our School: History of Ligon," accessed October 28, 2023, https://www.wcpss.net /Page/45919. John W. Ligon High School was desegregated and converted into a junior high in 1971.

34 Newbold, "Integration."

35 Sarah Caroline Thuesen, *Greater Than Equal: African American Struggles for Schools and Citizenship in North Carolina, 1919–1965* (Chapel Hill: University of North Carolina Press, 2013).

36 Kenneth Mack and Meira Levinson, "*Brown v. Board of Education* Explained," *Harvard Gazette*, video produced by Kai-Jae Wang, May 17, 2021, YouTube video, https://youtu.be/FwxprgouAYU. See also Annette Gordon-Reed, "*On Juneteenth* Historian Examines the Hope and Hostility Toward Emancipation," interview by Terry Gross, *Fresh Air*, NPR, May 25, 2021, https://www.npr.org/2021/05/25 /1000131568/on-juneteenth-historian-examines-the-hope-and-hostility-toward -emancipation.

37 See, for example, Tim Tyson, "Resegregation Is No Answer for Our Schools," *News & Observer*, January 19, 2010. Tyson warned against nostalgia for segregation, while also acknowledging the losses for Black communities when schools integrated. At the time of publication, Timothy B. Tyson was senior research scholar at the Center for Documentary Studies at Duke University, visiting professor of American Christianity and Southern Culture at Duke Divinity School, and adjunct professor of American Studies at UNC-Chapel Hill.

38 Nancy Petty, interview with the author, February 25, 2019.

39 William Barber describes various fusion coalitions throughout North Carolina history in *The Third Reconstruction: How a Moral Movement Is Overcoming the Politics of Division and Fear* (Boston, MA: Beacon Press, 2016). Others have referred to this same coalition of people as a "carpetbagger government." See William W. Peek, "The History of Education in North Carolina," Department of Public Instruction, 1993. "The new State Constitution, adopted in 1868, contained a relatively strong article on public education. Generally unpopular at the time because it was viewed as the product of a 'carpetbag government,' it was, nevertheless, a rather progressive document for that period and later came to be recognized as such" (10); WestEd, Learning Policy Institute, and Friday Institute for Educational Innovation at NC State University, *Sound Basic Education for All: An Action Plan for North Carolina*, WestEd, 2019; David Sciarra, "No More Excuses for Lawmakers When it Comes to Public Schools," *NC Policy Watch*, July 1, 2021, http://www.ncpolicywatch.com/2021/07/01/no-more-excuses-for-lawmakers -when-it-comes-to-public-schools/.

40 J. Morgan Kousser, "Progressivism—For Middle-Class Whites Only: North Carolina Education, 1880–1910," *Journal of Southern History* 46, no. 2 (May 1980): 173.

41 Kousser, "Progressivism," 177; Also from Kousser: "During the period of fusion rule (1896–1900), the proportion of funds going to Blacks increased by 6 percent, but after the restriction of suffrage, the ratio of Black to white expenditures per school-age child dropped 53 percent in ten years." (179)

42 David Zucchino, *Wilmington's Lie: The Murderous Coup of 1898 and the Rise of White Supremacy* (New York: Atlantic Monthly Press, 2020).

43 Ann McColl, "Moving past intentional inequities in education," *EdNC*, October 29, 2015, https://www.ednc.org/moving-past-intentional-inequities-in-education/. See, for example, this letter from James Joyner, superintendent of Public Instruction 1902–1919, to local NC superintendents: "The negro schools can be run for much less expense and should be. In most places it does not take more than one fourth as much to run the negro schools as it does to run the white schools for about the same number of children. The salaries paid teachers are very properly much smaller, the houses are cheaper, the number of teachers smaller . . . if quietly managed, the negroes will give no trouble about it." (Quoted in Kousser, "Progressivism," 186)

44 Although perhaps not the most egregious example of southern resistance to desegregation, North Carolina still resisted. Elizabeth Gillespie McRae writes specifically about the women who were segregation's "constant gardeners" in *Mothers of Massive Resistance: White Women and the Politics of White Supremacy* (New York: Oxford University Press, 2018).

45 Thomas J. Pearsall, Chairman, *Report of the North Carolina Advisory Committee on Education*, Raleigh, NC, April 5, 1956, 7–8.

46 Pearsall, *Report*, 10.

47 Pearsall, *Report*, 9. "We are proposing the building of a new school system on a new foundation—a foundation of no racial segregation by law, but assignment according to natural racial preference and the administrative determination of what is best for the child."

48 Pearsall, *Report*, 7.

49 John Drescher, "How a Courageous Southern Governor Broke Ranks with Segregationists in 1961," *Washington Post*, January 1, 2021, https://www.washingtonpost.com/history/2021/01/01/terry-sanford-north-carolina-race-segregation/.

50 Trip Stallings, "Jim Hunt: The Rise of an Education Governor," *EdNC*, June 8, 2015, https://www.ednc.org/jim-hunt-the-rise-of-an-education-governor/ Among many other accomplishments, Smart Start and the North Carolina School of Science and Math (NCSSM) began under his leadership.

51 Opinion of the Court in No. 16-1468(L), *N.C. State Conference of the NAACP v. Patrick McCrory*, United States Court of Appeals for the Fourth Circuit, July 29, 2016, http://www.ca4.uscourts.gov/Opinions/Published/161468.P.pdf.

52 J.B. Buxton, "The Two Heroes of NC School Integration," *News & Observer*, November 22, 2014. "A typical example of what they faced was in Hyde County. Large numbers of white and Black parents had boycotted the schools for nearly a year. Causby and Flood were sent in to get children back to school. They arrived in Hyde to facilitate a meeting that included representatives from the local school board and county commissioners, the Black Panthers, Ku Klux Klan and local teachers and parents. The result: a joint resolution to reopen the schools—as integrated schools."

53 "Two into One—John Murphy Somehow Kept Tumult to a Minimum after the Merger of Raleigh and Wake County Schools," editorial, *News & Observer*,

August 12, 2011. "The tenure of John Murphy, and of his successors, is a testament to the wisdom of merger and its results. It worked. . . . Current school board members would do well to study Murphy's tenure, and the history he had to confront. There are good lessons there."

54 "A Community United," hosted by Debra Morgan, WRAL, 2006, accessed October 28, 2023, https://www.youtube.com/watch?v=cupH9MbyXW4.

55 This quote is from Walt Sherlin, a teacher at Ligon Junior High at the time of the merger. The 1975 Wake County Legislative Delegation included Al Adams, Ruth Cook, Bill Creech, Bob Farmer, Joe Johnson, and Wade Smith. The "Solid Six," as they called themselves, prepared and submitted the bill calling for merger of the former Raleigh City and Wake County school systems. Remarkably, no legislator who had supported the merger was defeated in the next election (according to those interviewed in the video).

56 Interview, October 2, 2018.

57 Interview, October 2, 2018.

58 Interview, September 20, 2018.

59 Interview, February 15, 2019.

60 McNeal specifically cited parents' discontent with students who were being bused to the suburbs from Raleigh: "I remember being invited to Garner once upon a time to come to the city council meeting, or town council meeting. And under the guise of something else to explain something, and what it really was an ambush from the town council to tell me about those children you're bringing. So, no, we had our moments." Bill McNeal, interview with the author, March 29, 2019.

61 McNeal, Interview.

62 Interview, May 3, 2019.

63 Interview, February 10, 2019.

64 The Pearsall committee, unable and unwilling to digest the full import of *Brown* (1954), clung to the separate but equal logic of *Plessy v. Ferguson* (1896).

65 Judy Swain Keener, letter to the editor, "Support Unreported," *News & Observer*, July 28, 2010.

66 Arlaine Niclas, letter to the editor, "Segregated Already," *News & Observer*, April 30, 2010.

67 Lisa Chappell, letter to the editor, "Timely Changes," *News & Observer*, January 16, 2010.

68 Interview, March 12, 2019.

69 James Ryan, *Five Miles Away*, 59. According to Ryan, all three branches of the federal government were committed to enforcing the legal requirements of *Brown* for a mere seven months, between the time of the U.S. Supreme Court's decision in *Green v. New Kent County* in May of 1968 and President Nixon's inauguration in January of 1969. "At every other point, from the time of *Brown* until today, at least one branch of the federal government either acted to limit the reach of *Brown* or did next to nothing to enhance the likelihood that black and white students would actually attend school together." (60)

70 Erika Wilson, "The New White Flight," *Duke Journal of Constitutional Law & Public Policy* 14, no. 1 (2019): 237, 244. The U.S. Supreme Court's decision in *Parents Involved* suggested alternatives to race-based assignments: "School boards may pursue the goal of bringing together students of diverse backgrounds and races through other means, including strategic site selection of new schools; drawing attendance zones with general recognition of the demographics of

neighborhoods; allocating resources for special programs; recruiting students and faculty in a targeted fashion; and tracking enrollments, performance, and other statistics by race."

71 Sarah Garland, *Divided We Fail: The Story of an African American Community That Ended the Era of School Desegregation* (Boston, MA: Beacon Press, 2013), x.

72 Garland, *Divided We Fail*, xi–xii.

73 Garland, *Divided We Fail*, xi–xii.

74 Roslyn Arlin Mickelson, Stephen Samuel Smith, and Amy Hawn Nelson, eds., *Yesterday, Today and Tomorrow: School Desegregation and Resegregation in Charlotte* (Cambridge, MA: Harvard Education Press, 2015), 24–25. Charlotte schools were largely integrated during the 1970s and 1980s. As in Wake, it was the result of hard work as well as mixed motives. One of the biggest motivations was economic development, but that takes nothing away from the significance of the accomplishment: Charlotte had integrated schools for a period of time and the community supported them.

75 Mickelson et al., *Yesterday*, 25.

76 The frenzied competition to get into coveted public high schools in New York City is a case in point: "A child's admission to a sought-after high school is rarely her success alone but one she shares with a driven mother or father, who has most likely put other obligations aside to do research, tour schools and strategize around the best chances for attaining the perfect fit. Texting with a friend earlier this week, I congratulated him on his son's acceptance to two top schools; he wrote back that the work had taken him the better part of the year." Ginia Bellafante, "N.Y.C. Tried to Fix High School Admissions, Some Parents Are Furious," *New York Times*, June 17, 2022, https://www.nytimes.com/2022/06/17/nyregion/high-school-admissions-nyc.html?smid=url-share.

77 Mary Patillo, "Everyday Politics of School Choice in the Black Community," *Du Bois Review* 12, no. 1 (2015): 41–71. "Concepts that have disappeared from and are even perhaps taboo in school reform debates. Words like provision, state responsibility, and entitlement all require the state to meet people where they are as opposed to requiring citizens to seek out, navigate, and work for public benefits." (63)

78 This is the author's application of Sharon Hays's concept of intensive mothering, as described in *The Cultural Contradictions of Motherhood* (New Haven, CT: Yale University Press, 1996).

79 Interview, March 13, 2019.

80 Wilson, *White Flight*, 239.

81 Wilson, *White Flight*, 263.

82 Themes related to school choice included "charters," "vouchers," "magnet schools," "choice as a benefit," "parents as consumers," and "privatization." Taken together, these themes represented nearly a fifth of all coded references.

83 Wake County reflects national disagreements. A recent PDK national poll shows disagreements over school funding and privatization measures falling along partisan lines, e.g., "About 5 in 10 Republicans and conservatives want a greater focus on the expansion of these [charter] schools, compared with 29% of Democrats and 26% of liberals." PDK Poll of the Public's Attitudes toward the Public Schools, "Public Schools Priorities in a Political Year," September 2020, accessed June 14, 2021, https://pdkpoll.org/wp-content/uploads/2020/08/Poll52-2020_PollSupplement.pdf.

84 Milton Friedman, "Public Schools: Make Them Private," *Education Economics* 5, no. 3, (1997): 341–344.

85 "Decline of post-secondary desegregation due to conservative backlash." Excerpt from Oral History Interview with Julius L. Chambers, June 18, 1990. Interview L-0127. Southern Oral History Program Collection (#4007). Documenting the American South. Chambers argued that "Reagan's administration, in particular, represented a sharp retreat from higher education desegregation."

86 Keeanga-Yamahtta Taylor, "What's at Stake in the Fight over Reopening Schools," *New Yorker*, February 9, 2021, https://www.newyorker.com/news/our-columnists /whats-at-stake-in-the-fight-over-reopening-schools.

87 "K-12 Education: School Districts Frequently Identified Multiple Building Systems Needing Updates or Replacement," U.S. Government Accountability Office, GAO-20-494, June 4, 2020. https://www.gao.gov/products/gao-20-494.

88 Kris Nordstrom, "Vetoed Budget Would Have Done Nothing for Education," *NC Policy Watch*, July 1, 2019, http://pulse.ncpolicywatch.org/2019/07/01/vetoed -education-budget-would-have-done-nothing-for-education/#sthash.vBfaldYY .dpbs.

89 "Making the Grade 2020: How Fair Is School Funding in Your State?," Education Law Center, https://edlawcenter.org/research/making-the-grade-2020.html.

90 The state budget signed into law in 2022 approved more money for vouchers.

91 T. Keung Hui, "NC House Backs Expanding School Vouchers. Attack on Public Schools or More Choice?," *News & Observer*, April 13, 2021, https://www .newsobserver.com/news/politics-government/article250629959.html.

92 "NC School Vouchers Fact Sheet," Public Schools First NC, September 2022, https://www.publicschoolsfirstnc.org/resources/fact-sheets/the-facts-about-school -vouchers/.

93 "The Facts on Charter Schools," Public Schools First NC, December 2021, https://www.publicschoolsfirstnc.org/resources/fact-sheets/quick-facts-on-charter -schools/.

94 Interview, March 15, 2019.

95 Other strategies of privatization include things like using A–F school grading, which tends to stigmatize low-performing or low-income public schools; the state legislature's decision to keep public school teacher pay well below the national average, etc.

96 Wilson, *White Flight*, 271–272.

97 Interview, March 13, 2019.

98 Interview, September 11, 2018.

99 Helen F. Ladd and Mavzuna Turaeva, "Parental Preferences for Charter Schools in North Carolina: Implications for Racial Segregation and Isolation," (Working Paper 243, National Center for the Study of Privatization in Education, Teachers College, Columbia University, New York, September 29, 2020).

100 Wilson, *White Flight*, 257.

101 Patillo, "Everyday Politics," 41.

102 Terry Stoops, "Busing Isn't the Answer, Choice Is," *New York Times*, May 21, 2012.

103 Terry Stoops, interview with the author, May 14, 2019.

104 Stoops, interview.

105 As we saw in chapter 2, letters and op-eds from parents of color emphasized the importance of obtaining a good education, regardless of the demographics of a school. From Gerald Grant: "Black parents who participated in the Boston busing

experiment (METCO) in the 1960s and 70s, though they valued diversity, overwhelmingly ranked the suburban schools' academic excellence as the most important reason for participating." *Hope and Despair in the American City: Why There Are No Bad Schools in Raleigh* (Cambridge, MA: Harvard University Press, 2009), 21.

106 Quoted in Ryan, *Five Miles Away*, 29. Original source: W.E.B. Du Bois, "The Courts and the Negro Separate School," *Journal of Negro Education* 4, no. 3 (July 1935): 335.

107 Stoops, interview.

108 Stoops, interview.

109 Rob Schofield, interview with the author, April 12, 2019.

110 Martha Minow, "Confronting the Seduction of Choice: Law, Education, and American Pluralism," *Yale Law Journal* 120, no. 4 (January 2011): 814–848.

111 Steve Suitts, "Segregationists, Libertarians, and the Modern 'School Choice' Movement," *Southern Spaces*, June 4, 2019, 33, https://southernspaces.org/2019/segregationists-libertarians-and-modern-school-choice-movement/.

112 Yvonne Brannon, interview with the author, January 11, 2019.

113 Brannon, interview.

114 Brannon, interview.

115 Barber, *The Third Reconstruction*, 124.

Chapter 5   Moral Logics and the Case for True Integration

1 Chana Joffe-Walt, "Episode One: The Book of Statuses," July 30, 2020, in *Nice White Parents*, produced by Julie Snyder, podcast from *Serial* and the *New York Times*, https://www.nytimes.com/2020/07/30/podcasts/nice-white-parents-serial.html. Full quote: "Horace Mann believed public schools would make us equal, but it doesn't work. I'm not sure how to fix that, but I want to lay out the story, the whole story of this one American public school, because what I am sure of is that in order to address inequality in our public schools, we are going to need a shared sense of reality. At the very least, it's a place to start."

2 Nikole Hannah-Jones, keynote address, October 2, 2018, Public School Forum of North Carolina, Color of Education 2018, https://colorofeducation.org/events/color-of-education-an-evening-with-nikole-hannah-jones/. See also Nikole Hannah-Jones and Jonathan Kozol, "Confronting the Truth about Inequalities in America's Schools," April 21, 2021, Vernon L. Pack Distinguished Lecture Series at Otterbein University, webinar discussion, https://digitalcommons.otterbein.edu/vernonpack/6/.

3 Heather McGhee, *The Sum of Us: What Racism Costs Everyone and How We Can Prosper Together* (New York: One World, 2021).

4 See, for example, Jennifer Berkshire and Jack Schneider, "If You Think Republicans Are Overplaying Schools, You Aren't Paying Attention," *New York Times*, March 21, 2022, https://www.nytimes.com/2022/03/21/opinion/democrats-public-education-culture-wars.html.

5 Ginia Bellafante, "N.Y.C. Tried to Fix High School Admissions. Some Parents Are Furious," *New York Times*, June 17, 2022, https://www.nytimes.com/2022/06/17/nyregion/high-school-admissions-nyc.html.

6 Hannah Natanson, "Parental Say in Schools, Resonant in VA Governor's Race, Bound for GOP National Playbook," *Washington Post*, November 3, 2021,

https://www.washingtonpost.com/local/education/parent-control-schools
-republican-virginia/2021/11/03/313e8a68-3cc3-11ec-a493-51b0252deaoc_story
.html; Lisa Lerer, "The Unlikely Issue Shaping the Virginia Governor's Race:
Schools," *New York Times*, October 12, 2021, https://www.nytimes.com/2021/10
/12/us/politics/virginia-governor-republicans-schools.html.

7 Gene Demby, "Two Justices Debate the Doctrine of Colorblindness," *Code Switch*,
NPR, April 23, 2014, https://www.npr.org/sections/codeswitch/2014/04/23
/306173835/two-justices-debate-the-doctrine-of-colorblindness.

8 Nikole Hannah-Jones, "Choosing a School for My Daughter in a Segregated
City," *New York Times Magazine*, June 9, 2016, https://www.nytimes.com/2016
/06/12/magazine/choosing-a-school-for-my-daughter-in-a-segregated-city.html.

9 Hannah Sampson, "Airlines Have Seen an Unprecedented Rise in Disruptive
Passengers," *Washington Post*, June 11, 2021, https://www.washingtonpost.com
/travel/2021/06/11/flights-mask-incidents-faa-fines/.

10 Geoff Brumfiel, "Vaccine Refusal May Put Herd Immunity at Risk, Researchers
Warn," NPR, April 7, 2021, https://www.npr.org/sections/health-shots/2021/04
/07/984697573/vaccine-refusal-may-put-herd-immunity-at-risk-researchers-warn.

11 Kayla Ruble and Robert Klemko, "The Other Rebellion: Dozens of Michigan
Restaurants Defy State Coronavirus Order," *Washington Post*, January 30, 2021,
https://www.washingtonpost.com/national/michigan-restaurants-covid
-restrictions/2021/01/30/e97b53ba-5b49-11eb-a976-bad6431e03e2_story.html.

12 Theresa Opeka, "Parents Rally to End Mask Mandate in Wake County Schools,"
Carolina Journal, February 16, 2022, https://www.carolinajournal.com/parents
-rally-to-end-mask-mandate-in-wake-county-schools/; Julia Carrie Wong, "Masks
Off: How US School Boards Became 'Perfect Battlegrounds' for Vicious Culture
Wars," *The Guardian*, August 24, 2021, https://www.theguardian.com/us-news
/2021/aug/24/mask-mandates-covid-school-boards; Deepa Shivaram, "The Topic
of Masks in Schools Is Polarizing Some Parents to the Point of Violence," NPR,
August 20, 2021, https://www.npr.org/sections/back-to-school-live-updates/2021
/08/20/1028841279/mask-mandates-school-protests-teachers.

13 In 2022, the United States Supreme Court handed down remarkable decisions
pertaining to individual freedom, expanding gun rights while restricting access to
abortion. The *NYSRPA v. Bruen* decision overturned a New York state gun safety
law. The *Dobbs v. Jackson Women's Health Organization* decision took away the
constitutionally protected right to abortion that women have enjoyed for nearly
fifty years.

14 Interview, May 10, 2019.

15 Steve Suitts, "Segregationists, Libertarians, and the Modern 'School Choice'
Movement," *Southern Spaces*, June 4, 2019, 32, https://southernspaces.org/2019
/segregationists-libertarians-and-modern-school-choice-movement/.

16 Interview, March 13, 2019.

17 For a discussion of the different intellectual foundations underlying different
approaches to school choice, see Virginia Riel, Roslyn Arlin Mickelson, and
Stephen Samuel Smith, "Who Favors Magnets and Who Favors Charters? Political
Ideology, Social Purpose Politics, and School Choice in the Upper South,"
American Behavioral Scientist 66, no. 6 (May 2022): 717–743, https://doi-org.prox
.lib.ncsu.edu/10.1177/00027642211033288. Specifically: "The fact that Republicans
and conservatives favor charters, while those who support social purpose politics
favor magnets, is strongly consistent with the different intellectual foundations of

the two school forms: market theory of choice supporting charters and social integration theory of choice supporting magnets." (735)

18 Both Bill McNeal and a prominent Raleigh business leader made the point that competition can be healthy and beneficial.

19 Both Sheneka Williams (2012) and Deven Carlson et al. (2020) make the point that voluntariness is more politically sustainable.

20 Jill Filipovic, "Women Are Having Fewer Babies Because They Have More Choices," *New York Times*, June 27, 2021, https://www.nytimes.com/2021/06/27/opinion/falling-birthrate-women-babies.html.

21 "North Carolina Charter Schools at 25," John Locke Foundation, June 28, 2021, webinar, https://www.johnlocke.org/events/north-carolina-charter-schools-at-25/. Panelists included Terry Stoops, John Locke Foundation; Lindalyn Kakadelis, NC Coalition for Charter Schools; Dave Machado, NC Department of Public Instruction; and Rhonda Dillingham, NC Association for Public Charter Schools.

22 Judith Jarvis Thomson, "A Defense of Abortion," *Philosophy & Public Affairs* 1, no. 1 (Autumn 1971): 47–66. "No one in any country in the world is legally required to do anywhere near as much as this for anyone else." (63)

23 John Dewey, "Chapter 1: The School and Social Progress," in *The School and Society* (Chicago: University of Chicago Press, 1915), 19–20.

24 Rob Schofield, interview with the author, April 12, 2019. Full quote:
    I remember [Raleigh business leader] saying to me one time, something like, "So what we have to do, is we have to convince people they have to take one for the team sometimes." I was like, I guess, I mean that seems a little . . . Maybe we can make it sound a little more, a little grander than that, or a little more positive spirit, but there's something to that, I guess. I mean, that's what I was trying to tell my kids. It's like, you know, it's not just about the short term and what you can get for yourself.

25 See discussion in Chapter 1 of this case study: Jenni Owen and Megan Kauff-mann, "The End of a Diversity Policy? Wake County Public Schools and Student Assignment Case," E-PARCC Collaborative Governance Initiative, PARCC, Syracuse University (2014), https://www.maxwell.syr.edu/research/program-for-the-advancement-research-on-conflict-collaboration/e-parcc/cases-simulations-syllabi/cases/the-end-of-diversity-policy-wake-county-public-schools-and-student-assignment.

26 John Rawls, *Political Liberalism* (New York: Columbia University Press, 1993).

27 John Dewey, "The Ethics of Democracy," in *The Early Works of John Dewey, 1882–1898* (Carbondale: Southern Illinois University Press, 1969), 231–232.

28 Matthew Festenstein, "Dewey's Political Philosophy," in *Stanford Encyclopedia of Philosophy*, accessed July 14, 2022, https://plato.stanford.edu/entries/dewey-political/.

29 Dewey, "The Ethics of Democracy," 231–232.

30 Derrick A. Bell, Jr., "*Brown v. Board of Education* and the Interest-Convergence Dilemma," *Harvard Law Review* 93, no. 3 (January 1980): 518–533. Bell described the principle of interest convergence as follows: "The interest of blacks in achieving racial equality will be accommodated only when it converges with the interests of whites. . . . The fourteenth amendment, standing alone, will not authorize a judicial remedy providing effective racial equality for blacks where the remedy sought threatens the superior social status of middle and upper class whites." (523)

31 Nikole Hannah-Jones and Jonathan Kozol, "Confronting the Truth about Inequalities in America's Schools," April 21, 2021, Vernon L. Pack Distinguished Lecture Series at Otterbein University, webinar discussion, https://digitalcommons.otterbein.edu/vernonpack/6/. Both Hannah-Jones and Kozol felt that white parents are too invested in an unequal system that benefits them and their children to tolerate fundamental change. Hannah-Jones expressed little faith in legislatures or school boards to effect change, as officials will be promptly voted out of office if they disrupt white privilege. It was a stark vision of entrenched white power. Still, she described what needs to change: funding mechanisms (do not fund schools based on local wealth) and municipal boundaries (do not wall off educational opportunities and enable hoarding).

32 W.E. Burghardt Du Bois, "Does the Negro Need Separate Schools?," *Journal of Negro Education* 4, no. 3 (July 1935): 335.

33 Gerald Grant, *Hope and Despair in the American City: Why There Are No Bad Schools in Raleigh* (Cambridge, MA: Harvard University Press, 2009), 21.

34 John Dewey, *The School and Society*, 19–20.

35 Wake County Board of Education Meeting, Part 6, March 23, 2010, *WRAL News*, minute mark 25–27, https://www.wral.com/news/education/video/7290295/.

36 Margaret Newbold, "We Can't Let Integration Slide," *News & Observer*, April 30, 2010.

37 Elizabeth Anderson, *The Imperative of Integration* (Princeton, NJ: Princeton University Press, 2010), 117.

38 Bill McNeal, interview with the author, March 29, 2019.

39 For example, Black and white students attending West Charlotte High School during the 1970s led their school's efforts to make integration work on the ground. See "The Battle for Busing: Retro Report," *New York Times*, September 9, 2013, YouTube video, https://www.youtube.com/watch?v=sld722slarw.

40 See, for example, Nikole Hannah-Jones's description of three generations of one family attending the same high school in Tuscaloosa, AL, in "Segregation Now," *The Atlantic*, May 2014, https://www.theatlantic.com/magazine/archive/2014/05/segregation-now/359813/.

41 Interview, April 10, 2019.

42 Amanda Lewis and John Diamond, *Despite the Best Intentions: How Racial Inequity Thrives in Good Schools* (New York: Oxford University Press, 2015), 163.

43 Lewis and Diamond, *Best Intentions*, 163.

44 Full quote, which comes from an interview: "Mr. Morris . . . commented that trying to do something about the achievement gap 'will be met with opposition' from white parents because 'folks who are benefitting from the gap really don't want the attention to be put on the gap because they want their kid to have the perfect education. These parents start planning and optimizing for kids in second grade, like it's war, preparing for battle." Lewis and Diamond, *Best Intentions*, 135.

45 Elizabeth Anderson, interview by John White, *Journal of Philosophy of Education* 53, no. 1 (2019): 8.

46 Anderson, *The Imperative of Integration*, 191.

47 Anderson, *The Imperative of Integration*, 176.

48 Anderson, *The Imperative of Integration*, 176.

49 Heather McGhee, *The Sum of Us: What Racism Costs Everyone and How We Can Prosper Together* (New York: One World, 2021).

50 Hannah-Jones, "Color of Education."

51 Hannah-Jones, "Choosing a School."

52 Posted June 23, 2022, to the NC Alliance for Equity & School Safety page on Facebook by Lindsay Boole as an "etiquette" question: "Those that purchased those Allem hepa filters for your kids' classrooms, did you ask for them back at the end of the school year so they can age-up with your child(ren)? Debating whether to ask K teacher for the >$600 one that we purchased, or consider it a gift." Many, but not all, of those who commented said she should take the air filter back rather than consider it a gift.

53 Anderson, *The Imperative of Integration*, 190.

54 Deven Carlson et al., "Socioeconomic-Based School Assignment Policy and Racial Segregation Levels: Evidence from the Wake County Public School System," *American Educational Research Journal* 57, no. 1 (February 2020): 261. Full quote with in-text citations:

> This line of work has found desegregation to increase Black educational achievement (Billings, Deming, & Rockoff, 2014; Card & Rothstein, 2007; Mickelson, Bottia, & Lambert, 2013) and attainment (Guryan, 2004; Johnson, 2011; Lutz, 2011; Reber, 2010).3 These studies also find desegregation to increase the later-life earnings of Black males (Ashenfelter, Collins, & Yoon, 2006; Johnson, 2011), improve Blacks' later-life health status (Johnson, 2011), reduce the probability of criminal behavior and victimization (Lafree & Arum, 2006; Weiner, Lutz, & Ludwig, 2009; see Bergman, 2016), and limit the likelihood of living in poverty as an adult (Johnson, 2011). Most of this work finds desegregation to have either no effects (Johnson, 2011) or small positive effects (Weiner et al., 2009) on White students' outcomes.

55 For a deeper discussion of this point, see Michael J. Dumas, "Against the Dark: Antiblackness in Education Policy and Discourse," *Theory Into Practice* 55, no. 1 (2016): 11–19.

56 Elizabeth Anderson, "Race, Culture, and Educational Opportunity," *Theory and Research in Education* 10, no. 2 (2012): 125.

57 Wake County Board of Education Meeting, Part 11, March 23, 2010, *WRAL News*, minute mark 29:01-31:03, https://www.wral.com/video/news/education/video/7291597/.

58 Nancy Petty, interview with the author, February 25, 2019.

59 Christine Kushner, interview with the author, September 11, 2018.

60 Anderson describes in much greater detail than I can summarize here the important democratic effects of "formal social integration," the third of four stages of integration. Specifically, it reduces discrimination and responds more effectively to the claims of the disadvantaged through two causal routes: *epistemic diversity* and *accountability*. "[Formal social integration] works through at least two causal routes—epistemic diversity, whereby members of disadvantaged groups bring relevant considerations to the attention of agents who would otherwise be ignorant of them, and accountability, whereby agents respond to the presence of diverse others by expanding the circle of justification to address them as well as in-group members. This results in a more deliberative, public and democratic politics." Anderson, *The Imperative of Integration*, 134.

61 Gordon Allport's contact hypothesis (1954) is relevant here: "Allport argued that four conditions were required for intergroup interaction to reduce prejudice: contact must be (1) frequent enough to lead to personal acquaintance, (2) be cooperative, in pursuit of shared goals, (3) be supported by institutional authorities, and (4) take place among participants of equal status (equal roles within the organization)." From Anderson, *The Imperative of Integration*, 123.
62 Milton Friedman, "The Role of Government in Education," in *Economics and the Public Interest*, ed. Robert A. Solo (New Brunswick, NJ: Rutgers University Press, 1955), 131, note 2.
63 Erika Wilson, "The New White Flight," *Duke Journal of Constitutional Law & Public Policy* 14 (2019): 282.
64 Genevieve Siegel-Hawley, "How Non-Minority Students Also Benefit from Racially Diverse Schools," *National Coalition on School Diversity*, Brief no. 8 (October 2012): 1–2, http://www.school-diversity.org/pdf/DiversityResearch BriefNo8.pdf.
65 Integrated Schools: Families Choosing Integration, accessed August 2, 2021, https://integratedschools.org/about/our-mission-vision/.
66 Interview, February 15, 2021.
67 "[*The Imperative of Integration*] reconstructs Dewey's integrationist vision of education for democracy in the 21st century. In that work I regard schools as one site of democratic education, along with workplaces and other institutions of civil society." Anderson, interview by White, 7.
68 Anderson, *The Imperative of Integration*, 112. "Group-based segregation is the linchpin of group inequality." Nothing is as effective as integration in creating a democratic society of equals.
69 Michael Sandel, *The Tyranny of Merit: What's Become of the Common Good* (New York: Farrar, Straus and Giroux), 145.
70 Sandel, *The Tyranny of Merit*, 120.
71 Sandel, *The Tyranny of Merit*, 224.
72 Michelle Burris and Stefan Lallinger, "Leaving Nice White Parents Behind in 2020: New Hopes for School Integration," Century Foundation, January 15, 2021, 2, https://tcf.org/content/commentary/leaving-nice-white-parents-behind-2020 -new-hopes-school-integration/.
73 Anderson, *The Imperative of Integration*, 188.
74 Interview, April 10, 2019.
75 Anthony Foxx, "The Ground on Which We Stand," Medium.com, June 18, 2020, https://medium.com/@anthonyrfoxx/the-ground-on-which-we-stand-2fef44c57087.

Index

achievement, academic: achievement gap, 33–35, 37, 155n65; in arguments for school choice, 94–95; as contested value, 29–30, 31, 33–35, 36–37, 38–39, 41; in the "golden age" of Wake County schools, 58–60, 61–62; impact of diversity policy on, 9, 11–12; in moral logics and the case for true integration, 116–117, 123, 126–127; as the purpose of education, 50, 54–55, 94–95; socioeconomic-based student assignment in, 11–12

"A Community United: Celebrating 30 Years of Courageous Leadership," 84–85

activism/activists: commitment to integration in, 118; as defenders of the faith, 46–47, 51–53, 55, 65–67; divergent interests of, 37–38; in fighting for the future, 86, 93, 97–99; in resisting anti-integration, 2–3

AdvancED, 149n52

advantages/disadvantages, socioeconomic: in contested values, 23–24, 30–31, 32–33, 35–36, 38–39; in moral logics and true integration, 101–102, 104, 105, 107–108, 120–121, 122–124, 126–127; in power over policy, 12; in priorities, 14–15; and the purpose of public education, 51. *See also* socioeconomic status

Allport, Gordon, 168n61

Anderson, Elizabeth, 32–33, 77, 81–82, 117, 121–122, 126

Apex, NC, 8–9

arts programs, 66–67

Ashley, Samuel, 82

Asian students, 5–6, 7–8

"at-risk" children, 35–36, 76–77

Aycock, Charles, 82

backgrounds, socioeconomic. *See* socioeconomic status

Backhouse, Allison, 41

Baltimore/Baltimore County, MD public schools, 6–7

Baptist dissenting tradition, 45–46

Barber, William J., II, 36, 46–47, 98–99

beliefs: in contested values, 28–29, 32–33; in moral logics, 105–106, 111, 117, 118; on the purpose of public education, 50, 51–52, 117, 118–120; in radical equality, 19, 105–106; of the WCPSS strategic plan, 2–3; of white parents, in priorities on integration, 14–15

Bellah, Robert, 15

benefits of integration: in case studies and scholarship, 12, 13–14, 15; community, 28, 40, 104, 124–125; in contested values, 28, 29, 35–36, 37–38, 40–41, 42; exposure to difference as, 52–53; generational, 148n49; in moral logics and the case for true integration, 101–102, 104, 105, 110–111, 123–126; and true inclusion, 66–67

169

best-interests of children, 28, 35, 40, 57–58, 67, 80–81, 82–83
biases, 14–15, 63–64, 65, 66, 68–69, 77
Black communities: costs of integration to, 13–14, 81–82, 88–89, 107, 123–124; pragmatism of, 115–116; reluctance to integrate of, 84–85
Black families: moral logics of, and the case for true integration, 105, 107, 115–116, 118–119; preference for all-Black schools of, 95; in the unraveling of desegregation, 88–89
Black schools, 81–82, 95. *See also* racially identifiable schools; students, Black; teachers: of color
"blueberry story, the," 51–52
"both/and" thinking, 67–68, 71
Bradley v. Richmond School Board, 145–146n12
Brannon, Yevonne, 51, 97–98
Breyer, Stephen, 156–157n18
Broughton High School, 79, 80–81, 117
Brown v. Board of Education, 14, 35, 77, 160n69
Burris, Michelle, 127
business of academics, 57–59, 95
busing: in *Capacchione v. Charlotte-Mecklenburg Schools*, and the unraveling of desegregation in the U.S., 89; and the case for true integration, 118–119, 121–122; competing facts on, 149n53; and contested values, 31–32, 34; and the "golden age" of Wake public schools, 59–60, 62; in the historical context of segregation, 74–76, 78–79
buy-in, 58, 63, 95, 96–97, 110–111

Campbell, Bill, 80–81
Capacchione v. Charlotte-Mecklenburg Schools, 31–32, 89
Carolinian, The (Raleigh), 26
case studies of WCPSS, 8–13
Causby, Gene, 84, 159n52
Chambers, Julius Le Vonne, 74–75, 117
Charlotte-Mecklenburg school district, 31–32, 35–36, 74–75, 77, 78–79, 89, 107, 121–122
charter schools: as competition, 3–4; in conceptions of equality and freedom, 33,

107, 110–111, 164–165n17; in the end of the "golden age," 62–63; in school choice and privatization, 90–91, 92–94, 95–96, 161n83; in self-segregation, 14; white charter school enclaves, 90–91, 93, 123–124. *See also* privatization; school choice movement
Churn, Peggy, 84–85
citizenship, 16, 17–18, 19–20, 54–55, 109–110, 116–118, 125, 126–127
civil rights: achievement in challenges to, 34–35; Civil Rights Act of 1964, 36, 67; Civil Rights Movement, 83–84; in the historical context of segregation, 74–75; Office of Civil Rights, U.S. Department of Education, 36, 56–57, 149n52; public education in, 51
Colbert, Stephen, 12–13
Collins, Kristin, 37, 40–41
color blindness, 19, 31, 76–77, 87, 106
commodification of public education, 21–22, 42, 51–52, 118–119
common good: as contested value, 28, 40–41, 42–43; in moral logics and the case for true integration, 101–102, 111–112, 119, 122–123, 126–127; and school choice, 94–95, 96. *See also* social goods
communitarianism: as contested value in Wake's debate, 24–25, 40–41, 42; in moral logics and true integration, 108–109, 114, 127; in reflections on diversity, 57–58; and school choice, 90, 96
Community of the Cross of Nails, 46
competition, interschool, 3–4, 60, 90, 91–93, 109, 110–111
constitution of North Carolina, 50–51, 82, 139n6, 152n10
consumerism, 61, 90, 91–92, 94–97, 109–110
costs: of integration, to Black students and communities, 48–49, 81–82, 122–124; of white supremacy, 122
COVID-19 pandemic, 71–72, 92, 108
creativity/creative potential in integration, 110–111, 126, 127–128
criminalization of non-residency, 22
critical race theory, 104
cultures/cultural appreciation, 52–53, 67–68, 88–89, 127–128

Daniels, Josephus, 82

de Blasio, Bill, 22–23

democracy/democratic ideals: as contested value, 9–10, 18, 21, 42–43; in moral logics and the case for true integration, 103–104, 111–112, 113, 116–117, 118, 121, 126, 167n60; multicultural, and fully-funded public education, 98–99; multiracial power-sharing in, 103, 118; in reflections on diversity, 51, 54–55

Democrats/Democratic Party, 2–3, 36–37, 40–41, 61–62, 82, 97–98

desegregation: benefits of, in framing true integration, 123; in contested values, 23, 145–146n12; history and future of, 81, 84, 88–91, 98; measuring Wake's success in, 11–12; moral logics of, 109–111; in reflections on diversity, 45–46

Detroit, MI, 23

Dewey, John, 42–43, 111–112, 113

Diamond, John, 120–121

difference, human (socioeconomic/ethnic/cultural): in conceptions of equality, 30–31, 32, 103–108; exposure to and appreciation of, 52, 124, 127–128; in scholarship on integration, 14–15; socioeconomic, and equality of treatment, 76–77

"Directive for Community-Based Assignment," 73–78

discrimination: effects of, in competing conceptions of equality, 106; in racial inequity and internal segregation, 63–64. See also biases; racism

disenfranchisement of Black citizens, 82, 83–84

diversity policy: in case studies of Wake public schools, 8–9, 11–12; dismantling of, 2–3, 88–90; diversity as priority in, 2, 67; effects of reassignment, 10; free-and-reduced lunch as benchmark in, 3–6; impact of policy decisions on, 8–13; in reflections on diversity, 55, 64–65, 67; socioeconomic status in, 75–76, 77–78; in Wake's debate, 23–24, 36

Du Bois, W.E.B., 115

Dula, Gretta, 68–69

enclaves, homogeneous and segregated, 39, 63, 90–91, 93, 106, 123–124, 127

End-of-Grade (EOG) tests, 58

engagement, civic, 3, 26–27, 30, 113, 118

Enloe High School, 38, 64, 68–69, 126

enrollment, WCPSS, 3–4, 8–9, 31–32, 33, 56–57, 63–64, 108–109

equality/inequality: competing conceptions of, 28, 29–33, 41, 103–108, 112, 117–118, 122–123, 126; in democratic values, 18; racial, in the history of NC, 19; radical, 19, 105–106, 107–108, 126; in reflections on diversity, 71; structural, 14, 31, 105; in true integration, 117–118, 126, 127

equity/inequity: and conceptions of equality, 32–33, 105, 107–108; in the historical context of segregation, 81, 82, 84, 96; organizations supporting, 3; in reflections on diversity, 57, 63–69; of schools within schools, 63–69; in true integration, 118, 125

excellence, academic, 1–2, 30, 38–39, 42, 59–60, 84–85, 116–117

exposure, sociocultural, 12, 52–53, 81, 124–125

Fairmont United Methodist Church meeting, 17–18

fairness, 28, 30–33, 35, 39–40, 55, 103–105, 112, 122

faith leaders. See leaders/leadership

Festenstein, Matthew, 113

Finlator, William Wallace, 45–46

Flood, Dudley, 84, 159n52

Ford, Steve, 32–33, 41

Foxx, Anthony, 128

free and reduced-price lunch (FRL), 3–6, 7, 8

freedom: of choice, 23–24, 48–49, 90–91, 116; competing conceptions of, 102–103, 104, 108–12, 114, 116; as contested value, 23–24; and true integration, 127. See also school choice movement

free market, 90, 91–92, 109, 114

Friedman, Milton, 91–92, 125

friendships, interracial, 52–53, 126

funding, educational: funding effort, 92; in the historical context of segregation, 82, 83–84; per-student, 7–8, 159n41; in published opinions, 35–36; school choice and privatization in defunding, 92–93

fusion coalitions, 82, 97–99, 144n64, 158n39, 159n41
fusion rule, 82, 159n41

Garland, Sarah, 88
Geary, Bob, 26
gerrymandering, 82, 83–84, 119
ghettoization, 39
gifted and talented/academically gifted programming, 66, 104
globalization/global society, 52–53, 67–68
goals: collective, individualism in denigrating, 115; contested values in, 24, 36; Goal 2003 (95% goal), 58, 60; in reflections on diversity, 54–55, 58–59; of school choice and communitarianism, 94–95, 96; shared, in contact hypothesis, 168n61
"golden age" of Wake County schools, 55–64, 121–122
governance, 39–40, 77–78
Government Accountability Office, U.S., 92
"government schools," 91–92, 110–111
Grant, Gerald, 9–10
Great Schools in Wake, 17–18, 97–98, 144n64
Green v. New Kent County, 160n69
Greenwich, Connecticut, 22

Hannah-Jones, Nikole, 43, 107–108, 114–115, 122–123
Hargens, Donna, 73
HBCUs (Historically Black Colleges and Universities), 107
healthy schools index, 61–62, 108–109
hierarchy, social, 121, 122, 126
high-poverty schools: in contested values, 31–32, 33, 34–36, 37, 149n56; free and reduced lunch program numbers in, 3–7; in the historical context of segregation, 75, 79–80, 92; in moral logics and the case for true integration, 105, 107, 123–124; in reflections on diversity, 56, 57–58, 67, 153n38. See also low-income students/neighborhoods; poverty
Hispanic students and parents, 5–6, 34–35, 37–38, 116, 150n73

history/historical context: in activism for the future, 86, 93, 97–99; as argument against community-based assignments, 74–75; in case studies, 13–14; of the choice movement, 89, 90–97; in competing conceptions of freedom, 108–109; disagreements over, in Wake County, 85–88; of segregation, 19, 78–85, 87–88, 97; in the unraveling of desegregation, 88–90; in Wake's commitment to integration, 118–119
Holden, William Woods, 82
Holt, Joe, Jr., 80–81
homeowners/ownership, 21–23, 77–78. See also property rights (private property)
homogeneity, 13, 53, 62–63, 106, 127–128, 153n38. See also enclaves, homogeneous and segregated
housing: in the case for true integration, 122; in conceptions of equality, 105; in contested values, 22–23, 39; in published opinions, 39; redlining in segregation of, 13–14, 23, 105
Hui, T. Keung, 25–26
human right, education as, 51, 105–106
Hunt, Jim, 83–84
Hunter Elementary School, 61
Hyde County, 159n52

idealism, civic: as contested value, 28; in moral logics and true integration, 19, 102–103, 109–110, 117–118, 120, 122–123, 127; in reflections on diversity, 48, 50–51, 56, 71–72
ideology, 21–25, 35–37, 84, 87–88, 90, 110–111, 118–119
inclusion: and internal segregation, 66–67, 69; in moral logics and true integration, 103, 111–112, 117, 120, 124, 125–126
individual (private) goods: and competing conceptions of equality, 104; in contested values, 23–25, 28, 30, 40–41, 42–43; education as consumer good in framework of, 90; in moral logics and the case for true integration, 101–102, 104, 105–106, 108, 109, 111–112, 116–117, 118–119; and rational self-interest, 108, 126; in reflections on diversity, 50–53, 54–55

individualism/individualistic approach: in contested values, 42–43; and integration, 118–119, 120, 121, 122; in moral logics, 104, 107, 108–109, 111–112, 113–115, 116–117; in school choice, 90, 96–97. *See also* preferences, individual

insiders, 78, 81–82, 86–87, 88

instrumental good/value, 52, 71, 115–116

Integrated Schools: Families Choosing Integration, 125–126

integration: the case for true integration, 120–28; as ordeal for Black students and communities, 81–82, 88–89, 107, 123–124; scholarship on, 13–15; "school within a school" problem in, 63–69; voluntary, 31–32; Wake's commitment to, 118–120

intensive parenting, 90, 96–97

interest convergence/divergence, 37–38, 114–115, 125–126, 165n30

internal segregation, 63–69

isolation, racial and social, 12, 66–67, 75, 113, 123–124

Jenkins, Jim, 80–81

Joffe-Walt, Chana, 101–102

Johnson, Rucker C., 2–3

Jones, Benita, 75, 117

Joyner, James, 159n43

justice: in conceptions of equality, 32, 104–105, 107–108; in contested values, 32, 42; distributive, 105; egalitarian, 32; moral logics of, and the case for true integration, 104–105, 107–108, 112–113, 122–123; social, in reflections on diversity, 46; substantive, in *Parents Involved*, 77

King, Martin Luther, Jr., 127, 128

Kozol, Jonathan, 114–115

Kushner, Christine, 70–71, 124

Ladd, Helen, 93

Lallinger, Stefan, 127

leaders/leadership: competing conceptions of equality of, 105–6; on the "golden age" of Wake County schools, 55–63; in the historical context of segregation, 84–85; on past and present in Wake County,

85–88; on the purpose of higher education, 50–55; on racial inequity and the "school within a school," 63–69; in true integration, 117–118, 121–122

Leandro v. State, 139n6

legislature, North Carolina, 3–4, 62–63, 83–85, 92–93, 122, 139–140n8

Lewis, Amanda, 120–121

Ligon Middle School/John W. Ligon High School, 61, 80–81

Louisville, Kentucky, 2–3

low-income students/neighborhoods: and contested values, in Wake's debate, 24–25, 32–33; in the historical context of segregation, 79–80, 86–87, 90–91, 92, 94; and the school-within-a-school problem, 64; and separate-but-equal, 35–36, 107. *See also* high-poverty schools; poverty

low-performing students/schools, 38–39

Luebke, Bob, 36

magnet schools: in the case for true integration, 125, 126; in contested values, 31–32, 38; impact of, in racial balance, 8–9; and moral logics, 110–111, 115–116; racial inequity and internal segregation in, 63–65, 66–68; in reflections on diversity, 60–61, 63–65, 66–68; and school choice, 90–91, 110–111

Majestic, Ann, 73

Making Caring Common (Harvard Graduate School of Education), 14–15

Malone, Vernon, 84–85

Margiotta, Ron, 1–3, 76–78

Marks, Walter, 60

Martinez, Rick, 30, 34–35

Martin Middle School, 54, 64

Massive Resistance campaign, 82–83

McGhee, Heather, 122–123

McNeal, Bill, 55–63, 86, 95, 117–118

Meeker, Charles, 78, 157n23

merger of Wake County and Raleigh City schools, 56–57, 61–62, 84–85, 97–99, 108–109, 117–118, 121–122

Merhige, Robert H., 145–146n12

meritocracy, 124–25, 126–27

Michaels, Cash, 26

Mickelson, Roslyn, 89

Mill, John Stuart, 108
Milliken v. Bradley, 23, 88
Minow, Martha, 96–97
mobility, social, 50, 51, 126–127
moral logics: in challenges to integrated schools, 14; civic idealism as, 19, 102–103, 109–110, 117–118, 120, 122–123, 127; in commitment to true integration, 118–120; conceptions of equality as, 103–108, 112, 117–118, 122–123, 126; conceptions of freedom as, 102–103, 104, 108–112, 114, 116; in conceptions of "good," 101–102, 112–113; core, in the debate over diversity policy, 113–118; in identifying Wake County's normative values, 16; of individualism, 102–103, 108–109, 111–112, 113–115, 116–117, 118, 120, 121; pragmatism as, 19, 102–103, 112–113, 115–117; on school integration, 15. *See also* equality/inequality; freedom
Moral Monday Movement, 47
Morrison, Carolyn, 2
Murphey School, 80–81, 83–84
Murphy, John, 84–85

NAACP (National Association for the Advancement of Colored People), 67–68, 149n52
National Center for Education Statistics (NCES), 140n13
NC HEAT (Heroes Emerging Among Teens), 67–68
neighborhoods/neighborhood schools: contested value of, in Wake's debate, 21–23, 24–25, 33–34, 36, 38, 40–41; in the "Directive for Community-Based Assignments," 73, 75–76; in the historical context of segregation, 74–76, 79, 84, 87–88, 90–91, 94–95; in moral logics and the case for true integration, 105, 115, 119, 122; in reflections on diversity, 46–47, 62–63, 64; socioeconomic class in support for, 10–11
Newbold, Margaret, 81
Newbold, Nathan Carter, 81
newcomers, 2, 11, 85–86, 89. *See also* outsiders
News & Observer, 13, 16–17, 19, 37–41, 82
New York City, 22–23, 161n76

New York Times, 12–13
Nice White Parents podcast, 101–2, 120–121, 127
No Child Left Behind Act, 39, 58, 60. *See also* testing
North Carolina General Assembly, 62–63, 93, 139–140n8. *See also* legislature, North Carolina

openness: to change, in reflections on diversity, 68–69; to change, in true integration, 117, 120–121; to civic engagement, in Wake's debate, 30; to education as civic and social good, 96
opportunity: equality of, as contested value, 21–22, 30–33, 41; equality of, in reflections on diversity, 50–51, 70, 74–75; and internal segregation, 65, 67–68; in moral logics and the case for true integration, 107, 114, 116, 120–121, 122; opportunity-based hoarding, 107, 120–121, 122; for socialization, in reflections on diversity, 53
organizations supporting public education, 3
outcomes, academic: as contested value, in Wake's debate, 29, 30–31, 33–36; in framing integration, 123, 125; and the problem of racial inequity, 67; and school choice, 94–95; studies on, 14. *See also* achievement, academic
outcomes of integration/segregation, 31–32, 107, 123, 148n49
outsiders, 78, 84, 85–86, 88, 118–119. *See also* newcomers
Oxholm, Tom, 40

Parcel, Toby, 10–11
parents, Black: interests and voices of, 37–38, 89–90; moral logics of, and the case for true integration, 115–116, 118–119, 123–125; in reflections on diversity, 65, 88–90, 94, 95, 159n52
parents, white: beliefs and biases of, in priorities on integration, 14–15; interests and voices of, 37–38, 42, 89–90; moral logics of, and the case for true integration, 101–102, 103, 107, 114–115, 118–124, 127; power of, 101–102, 103, 119–123; in

privatization and school choice, 90–91,
93–94; in reflections on diversity, 65–66;
in resistance to integration, 82–83; value
of integrated schools to, 14–15
Parents Involved v. Seattle School District,
61–62, 77, 88–89, 110, 156n18,
160–161n70
Patillo, Mary, 94
Pearsall Plan, 82–83, 87
performance, student. *See* achievement,
academic; outcomes, academic
Petty, Nancy E., 45, 46–49, 70–71, 124
Plainfield, New Jersey school district, 7–8
Plessy v. Ferguson, 35. *See also* separate but
equal/separate and unequal
polarization, 6–7, 77–78, 106, 161n83
Policy 6200/Wake student assignment
policy. *See* diversity policy
Pope, Claude, Jr., 31
population growth, Wake County, 3–4,
8–10
Poteat, Edwin McNeill, Jr., 45–46
poverty, 3–7, 33, 76–77. *See also* low-income
students/neighborhoods
power: of advantaged families, 12; of fusion
coalitions, in fighting for the future,
97–98; and school choice, 93; and true
integration, 103–104, 117–121, 126, 127;
and the unraveling of desegregation,
88–90; white power structures, in local
history, 80–81, 82–83
pragmatism: of defenders of the faith, 71;
on internal segregation, 67–68; as moral
logic, 19, 102–103, 112–113, 115–117; in
reflections on diversity, 50–51, 52–53,
56–57; in true integration, 117–118
preferences, individual, 87–89, 90–92,
93–94, 95–96, 104, 107, 114–115. *See also*
individualism/individualistic approach
principals, 56, 60–61, 68, 81–82, 118
private schools: as contested value, in
Wake's debate, 23–24; private school
vouchers, 3–4, 82–83, 92; in reflections
on diversity, 53, 71–72; vouchers for, in
the end of the "golden age," 62–63.
See also school choice movement
privatization, 13, 14, 19, 90–94, 110, 122,
161n83. *See also* school choice movement
profiling of students, 76–77, 106

property rights (private property), 21–25,
42, 77–78, 114
Pullen Memorial Baptist Church, 45–46
purposes of public education, 50–55, 94–95,
117, 118–120

quality of schools: and competing
conceptions of equality, 107; as contested
value, 22–23, 30; in moral logics and the
case for integration, 104, 109, 114–115,
116; as priority of white parents, 14–15; in
reflections on diversity, 57, 59–60, 61–62,
63, 67–68; and school choice, 90, 91–92,
95

race: color blindness, 19, 31, 76–77, 87, 106;
as factor, in integration, 61–62; "natural"
separation by, in the historical context of
segregation, 87; race-based student
assignment, 61–62, 88–89, 156n18; racial
quotas, 88–89; and wealth of schools, 5–6
racially identifiable schools, 63, 67, 75,
79–80, 81–82, 95
racism: and the Margiotta school board
majority, 149n52; persistence of, 84;
structural, 97, 101–102, 121, 124–125;
systemic, and competing conceptions of
equality, 105
Radical Reconstructionists, 82
Rawls, John, 112–113
Reagan, Ronald, and administration,
78–79, 91–92
reassignment of students, 2, 10, 24, 25, 67,
86–87
reproductive choice, 111
Republicans/Republican Party: contested
values of, 25, 31, 36, 41; and fusion
coalitions, 97–98; and the history of
segregation, 83–84, 86–87, 159n52;
national media on policies of, 12–13; in
reflections on diversity, 53, 61–63; school
board takeover by, 1–3; in school choice
and privatization, 92
resegregation: in Charlotte-Mecklenburg,
31–32, 74; and contested values, in
Wake's debate, 26–27, 33, 34–35, 36–37;
in historical context, 74–75, 76–77,
79–80; rhetoric of, in historical context,
79–80

residency, 11–12, 22
resistance: fusion coalitions in, 97–99; to
    integration, 80–81, 82–83, 90–91, 122,
    159n52; to segregation, 2–3
responsibility, individual, 31, 90, 103, 113,
    120–123, 126–127
Roberts, John, 77, 106
Roe v. Wade, 111
Ryan, James, 145–146n12

Sandel, Michael, 126–127
Sanford, Terry, 83–84
Schofield, Rob, 54, 66, 70
school board, Wake County: causes of
    2009 takeover of, 70; disinterest in
    history of segregation of, 85; in-person
    comment periods, 26; letters to the
    editor on, 6–7; March 23, 2010 meeting
    of, 73–78; polarization of, 77–78; quality
    of governance by, 39–40; Republican
    takeover of, 1–3
school choice movement, 11, 13, 28, 89,
    90–97, 109–111, 114. *See also* private
    schools; privatization
school equity teams, internal, 3, 69
school-to-prison pipeline, 63–64
school-within-a-school problem, 63–69
secession, voluntary, 13, 93–94, 115–116
segregation: de facto, 23–24, 82–83, 110,
    145–146n12, de jure, 23, 82–83, 145–
    146n12; in historical context, 19, 79–85,
    87–88, 97; internal, 63–69; persistence
    of, in the U.S., 118–119; self-segregation,
    14, 63–64, 94, 106; in Westfield, NJ, 7–8
segregation academies. *See* private schools
self-interest (individual good). *See*
    individual (private) goods
separate but equal/separate and unequal,
    14, 28, 35–37, 77, 81, 87–88, 106–108
Silberman, Todd, 8–9
social capital theory, 10
social contact theory, 126, 168n61
"social engineering," 12–13, 104, 115
social goods, 42–43, 50–52, 96, 111–112.
    See also common good
socialism, 111–112
social-psychological benefits of integration,
    125
social purpose politics, 24–25, 164–165n17

socioeconomic status: as alternative to race,
    160–161n70; in competing conceptions
    of equality, 30–31, 32–33, 104–105; in
    contested values, 31; in the historical
    context of segregation, 76–77; in impact
    of reassignment and school proximity,
    10; in polarization, 6–7; in reflections on
    diversity, 52, 58; in scholarship on
    integration, 14; in student assignment
    policies, 8–9, 11–13; student interactions
    with, in the case for true integration,
    126; in student reassignments, 11–12,
    86–87
solidarity: community, in the future of
    public education, 97–98; in moral logics
    and true integration, 101–102, 103,
    105–106, 108, 117–118, 120, 126–127, 128;
    in opposing the dissolution of diversity
    policy, 17–18; in reflections on diversity,
    57–58; solidarity dividends, 101–102;
    value of, 41
Sotomayor, Sonia, 106
spending. *See* funding, educational
stability of student assignments: in the
    "Directive for Community-Based
    Assignments," 73; in dismantling of
    diversity policy, 2; of inequalities,
    119–20; of student assignments in
    diversity policy support, 11; value of vis
    diversity, 12, 19, 73, 77–78, 86–87, 112
Stoops, Terry, 54–55, 94–96
strategic plan, WCPSS, 2–3
striving. *See* meritocracy
structures: formal, in competing concep-
    tions of equality, 104; of inequality and
    inequity, 14, 82; racial, and school
    choice, 97; racial, in the case for true
    integration, 121, 124–125; structural
    disadvantage and conceptions of
    equality, 30–31, 105; of white supremacy,
    in American public education, 23–124
student assignment policies. *See* Policy
    6200/Wake student assignment policy;
    stability of student assignments
students, Black: concentration of, in
    high-poverty schools, 33; distribution of,
    across wealthy/poor schools, 5–6; harm
    of high-poverty schools and racial
    isolation to, 123–124; in the historical

context of segregation, 81–82, 90–91; improved outcomes and generational benefits of integration for, 9, 33–35, 75–76, 148n49; over disciplining of, 63–64, 69; rise in test scores of, 9; socioeconomic status in policy impact on, 10; tracking and racial inequity for, in integrated schools, 63–69

students, white: and contested values, 31–32, 37–38, 41; distribution of, across the district, 5–6, 7–8; falling public school enrollment of, 142–143n46; harm of majority-white environments to, 123–125; in reflections on diversity, 61, 63–64, 65; rise in test scores of, 9; and school choice, 88–89, 90–91

Supreme Court, U.S., 13, 106, 111, 122. *See also under case name*

Supreme Court of North Carolina, 139n6

Sutton, Keith, 76–78

Swann v. Charlotte-Mecklenburg Board of Education, 74–75, 77, 121–122

Syracuse, NY public schools, 9–10

Tata, Anthony, 39–40, 62–63, 154n50

taxes/taxpayers, 22, 79, 83–84, 85–87, 92. *See also* homeowners/ownership

Taylor, Andrew, 10–11

teachers: of color, 68–69, 81–82, 118; as contested value, 29, 34, 36, 42–43; in the local history of desegregation, 81–82, 83–84; and privatization, 92; race-based salaries of, 159n43; in reflections on diversity, 48, 51–52, 56, 58–60, 61–63, 66, 67, 68–69; white, 66, 68

Tedesco, John, 12–13, 39, 76–77

testing, 58, 60, 65–66. *See also* No Child Left Behind Act

Torres, E., 14–15

tracking, academic, 14, 63–66, 118, 121

transactionalism, 96, 109–110

transplants, northern, 64–65, 68–69, 78–79, 85–86, 157n23

treatment, equal, 30, 32–33, 48–49, 76–77, 103–105, 106

Turaeva, Mavzuna, 93–94

Tyson, Timothy B., 46–47, 158n37

underestimation of abilities, 65–67

values, contested: achievement as, 29–30, 31, 33–35, 36–37, 38–39, 41; and challenges to integrated schools, 14–15; in clashes over assignment policies, 12; and competing conceptions of equality, 30–33, 104; democratic, equality as, 18; interviews and public moral arguments in identifying, 16; as motivation of people and policy, 102; in themes of published opinions, 27–41; in Wake's debate, 21–27

WakeEd blog (*News and Observer*), 25–26

Wallace, George, 83–84

Ward, Jason Morgan, 79–80

Washington Post, 12–13

wealth gap, 105. *See also* socioeconomic status

Weissbourd, R., 14–15

well-being, 13, 28–29, 37–38, 108–109

Westfield, NJ school district, 7–8

white flight, 57, 88, 90–91, 93–94, 122

white privilege, 93–94, 120–121, 123–125, 166n31

white supremacy, 23–24, 122

Williams, Mary, 47–48

Williams, Sheneka, 11

Wilson, Erika, 90–91, 93–94, 125

year-round schools, 10–11, 108–109, 148n39

zero-sum game, 43, 90, 105–106, 122, 126–127

About the Author

KAREY HARWOOD is an associate professor of religious studies in the Department of Philosophy and Religious Studies with a joint appointment in Women's, Gender, and Sexuality Studies at North Carolina State University in Raleigh, North Carolina. Her work focuses on questions of ethics and values in human reproduction, parenthood, and education. She is the author of *The Infertility Treadmill: Feminist Ethics, Personal Choice, and the Use of Reproductive Technologies*. A parent of children attending Wake County Public Schools over the course of twenty years, she helped launch a statewide nonprofit supporting public education.

Printed and bound by CPI Group (UK) Ltd, Croydon, CR0 4YY

09/06/2025

14685732-0001